LUCY B

RUNNING A CREATIVE
COMPANY IN THE DIGITAL AGE

creative ESSENTIALS

First published in 2017 by Kamera Books
an imprint of Oldcastle Books,
PO Box 394, Harpenden, Herts, AL5 1XJ
www.kamerabooks.com

A CIP catalogue record for this book is available from the British Library.

ISBN
978-1-84344-926-3   (Print)
978-1-84344-927-0   (epub)

2 4 6 8 10 9 7 5 3 1

Typeset by Elsa Mathern in Franklin Gothic 9 pt
Printed and bound in Great Britain by Clays Ltd, St Ives Plc

CONTENTS

INTRODUCTION

I chose to call this book *Running a Creative Company in the Digital Age*, rather than *Running a Production Company* or *Running a Digital Agency*, because the concept of what a 'creative' company is, and what it does, has become much more fluid in the last ten years.

As the digital age beds in, entirely new ways of working and creating have evolved. Traditional models of ideas generation, collaboration, funding, production, distribution and consumption are disappearing or morphing into something else. These new ways have been built from a truly digital native foundation, rather than with one foot in the old world of analogue and hard copy. This means they are unprecedented, unpredictable and exciting as well as a bit scary for anyone who grew up with more traditional models – which means pretty much anyone over 35 who isn't involved in digital innovation already.

The landscape of work is changing, too, with more flexible working cultures and structures emerging, and large corporations hoovering up smaller rivals and promising start-ups in a bid to secure their global content kingdom.

The focus of the book is primarily on digital visual content, meaning digital video, animation, film and TV and to a lesser extent gaming and creative tech. Some of what is covered may also be true across the worlds of publishing, social enterprise, live performance and music. I generally use the term 'content' rather than referring specifically to TV programmes, films, business promos or campaign videos, because so many of these things overlap in the digital space.

My background is in independent film and TV drama initially, then factual content including documentaries, specialist factual, news and current affairs, digital education projects, new talent and promos for brands and businesses, so much of what I talk about will be directly relevant to these areas.

I have tried to maintain a wider overview when possible, though, precisely because the lines are so blurred these days. The digital revolution has created a landscape where collaboration is widespread and innovation so prolific that when starting up a creative company you could find yourself working within the arenas of digital technology development, artificial intelligence, virtual reality, biotech or gaming as part of any wider creative project.

I also wanted to write a nuts and bolts guide to setting up and running a creative company that can be a one-stop shop for aspiring creative entrepreneurs, because it seems to me that such a guide is sorely needed. It's something I could definitely have used when I was starting out, full of ideas and ambition but blissfully unaware of the potential pitfalls! Although I learned a lot from running my small production company, Mandrake Films, for eight years, it was mostly on the job with a lot of trial and error, and cobbled together from different and frequently baffling sources. Wading through the incomprehensible jargon and doublespeak of officialdom and having surreal, contradictory conversations with different government departments was a dominant feature of the early years; perhaps this book will save others that considerable pain and frustration.

As digital content production becomes cheaper and more accessible, it's becoming more attractive, and theoretically more possible, to do things your own way. But many creative endeavours end up stalling because they lack the foundation in business administration, finance, company legals and market awareness needed to give ideas a chance.

Ambitious, talented creatives often burn out and feel frustrated because they can't get things off the ground, without realising they need some basic knowledge and training to make a company work and to partner up with others who have the skills and interests they lack. Similarly, those with business, legal or finance training often view creatives as 'other' from them, or exclude them from important processes. Other industries are aware that such training and structure is essential as a starting point but many of the 'creative industries' seem to be somehow exempt from this, as though what we are doing is in the realms of the amateur rather than the professional.

I think this has often led to casual exploitation of hard-working filmmakers, artists, musicians, ideas generators and writers by those who are gatekeepers and therefore have the power to marginalise them, or simply have the training to control the purse strings and write the contracts. Often key creatives are not paid enough to make a living, and that is not acceptable when they contribute so much to our creative economy.

The three parts cover the life cycle of a company from setting up and kicking off through growth and diversification and finally selling, merging, buying up or moving on. For the most part I am referring to a private limited company incorporated by shares, although part one outlines other company structures such as LLPs and non-profit companies, and a lot of the information contained in this book can also be applied to them.

Part one looks at company identity and structure, executive roles, paying yourself, shareholders and boards, start-up funding and all the nitty-gritty practical things you need to consider in the first year of running your business.

Part two covers topics such as publicity and advertising, dealing with staff, pitching for business, running your projects and whether or not it's actually possible to protect your ideas.

Part three is all about growth, maturity and working out what the best future for you and your company might be.

Throughout are case studies from a range of creative companies and interviews with media lawyers and accountants, company MDs, the founder of Crowdcube, the CEO of an investment fund, international broadcasters, pioneers in flexible working and the head of the Channel 4 Growth Fund, all of whom have their own take on what being a creative company today is all about.

There is also a section about the possible effects of a British exit from the European Union, or Brexit, which came so suddenly upon us in June 2016.

All parts contain my random musings and some brief rants, as well as practical examples and anecdotes from years of experience working in the production industry.

I hope this book will help people with ideas and ambition to have the confidence to go their own way, find the right collaborators, innovate change and take their place in an industry they love. Many more women, and many more people from a range of socio-economic, gender and ethnic backgrounds, need to set up shop in our creative industries and thrive there. We need their contribution to and representation in our culture. And I hope the scores of students I have encouraged to set up on their own over the years will be newly inspired to do so after reading these pages. Because, despite the challenges, running a creative company is inspiring, horizon-broadening, life-affirming and, above all, fun!

PART **ONE**

GETTING **STARTED**

YOUR **USP**

So who are you, why are you here and why should audiences and funders care about you?

Fundamental questions you need to ask yourself when setting up a creative company are: what makes you tick and how do you want to influence, educate and entertain others? Take some time to think about the things you really enjoy. Do campaigning virals make you think about the world in new ways? Or do longer documentaries help you to engage with the human story? Are you a gamer who interacts more online than in real life and, if so, what would you do differently or innovate with? Is there a disruptive technology idea that has been brewing in your head? Do you want to work in animation, live action, factual? Do you want to tell audiences stories directly by making and appearing in films yourself, or oversee the process from behind the scenes? Do you want to help businesses tell their stories?

It is also vitally important to know the landscape. Find out who is out there already doing what you want to do. Who made the content you have engaged with the most in the last year? Don't know? Find out and do some research on them. If they seem approachable you could ask them to meet for a coffee – or alternatively stalk them online until you understand exactly how they got to where they are today.

EXPERIENCE LEVEL

Media production, and the 'creative industries' in general, has always been one of the most popular career choices and also one of the most vague. Even if you have done a relevant degree in film, media studies, digital content production or broadcast journalism, it's so fiercely competitive out there that it could take years of free work before you get your dream paid job.

Broadcasters, production companies, digital agencies, technology and creative corporations are frequently approached by hopeful graduates and non-graduates alike.

Being a digital native obviously helps. Thousands of employed people have to retrain in digital skills including social media, web development and project management tools such as Javascript, Flash, Agile, JIRA, Waterfall (and many more) to get hired nowadays. You need to know some of this stuff to set up and run a company, too. There are myriad digital courses that can be done online, and organisations such as Digital Mums are aimed at people returning to work and a bit mystified by the world of digital media. Things move so fast now that you only need a few months not using these platforms to be out of touch. Those of you who are young enough to have been born into the digital age already have a great skills base to start from, but if you don't, never fear – there are plenty of training options out there and people you can partner up with.

The best way to get noticed now is to create a profile online using free platforms. For video, these would be content platforms such as Vimeo (or Vimeo Pro at a small fee with much larger storage), YouTube or Dailymotion, showcasing any work you have done, so that any approaches you make are backed up with an easy link that shows your identity as a content creator.

My advice would be to do this in the first instance and get some years of industry experience behind you as a freelancer in the creative industry you aspire to, before setting up a company. In parallel, create your own content and put it out there into the world.

If you are a novice and want to set up a company, first find a business partner who knows the industry ropes and will set up the company with you. This should be an experienced producer or executive producer, head of talent, head of development, chief technical officer or finance director depending on your individual company needs and the kind of creative enterprise that interests you.

WHAT IS A CREATIVE BUSINESS?

Running a business involves a huge amount of creativity. That doesn't mean it isn't for you. It just means that sometimes you have to rediscover yourself and what makes you tick, after functioning in a society and education system that values conformity.

The advent of the digital age has meant that things change faster than ever before in history. In almost any industry today, and certainly in the creative industries, 'Innovate or Die' is an apt phrase. Keeping on top of things is hard enough; keeping ahead of the curve nigh on impossible. The Silicon Valley generation, which opened the door to our digital age, taking notice of the crazy ideas and developing them, was often buoyed up by the hope and innocence of youth and had bypassed the traditional education system.

The Western education system is not, alas, always the friend of creativity. Much of it is stuck in the Industrial Revolution of the nineteenth century with large classes behind rigid rows of desks, listening to a teacher by the whiteboard, anxiously waiting to be singled out. Although schools vary in terms of teaching style, learning by rote is still often used for children in primary school. Uniforms, rigid rules, timetables, punishments, obedience: conformity is key and it is often at the expense of creative expression and allowing individuals to develop their talents and capacities. How can we make new, exciting connections, forge new brain pathways through free exploration that lead to profound innovation, when the ability to do so has been educated out of us? As is often mentioned by those encouraging an entrepreneurial spirit, some of the biggest tech and media tycoons are school or university dropouts; Steve Jobs at Apple, Bill Gates at Microsoft, Richard Branson at Virgin, David Karp at Tumblr, Mark Zuckerberg at Facebook, to name a few.

Finland offers hope for the future of our education system. It has banned subjects completely post-16, in favour of an integrated curriculum which follows the specific interests of students. Instead of individual subjects, students will study events and phenomena in an interdisciplinary format. The goal is that students choose for themselves which topic or phenomenon they want to study, according to their ambitions for the future and their capabilities. Students will no longer sit behind school desks. Instead, they will work together in small groups to discuss problems. The head of the Department of Education in Helsinki, Marjo Kyllonen, says: 'There are schools that are teaching in the old-fashioned way which was of benefit in the beginning of the 1900s – but the needs are not the same, and we need something fit for the 21st century.' Let's hope it catches on!

The stereotype of the 'creative' as useless at business, often peddled by creatives themselves as well as those around them, helps maintain a convenient distance between the number crunchers (and profit takers) and those doing the content creation. It has allowed middle and senior management to cream profits off the top for generations – stories abound of musicians, painters, filmmakers and writers being fleeced by their management through time immemorial. It still means that, for example, in documentary feature film production today, directors and originators are the people who make the least cash out of the finished product.

Of course, sometimes it's true that an individual is terrible at running a business, but just because you create the content doesn't mean you can't grasp the fundamentals of business and finance. You just have to learn, and not sell yourself short. A 2016 report by RealScreen called *Documentary Pays? The Price of Filmmaking* was a candid look at how directors in particular are selling themselves short while everyone around them makes the cash. In the report, documentary filmmaker Emily James is quoted as saying:

> *We're exploiting ourselves, but we're also being exploited by all the people around us who are making a proper living from what they're doing, and using our work as the center of that ... Nobody ever pays you back for all of that effort you put into [development]. But then, if the film is good, you suddenly have all of these other people that are working for distributors, festivals and broadcasters – who are being paid a waged job – and they're using the work that we've created as the central commodity of their industry without ever repaying the people that took the major risk at the beginning.*

It's incumbent upon everyone to take creative roles seriously and allot to them a decent salary, and also upon creatives to understand their worth.

I remember being labelled 'artsy' at school. This meant I could not be 'mathsy' or 'sciencey', and indeed I was useless at science and maths while being good at writing, art and the humanities. But before that, at primary school, I was among the top of my class at maths and science. And after working as a producer on various science and medical films and programmes on subjects like particle physics, autism, intensive farming and heart surgery, I became passionate about scientific ideas and came to view them as intensely creative. Alas, I still lack the foundation in science that might have allowed me to appreciate them fully, because I was shooed away from it at school. What I'm saying is, don't judge yourself as not up to the task without giving yourself a chance. The old adage 'The more you do, the more you can do' is true. Boardrooms are full of financiers, lawyers and administrators who think they know best and keep the 'creatives' out of the room. You can help change that by appreciating that we can be multifaceted and having the gumption to do your homework and stand up for yourself.

TEN FOUNDING AND GUIDING PRINCIPLES FOR YOUR CREATIVE COMPANY

1. Follow the Passion, Not the Money

This might sound rather quaint in today's profit-orientated landscape, where turnover is so much more important than quality. In the creative arena, in my experience, you are far better doing the things you care about – and if you get to know the landscape and the basic rules you will eventually be savvy enough to make it lucrative, too. When I have tried to follow the money, it has only got me lost and made me question why I wanted to do this in the first place. That said, you need to be practical, too. If your main passion will never bring more than a trickle of funding in, think about what else floats your boat and how you can diversify to bump up your turnover. Even better, find a business partner whose job it is to follow the money for you!

2. Know Your Talents and Know Your Limits

No one is brilliant at everything, so work out what you are great at and what you are not so great at – and identify the people you know and trust that can do the things you can't and are interested in the things that bore you to tears.

3. Know the Landscape

Find out who is out there already doing what you want to do. Who made the content you have engaged with the most in the last year? Don't know? Find out and do some research on them. If they seem approachable you could ask them to meet for a coffee – or, alternatively, stalk them online until you understand exactly how they got to where they are today.

4. Do Not Max Out Your Credit Card

You may believe in your passion project, and that's great – in fact, without that passion and belief, you won't get very far. But you need to be practical, too, and take all the variables into consideration. So when you're starting your company with a project in mind, get some backing, and some opinions first – and don't use your own cash, unless you can afford to lose it. It all depends how much stress you want in your life! I know some creatives will disagree with me on this, because they have taken a punt with their own cash and it has paid off. If you are starting something that you have a lot of experience in already and you have a couple of business partners who are also fronting up some cash, it may fly – but the truth is, these people are in the minority.

5. Surround Yourself with People Who Know What They're Doing

It can sometimes be tempting, because it feels more comfortable and less intimidating, to work with mates or people you know are not the best in the world but are fun and easy to get on with. This can be a mistake and it's a rut you might find yourself in for some time until you branch out and approach people outside of your circle. Make sure you have a business partner who complements your skillset. In other words, someone who knows the stuff you don't know, inside out. More often than not with creative companies, this means getting someone in who is comfortable with the numbers.

6. Be Collaborative

The digital age has heralded a new and in my view very welcome shift in attitude towards collaboration and sharing rather than competition and suspiciously holding your cards to your chest. Cooperatives are popping up everywhere, and the sharing economy means that you can swap skills rather than money when you are cash-strapped, and often use material for free via platforms like Creative Commons. I believe that collaboration and openness lead to a more interesting, diverse and exciting creative landscape.

7. Don't Be Too Down to Earth

Although I advise being practical in some instances, you also have to allow yourself time to be the opposite way. Where I grew up, the biggest compliment you can pay to someone's character is that they are 'down to earth', meaning they are grounded, realistic, and not too big for their boots. Sometimes this can be a limiting idea, creatively. It's a kind of Tall Poppy Syndrome where people who try to stand out or do something differently feel exposed and ridiculed. Like our education system, it's all about conformity. We all absorb the culture in which we grow up and live. So allow yourself to have absurd flights of fancy, objectively unachievable ambitions and ridiculous ideas from time to time. Have collaborators with whom you can while away afternoons in the pub planning world domination. Dare to Dream. As the old Apple ad used to say: 'Here's to the Crazy Ones!'

8. Have Heroes

It's both helpful and important to have role models and heroes you aspire to be like. It's even better if you can make contact with them and ask for their guidance; it's very flattering to be asked and you may be surprised at how receptive they are.

9. Be Adaptable

Once you get a moderate amount of success and a couple of big clients, it can be tempting to kick back and coast for a while. Unfortunately, this can quickly become a habit. Don't assume you are indispensable. Keep abreast of changes in working methods and workflow, technology, industry trends. Keep abreast of staff changes within your clients' companies and stay in touch constantly.

10. Keep Doing What You Enjoy

Too many of us soldier on in life doing what other people think we should be doing, or what we were doing before, when we have changed as people. If you suddenly realise that you'd rather be a midwife in Peru, so what? It's your business and your choice. A life well lived can mean different things to different people.

THE MANDRAKE FILMS USP

I'd like to say I set up Mandrake with a clear five-year plan but, to be honest, the first couple of years were trial and error. I started with some funding from the Irish Film Board, a start-up grant and free administration help from the Innovatory Fund in East London and a commission from the Wellcome Trust. This was enough to get me through the first several months, pay myself a small salary from projects run from home, hire freelance crew and work out what to do next. I was also lucky enough to have contacts who were media lawyers and could advise me for free on some company law, but essentially I was learning on the job and pitching and networking like crazy.

This was an exciting time of intense creativity and energy, with scores of ideas simmering, and I made some great contacts and also partnerships that, with hindsight, were probably not the best idea. My first business partner and co-director was a fiction film director and personal friend with whom I had a few drama projects in development. We came to realise after the first year that we were going in different directions and did not have complementary skills. It was a rather messy process to part ways and taught me some valuable lessons. It also gave me a clearer focus about the direction I wanted the company to go in. Around this time I managed to find a private investor, a contact made through one of our drama projects, who was willing to take a small share in the company to help us drive forward. This allowed for some freedom to hire longer-term development and production staff to keep the momentum going, and realise some ideas.

Having straddled drama and factual during my career up to that point, and done some drama at Mandrake, I realised that I was feeling more excited about the educational factual content, documentary and current affairs we had done and had in development than I was about the very long and arduous process of fiction development. So at this point I made a three-year creative and financial plan to go in that direction.

Our first website was pretty difficult, too. Designed for free by a friend, it was less than perfect and there was a battle to get any updates or amendments done after the initial work – which also put strain on our personal relationship. I decided to pay to get it updated professionally and that small outlay was definitely worth the money. It also meant I could take as long as was necessary to get it perfect and bug the developers as much as I needed to as they were getting paid!

At this point I was hiring enough freelance staff to start thinking about how I wanted to be as a boss, and the structure the organisation should take. Things grew organically and I realised I was more of a collaborative and non-hierarchical boss than a 'Big Cheese' type. This was partly the result of experience and growing confidence. When I first started out working on feature films and dramas as a production manager and line producer looking after large crews, I was probably a lot less approachable, because I was more insecure. However, as someone who works a lot better in small groups or one on one, it was easier for me to have a small, friendly, intimate group to work with than a larger one. With creative and business endeavours, much depends on individual personality – of the founder/managing director and of the team.

After the first three years we had a much clearer USP. Our brand was educational, human rights, specialist factual and youth-orientated as well as business-to-business content. But we could have come to this brand identity more quickly, and less painfully, with more detailed forward planning and deeper thought about appropriate partnerships.

IS THERE A RIGHT TIME TO START A BUSINESS?

When I set up in 2008, it was at the beginning of a recession in the UK after a catastrophic financial crash. Funders, investors and broadcasters were even more cautious about spending money than usual and if you had a turnover under a million, the banks didn't want to know (alas, this seems to be the case even today with many banks – no matter how much they claim to be pro small businesses). Bizarrely, this had very little influence on my decision whether to start up or not. I felt it was 'now or never' and the challenging financial times probably meant I had to be more resourceful and imaginative.

The digital age had begun, but not truly taken hold in the media industry. The prevailing attitude, at least in TV and film, was competition, hierarchy, exclusivity and keeping your cards close to your chest. The industry had its gatekeepers and cliques, commissioning editors were king, and it was still very difficult to break down social and cultural barriers. When I was a freelancer working in medium-to-large production companies between 2001 and 2006, managing directors had their top office and didn't mix much with the hoi polloi. It wasn't till I worked in a smaller company, Mosaic Films, that I saw the spirit of collaboration and community at play. Diversity was not yet a watchword, although it was very much on the radar.

Although some of this is still true in some sections of the creative industries, things are rapidly changing. Attitudes to collaboration inside businesses and between businesses are now, happily, more fluid and company structures are more influenced by non-hierarchical models. There are more opportunities to get yourself heard although, of course, this does mean you have to shout even louder. The sheer scale and volume of digital creative content has meant that the traditional gatekeepers are running to catch up and have had to let go of some of that arrogant authority. The ease of production has led to a natural increase in social, ethnic and gender diversity, which traditional media giants have had to embrace and reflect in order to survive. This has begun to trickle down throughout the industry, slowly, and also emerge itself, organically and in parallel to traditional media – although much work still needs to be done on that score.

All that being said, you have to think about how you want to structure your company based on who will be in it – numbers, job roles, levels of seniority and autonomy, and what your ultimate goals are.

PRIORITISING DIVERSITY

This is something close to my heart and so important for creative businesses today, so I wanted to put it right up front. It is something you should be thinking about when forming your company. In my view, creative industries should reflect the global community as well as the local one and give a voice to all ethnicities, social and economic groups, gender and sexual identities, religions and non-religions, able-bodied and those with disabilities – where possible. Our culture tends to do this more naturally now that the digital age has truly bedded in, because it's simply easier for people to access technology – but in the creative industries generally, and especially in more mainstream ones, we are nowhere near where we need to be yet.

Of course, socio-economic factors and disenfranchised, marginalised or stigmatised groups within all cultures still make it difficult for some people to speak, creatively or otherwise. I come from a Western cultural perspective, because that is the one I know and have mostly worked in. There are variations. But creativity itself is universal, and all industries include some element of it – not just the official 'creative industries' such as digital content, film and TV, music, publishing, theatre and art. The huge global popularity of these officially sanctioned creative careers, however, means they have a chance to lead the way in reflecting and discussing who we are in the twenty-first century.

There has been a feeling of lip service to diversity from the media industry over the last ten years but now digital content has moved on from 'observing' or telling stories about marginalised communities, to those people telling their own stories in their own voice. Within digital film and TV, networks such as Al Jazeera English and Vice have led the way, in using reporters who live in the regions they are reporting on, rather than flying a Western journalist in to tell their story.

Online channels, like My Genderation by Fox Fisher, feature films made by, as well as just looking at, the LGBTQI community, which is an important shift. UK channels like Channel 4 have used their Diversity Fund and diversity department to great effect, reaching out to smaller companies and those outside the London capital, as well as diverse ethnic and underrepresented communities, including disabled creatives and presenters. Ade Rawcliffe, creative diversity manager at C4, and Lara Akeju, project lead events and Paralympics, are constantly working on projects that broaden our outlook and horizons.

Directors UK released a report in May 2016, 'Cut Out of the Picture', about the disparity between male and female directors across genres, which has some shocking statistics. In digital agencies and the games industry, there is also a notable lack of gender diversity. Organisations such as Raising Films are tackling these issues, and have finally given an industry voice to mothers who want flexibility in their work because of childcare or just shifting priorities. Women in Film and Television have done a brilliant job of encouraging women in the film and TV industry through large networks, events and initiatives like their mentoring scheme, led by Nicola Lees, which is aimed at mid-career-level women who have already established themselves but want to make a change and support each other through their careers. Having been briefly involved with this scheme myself, I know what a fantastic support network it offers.

The Creative Diversity Network (CDN) has highlighted the importance of featuring different ethnicities on-screen and behind it and in 2016 they launched Project Diamond, which is, their website states:

> a new industry-wide diversity monitoring system created by broadcasters BBC, Channel 4, ITV and Sky, and supported by Pact and Creative Skillset, through the CDN. It will provide detailed, consistent and comprehensive monitoring and reporting of diversity ... TV needs diversity at its very core to reflect society.

....

CASE STUDY:
FEMALE-LED START-UP AEGIS FILM PRODUCTIONS LTD

Athena Mandis is convenor of the documentary MA and lecturer in screenwriting at Queen Mary, University of London. She set up production company Aegis Film Productions as a funding vehicle for personally generated film, corporate and charity work. Being accepted onto a film scheme specifically targeted at female directors, producers and writers gave her the confidence to set up a limited company after doing projects as a freelancer or through the university for years. Athena says:

> I was fortunate to be selected as one of 12 female filmmakers on the Filmonomics Programme 2015 run by Mia Bays. This group of women have provided a network of collaborators but more importantly they have made me feel part of a supportive, dynamic filmmaking community. As a mother, it can be difficult starting up a business. A lot of events happen in the evening, so it is not always easy to attend because of childcare issues. I would personally like more events to be held during the daytime. I have also faced personal challenges to do with lack of belief in myself, which the Filmonomics scheme really helped me with.

Currently Aegis are producing a documentary on UK Armenians and World War I and have two features in development: one (*Anatolian Skies*) has been shortlisted for the Sundance Screenwriters Lab 2017; the other (*Greek Lanes*) has a proof-of-concept short (*Southgate to Brighton*) in production.

....

YOUR ORGANISATIONAL STRUCTURE

Traditionally, companies have been structured in quite a rigid, hierarchical way called the 'pyramid structure'. This means a narrow concentration of power at the top that trickles down to the subordinate levels – in other words, power, authority and input are centralised around the MD/CEO and board-level directors. This is still the case with many large, medium and small companies today but, in the digital age, non-hierarchical structures are much more popular, too. Non-hierarchical leadership flattens the pyramid to form a structure with decentralised authority and fewer levels – allowing more employees to have input into company ideas, and more responsibility for their roles.

Steve Jobs at Apple famously based his company structure on that of the Walt Disney Company because he thought it was the best way to maximise creativity. Although there is still a hierarchy with this model, it is a more organic and overlapping structure that allows employees to have input into company ideas and USP. Most digital companies function this way today.

Of course, many of the smaller, more agile creative companies that exist today work much better with an organic, collaborative structure because there are fewer staff involved anyway.

Think about the personalities of the key players here, too. Do they work better on their own, or as a team? Is your job the kind that needs a lot of concentrated thinking and planning time, or is it more front of house, interacting with staff? How do staff feel about the company structure?

Google headquarters in Dublin, Ireland have a 'nested' approach to work spaces, with closed rooms of between six and eight people as well as more open areas. They are taking a lead from anthropological research which indicates that seven people is the ideal number for a sense of community, security, belonging and productive collaboration within work culture without the need for a strict hierarchy. These smaller groups function within larger 'tribes' of up to 150 people in the building.

RISKS AND REWARDS WITH BOTH STRUCTURES

The advantage of the more traditional hierarchical structure is that the power belongs to the office more than the individual – meaning that if those at the top are not doing their jobs properly, they are more likely to be made accountable for it and less likely to abuse their power. Also, roles are very clearly defined, and career pathways clear. Accountability and chain of command are obvious, giving a certain amount of security and less big responsibility to employees who may not be comfortable with it. There is less opportunity for collaboration and openness and feeling part of the company as a whole, because each person is working within their established niche and this can breed competition, cliques and infighting.

With a less formal, more collaborative structure there is a lot more opportunity for diversity of thought and therefore creativity. Employees feel valued as parts of the whole rather than just working within their niche, which may embolden them to contribute things the MD and senior team hadn't thought of. Younger people, such as graduate interns or assistants, can be invaluable here because they are tapped into networks within their age demographic that more senior people may have lost touch with. Resources can be shared openly and can sometimes lead to unexpected leaps forward. However, these structures can lead to a corrosive lack of clarity and direction, or employees and directors overstepping the mark, unless the MD and senior team can clearly communicate boundaries at the same time as being democratic and open. Sometimes too much responsibility for a project on more junior staff members makes them self-sabotage because they are not ready for it. As a founder/MD, you need to look out for this stuff, deal with it immediately and manage it well on an ongoing basis.

In all cases, it is wise to have an experienced, independent board behind you. I will talk about company boards in the next chapter.

INTERVIEW WITH JAKE DUBBINS,
CO-FOUNDER AND MD OF DIGITAL BRAND ENTERTAINMENT AGENCY MEDIA BOUNTY

When did you set up Media Bounty and what do you do?

We started in 2008 with three founding partners who are still the board and we've morphed from a bespoke PR company to being a brand entertainment agency, effectively a modern ad agency. We do video, audiovisual content and social media for a bunch of big brands and then get the content seen across various platforms by the right person at the right time.

We all came out of a business that went bust so there was a decision to be made as to whether we go and get jobs or whether three crucial people in that business go and set up themselves. Over a pint and several glasses of wine we decided we could probably do this better than it's being done at the moment. We had an accountant that we knew, he introduced us to a lawyer and we set up the URLs and started trading very quickly, with a couple of clients we'd known for a long time. So we already had an element of revenue.

Because it was 2008 and banks were not lending money, we all went for personal loans. I went and said I needed money for a new car, my colleague said she needed money for home improvements, and my other partner and founder went to the Bank of Mum and Dad. So we had three months of cash from this and, obviously, if it had all gone wrong we would be in a lot of bother – but fortunately it went right!

You've got to do what it takes, if you have no other route. We went to friends who had more money than we did; we investigated getting a business loan but the climate wasn't there, so if we hadn't taken a personal risk it couldn't have happened.

Because it had come from somewhere you knew it was viable; it wasn't a complete unknown.

Yes, but I don't think many people set up a business that they don't think is viable; it's got to be a calculated risk as opposed to 'fuck it, I don't know what's going to happen' – otherwise you run out of money very quickly.

So were your co-founders colleagues, friends or both?

Colleagues in the previous business. One was a university friend whom I had recruited into the previous business, and Emma I had worked with for the best part of six years. So I knew them both well.

Do you feel that your roles complement each other and it all works, or did it take a bit of developing over the years?

It's taken some sorting out over the years. We ran by committee at first and, sometimes, when you run something with no structure at board level you run the risk of inertia, because the person who says no is de facto running the company.

When you say there was no structure, what exactly do you mean?

It was three directors on an even keel. So there was a consultant that approached us and he came in and did a lot of personality profiles, interviewed us all to then make a pretty strong recommendation as to how we should structure ourselves.

So have you picked someone to be in charge?

Yes

And that's you?

Yes

And has that worked? It's a tricky transition!

It has but it took time. People need to think about that as early as possible, i.e. how something is structured, because if you do it halfway through there are always going to be challenges because there's history. I would do that earlier if I was to do it again.

So what are your official roles now?

I'm MD, Matt is client services director and Emma is a hybrid of insights director, HR director and operations director.

Would you recommend, if someone is setting up with their mates, getting a consultant in to do that because it's an objective opinion?

Yes, definitely. When you set up you've got to park your egos at the door and say 'what is the best make-up of the characters in the business?' Because it could end up as a competition between you. Objective advice from somebody who has been in business for a few years and so can give good advice – that's a good starting position. We only did job descriptions three years ago and if we had done that earlier it would have been a clearer way of working.

What was your vision at the beginning?

Naively, we did what we knew, so we had run a lot of media competitions and radio interviews and the naive vision was 'this will probably work, we will probably be able to sell it in five years'. We are now seven and a half years in, have changed the business immensely and are now in a good position to work with big brands at a higher level because we're offering a much more strategic and creative package rather than a tactical, short-term 'solve a problem here and now'. It's more about the whole business or brand and communicating that to the target audience.

Unless you've got a piece of tech, it takes time to get to exit – the FBs, Twitters, Snapchats are very few and far between where they sell very quickly and make lots of money. When you're in your late twenties and quite naive about business you think it's going to be easy – and it ain't. You've got to find your feet.

Do you still aim to sell in the future or will you stay with the company?

Possibly. I'm open-minded about it – it's a judgement call if and when that happens. We're still in the process of trying to grow the business but I'd be lying if I said that if a good offer was put on the table I wouldn't consider it. I can't see that happening for the next few years.

Talk about your team now – who else is there in the office?

There's a senior team of five: head of strategy, two account directors, HOD in charge of audiovisual, and head of media. There's also a client services team and we're now 23 people. Building that senior team has been critical. Once you start growing you can't manage everybody so you need senior people whom you trust but who do parts of the job better than you do, so you've got that mix of skills that frees up people like me to work on the business rather than just in the business. If you don't have people you trust that do a great job and give a shit then it's very difficult to work on the business – you end up spending all your time working in the business. I'm trying to grow the business and see the bigger picture as opposed to being constantly at the coalface.

Did you have job descriptions for all those people or was it more organic?

Bit of both. We made quite a lot of mistakes. Mainly we hired the right people and those people are still there but we also hired the wrong people, too, and had to part company. Part of growing a business is that some of it you'll get right and some of it you'll screw up – it's about learning from the screw-ups so you don't do it again. A lot of it has been organic because four out of the five senior people have been with us for more than two years and have been promoted into these more senior positions, so they know the business well.

Who are your main clients – and what is the spread of clients?

We used to over-rely on one or two clients; the spread is now a lot better. We've moved from being project-based to having longer-term relationships with some of our key clients. Clients include SCA

(Bodyform, Plenty, Tena), Velvet, Colgate, Palmolive, Direct Line, Boots, Siemens, Celetrens who distribute drinks brands, Luxado in Italy.

Did you make a conscious decision that the business was more stable with a spread of clients?

If you're complacent then you're much more at risk than if you're aware of it and work hard to grow other opportunities. If that client had walked out three or four years ago we'd have probably been bust or we'd have had to really downscale quickly, whereas now we're in a position where if we lost a big client we'd be fine. That allows you to lose less hair. It's a balance about making sure the relationships are with the right stakeholders within the businesses as well, because those people can change and affect the company's relation to the business. We need to know how the politics of big business works and how their external and internal structures work.

Our turnover is all client-based. No investors. We've put a lot of profit back into the business to make sure we've always had a buffer cash reserve. We've been very lucky in that we did that quite early and we've never had a situation where we're saying: 'how the hell are we going to pay people?'

What advice would you give in terms of retaining money in the business over the years when you're not getting a huge amount of turnover?

Between three and six months of admin cash or on your balance sheet to cover your run rate; easily digestible management accounts so you understand as quickly as possible whether you're overspending somewhere; a robust forecast and budget so you understand what's coming down the track. This is easy to say in hindsight and we've done it as we've gone along – but if I was to do it again those are the things I'd put in straight away. All about having the right information to be able to make the right decisions.

What is the culture of your company?

The culture is a bunch of people who are fun to work with and really care. It's not just a job. One of our values is we give a shit about people we work with and clients we work with. We have a charity partner. It's quite flat in terms of ideas and where they come from. We don't have a 'creative' department. There's no creative director so nobody has that ultimate responsibility. We run open creative sessions, in an ego-free environment, where no idea's a bad idea. Then we go back to present to the client three or four ideas from a brainstorm of 25. If creativity is always 'owned' by one department then you don't encourage creativity elsewhere.

How has the digital space changed since you've set up?

It's now changed to the point where platform is becoming irrelevant. If you produce good content that is then optimised for platforms, that's the trick. The mobile is where people now consume a lot of content – a certain demographic don't watch traditional broadcast TV any more, so whether you're making TV film or short-form ads it's about the quality of the content, then getting it distributed to people as opposed to hoping that, for example, C4 will just commission it. Rather than one or two gatekeepers, it's a much broader idea. It's very consumer-first – are they on Instagram, Snapchat, YouTube, etc. so you can have a suite of assets that are not just cutdowns but thought about in terms of story – beginning, middle and end – for that platform? Mobile, social networks on those devices, increasingly Snapchat; video is exploding and continues to do so because it has been the best way of delivering messages since the fifties when TV came out.

Who is your charity partner?

It's an organisation called World Land Trust. We did some consultancy for them, but for every piece of work we do, we fund the purchase of one or more acres of threatened habitat. They work with local NGOs globally. Its patrons are David Attenborough and Chris Packham. It's about making sure we're not just using the planet as a resource. They obviously had to vet us and make sure we're a viable business, because your logo is on their site, etc. Over years we've given tens of thousands of pounds to them.

What lessons have you learned running a business for several years?

Budget together as early as possible; make sure you're on top of expenditure to allow quick growth; the mantra for any business is surround yourself with successful people. Starting out, what you don't know is a lot more than what you do know and you can avoid making mistakes by talking to people who have done it before. If you think you know it all you'll screw it up pretty quickly. Don't be afraid to make mistakes and try new things. If you start a business you're taking a risk. The market does not stand still – change your offer as you go along.

What does the future hold for Media Bounty and is it a positive future for start-ups?

We will be producing more and more content, but the right content – not just content for the sake of it. The spirit of collaboration is very good at the moment. Bigger businesses are more monolithic and they're very protective whereas we've grown up a bit over the last seven years. Now, if we don't do something, we'll recommend partners to fill the gaps – a collaboration between two companies providing a solution rather than a one-stop shop claiming to do everything. You've got to understand the market but I think it's a good time to set up and then collaborate with the right people.

Collaboration is a much more positive culture. We've tried to do too much before focusing on what we're good at and then collaborating. If you work with businesses in a non-competitive way then everyone learns a lot.

SETTING UP YOUR LIMITED COMPANY;
BUSINESS PARTNERSHIPS;
COMPANY LEGAL STRUCTURES

Buying a company off the shelf in the UK couldn't be easier. It's simply a case of picking a name (checking first on the Companies House website to see if there are any other UK companies with this name before buying your web domain), nominating a secretary if you choose to have one, getting together your Memorandum and Articles, and paying £40 by post or a mere £12 online at Companies House to register your shiny new company.

How exciting! Now comes the hard bit. How will you structure your company, and who will be involved? A word of warning: think hard before setting up with your mates. When things get rocky or you simply can't agree about the creative or financial direction, it could affect your friendship. As discussed in the previous chapter, I've been there! What if the closeness of your relationship means you can't be honest with your business partner for fear of offending them? What if your shared history and intimacy allows for a degree of control over each other that is not healthy in a business context? Often a better option is a colleague whom you trust and get on with and who has the kind of experience that will add value.

You can be limited by shares or guarantee, or be a partnership. Make sure you research this thoroughly. Are you starting out with capital, and if so where is this coming from? You also have to decide how to divide ownership, who has voting rights and who doesn't, who is managing director and therefore responsible for the day-to-day running of the company, and many more details.

We will look at alternative company structures such as Limited Liability Partnerships and non-profit structures later in this chapter, and much of what is covered also applies to them. For the most part, though, I am speaking of private companies limited by shares because this is still how most small and medium-sized companies are structured.

The ease with which one can become a company director is pretty surprising and very risky. It is a hell of a responsibility and requires no qualification or experience whatsoever. The only restrictions are that you have to be over 16 and not bankrupt, in prison or with a criminal record.

THE PRIVATE LIMITED COMPANY

One of the first things to do before setting up any company is think of a name, and buy the domain name for your website and online presence – checking first that there are no companies with the same name. The quickest way to do this in the UK is to go onto the Companies House Webcheck service, where all existing companies are listed, and type in the desired name. Bear in mind that you can't use names that are too similar to an existing name either. Also do a quick Google check, in case there are established sole traders (individual freelancers doing similar work) working under the same name or a very large company in another country with subsidiaries in the UK. Next check that the domain name is free. For example, if you want to call yourselves Doolally Films, you check www.doolallyfilms. com or www.doolallyfilms.co.uk. If the name is free, buying your domain is relatively inexpensive, about £20 for two years. Next, check that the name of your company doesn't contain a word you will need permission to use, for example a 'sensitive' or 'offensive' word or one that connects you to the government or local authorities.

Avoid names that are too similar to existing companies, as those companies may complain and you may have to change the name. Also, think about the connotations around your name, anything that may be misconstrued. When I first started trading my company name was 'Whipping Boy Films', which I rather liked. Unfortunately, everyone else thought we were making porn.

NAMES AND TRADEMARKS

Registering a company or partnership name or using a business name doesn't mean it's protected as a trademark – you have to register trademarks separately. First, check the Trademark Register to make sure it's not already taken.

***

Next you need to think about who will be involved with your company, what their specific role will be and how much of a share, if any, they will take.

Private companies are so called because they cannot offer their shares to the public. A private limited company must have one issued share but there is no maximum limit on the number of shares the company can issue. Private companies must include the word 'limited' at the end of their name.

You should have a board of directors to whom the managing director or chief executive officer reports. At first this can consist of just the founder and managing director but it is worth electing a board as you expand as they can be a useful resource and means of accountability. They should be experienced in business and, crucially, in your particular area of business, but have complementary experience. For example, one might come from a finance background, one from an ideas and editorial background and one from a legal background. The board is elected by the company shareholders. We will look at the board, its members and its responsibilities a bit further on.

You can also appoint a secretary, although this is not now obligatory in the UK and often in start-ups the directors do these admin duties. A secretary is responsible for the basic administration of the company, for example, Companies House documents, company returns, paperwork for company directors and shareholders, taking minutes at board meetings, etc. They are not responsible for the accounting books.

Next, think about the role you will take in this new creation. Will you be managing director or CEO (chief executive officer – this designation is used in the US and, increasingly, here) and will you have a co-director, a chairperson, a non-executive director (NED), and a creative director?

Confusingly, the title 'director' does not always mean a company director. This title is sometimes bestowed on an employee as a designation of purely internal significance, for example, 'creative director', 'account director', etc. While these people could also be company directors, they are often not.

These roles have different connotations and should be thought about carefully. Here's a quick summary of each:

MANAGING DIRECTOR (MD) AND CHIEF EXECUTIVE OFFICER (CEO)

There can be slight differences in the roles of managing director and chief executive officer in larger companies. For example, a CEO is sometimes more hands-off, working on the business, not *in* the business, and giving broad leadership and directing strategy, whereas an MD works both in and on the business. For the purposes of this book, though, I am treating the roles as more or less equal because, in the case of small-to-medium-sized businesses in the UK, most have either an MD or a CEO; it is not unheard of to have both, but it is less usual. CEO has historically been a designation more popular in the United States, but is increasingly used in the UK.

A managing director or CEO is responsible for the day-to-day running of the company and is in charge of executive decision-making. Objectively speaking, the MD's role is to direct and control the company's operations and to give strategic direction to the board to ensure that the company achieves its goals in terms of quality, delivery and finance.

In the case of a creative start-up, the founder and MD pretty much does everything, at least for the first year or so. The founder/ managing director is the heart, soul and strength of the company in its infancy and their guardianship ensures the health, or otherwise, of the organisation as it grows.

I have taken on a wide variety of tasks in my own company over the years including company administration, investor and board relations, human resources, tax, VAT and PAYE, website development, office, building and computer maintenance, as well as bringing business in and producing, directing or executive producing content. The producing I was trained in; many of these 'extras' I learned on the job out of necessity. One of the many reasons it's a good idea to have a strong board with a variety of skills and experience or co-director by your side is that they can stop you from becoming too much of a control freak. It can become difficult to cede control when you alone have held the reins, even if someone else can take care of a particular area much better than you can. Anxiety about letting other people take care of things can mean you are struggling with complex tasks that you simply have no experience of. At a certain point, delegation will become key – but not yet. In the first couple of years no one can grow your new business quite like you can, but remember to always ask for help from those who know what they are doing!

The managing director and all other members of the board need to be well versed in both their rights and their responsibilities.

There are many advantages to running your own creative business and it affords wonderful freedom and flexibility as well as creative satisfaction and a sense of achievement, but don't forget that along with that come many liabilities. You are expected to manage the company lawfully and take responsibility for any financial or executive mismanagement. Increasingly, this means that even in a 'limited liability' company, you can find yourself personally responsible for debt and mismanagement. Banks now look for personal guarantees as a matter of course, which can get you into hot water. We will go into what this can mean for a company in the third part of this book.

CHAIRPERSON

Often, smaller companies don't bother with a chairperson, but it is something to consider as you grow or if you are starting the company off with a higher budget, longer-term projects or a group of private investors (and lucky you if so!). The chairperson primarily acts as a buffer, a facilitator between managing directors or CEOs, other board members and investors. For this reason it's important that they are seasoned professionals, skilled at people management, with abundant emotional intelligence and diplomacy as well as independent industry experience and strategic insight. Generally they will have been around the block, witnessed and managed various conflict situations within companies and learned a lot about human nature in the process. Equally important with a chairperson is that they have relevant industry experience – don't go for a high-profile 'rent-a-boss' if they have not already worked for years in the environment you are now entering. No amount of sage business advice from a famous property magnate will help you navigate the tricky world of media content production. The chairperson will also organise the structure and frequency of board meetings (frequent, short meetings are generally best) and ensure that governance is meeting legal standards and financial accounts are produced on time. Look for people who have previously taken the helm at production companies or digital agencies that are the size, shape and have the back catalogue you aspire to. Getting the balance right between chairperson and managing director or CEO is also important. The chairperson is a light-touch, part-time overseer and sounding board; he or she is not running the company.

NON-EXECUTIVE DIRECTOR

Non-executive directors are directors who do not have executive powers within a company; they act in an advisory capacity only. They have a relevant business background, and may attend board meetings to offer advice or sit on committees about the conduct and pay of company directors and other senior managers. They are sometimes paid a fee for their services, sometimes not. They are not regarded as employees of a company. They can usually vote at board meetings. Something to remember is that, although non-executive directors (or NEDs) are not employees of the limited company or part of the official management team, they do have the same legal responsibilities and liabilities within the company as executive directors do. This includes being jointly liable for debt if the company gets into financial trouble or if they are charged with fraud or misconduct. This is important for NEDs to bear in mind when they agree to become part of a company as the assumption is often that they are not liable for debt or mismanagement in the way executive directors are because they are involved in the company on a much more casual basis.

FINANCE DIRECTOR

This is a board member in charge of all financial aspects of the company. The exact detail of this director's role will be outlined in the Articles of the company and will be limited to financial arrangements, i.e. much more limited than the managing director.

COMMERCIAL DIRECTOR

Initially this role often overlaps with that of the finance director but, as a company grows, it becomes more distinct. Commercial directors will deal with complex client contracts and relations, international deals, managing products and second revenue streams, and promoting the company globally.

CO-DIRECTOR

This is a board member with specific responsibilities as set out in the Memorandum and Articles, complementing the role of the managing director but more limited. Appointing the right co-director can be the difference between surviving or not in the early years – if they complement you as the managing director and you can share ideas, anxieties and responsibilities without conflict or unhealthy competition, these people are a real boon. And apart from anything else, collaborating with someone is much more fun than struggling along on your own.

CREATIVE DIRECTOR

Often, medium-sized or large creative companies will have a 'creative director'; however, this is not generally an official board position so it can be a little misleading to use this term. Be careful that people are aware they are not dealing with a member of the board management team in this case but someone who is responsible for the creative direction of the content you produce.

CHIEF CREATIVE OFFICER

This role will vary slightly depending on the type of organisation and is also usually confined to medium- and larger-sized organisations. Broadly speaking it is the person in overall charge of the identity and vision of the creative brand of a company. This person should be accountable if the standard of creative content is falling, and congratulated if it is high.

CHIEF TECHNOLOGY OFFICER

In creative companies (again, usually medium or larger in scale), the CTO is across all the technical aspects of content, facilities and company structure. They will oversee technical teams and platforms, product development, and present the narrative of the company to investors, consumers and the media from a technology point of view.

CHIEF OPERATIONAL OFFICER

Often thought of as second in command to the chief executive officer, this is a role you come across a bit less in creative companies but it still exists in the larger ones. The day-to-day duties will vary according to the priorities of the CEO and the company but the COO is in charge of making sure the organisation operates well as a whole.

MEMORANDUM OF ASSOCIATION AND ARTICLES OF ASSOCIATION

These are the foundation documents of your company, setting out who runs it and how it will be run. You can get general templates for these from Companies House and gov.uk; however, it is worth working out the structure of your company and its members in detail before putting your Memorandum and Articles together, to keep ongoing company administration to a minimum.

The Memorandum of Association is a legal statement signed by all initial shareholders, agreeing to form the company.

The Articles of Association are the written rules about running the company, agreed by the shareholders, directors and company secretary if there is one. It details the roles of the founding directors, including the managing director, so should be quite detailed.

The Memorandum can never be changed once completed but the Articles can, on the agreement of the company shareholders.

Example documents can be downloaded from the Companies House website.

COMPANIES ACT 2006

In 2006, company legislation in the UK was tightened up and reviewed in an attempt to reflect the business environment of the twenty-first century. For example, it axed the need for a company secretary, acknowledged that most company business and administration is now done online, set out a much wider context for corporate responsibility and more detail on general duties and powers for company directors. The goal of this was to enable all companies to understand their legal duties more fully, which is helpful to smaller companies without the financial resources to hire lawyers – as long as they bother to read it. This Act covers all company structures including private limited companies, public companies, charities and partnerships. Private limited companies generally have directors but charities and partnerships may, for example, use the terms 'trustee' and 'partner'.

DIRECTOR RESPONSIBILITIES AND LIABILITIES

A company limited by shares, as most are, has both directors and shareholders, although often with creative start-ups the founders are both directors and shareholders. I will go into the differences between these two entities, and the problems that can arise, later in this chapter.

Officially, directors are appointed by the company shareholders and day-to-day management of the company is delegated to the directors by them, meaning that the directors make the executive decisions. This group of directors is called the board of directors. Existing directors can then appoint additional directors according to the limits set out in the Articles of Association of the company. Those executive decisions can be overridden by a majority of the board of shareholders in the event of a conflict.

The managing director takes overall responsibility for the day-to-day running of the company; however, company directors take decisions as a board, i.e. one director cannot act alone unless he or she is the sole director of the company. The board pass changes and make decisions on a majority vote at meetings, or by signing a written resolution if they cannot be available to meet.

A director's specific duties are laid out in the Articles of Association and will vary according to the type and size of company, and the industry.

DIRECTOR'S SERVICE AGREEMENTS

An executive director, for example the managing director, will usually have a written contract of employment. This is known as a Service Agreement. A Service Agreement isn't compulsory, i.e. there is no automatic legal requirement if you are simply a director carrying out basic duties as an executive officer and taking pure director's fees (fees for carrying out those basic duties). However, because MDs have such a key role in most companies, and take a taxable wage for their work from company turnover, there should be one in place. Even if a written contract doesn't exist, one will usually be implied in law if you have a pivotal role and do a lot in the company. There is another important reason why you should be an official employee of your company. An executive director who is an employee benefits from various employment laws, including the right to a statutory minimum notice period, the right to be paid at least the national minimum wage, the right not to be unfairly dismissed, maternity and paternity pay and protection from discrimination. As many are enshrined in EU employment law, let's hope they all remain in place post-Brexit!

There are certain basic duties that come with the office of company director and must be carried out appropriately. These are called Statutory Duties.

The Statutory Duties towards the company by the managing director, according to the Companies Act 2006, include:

1. Duty to act within powers (section 171)
2. Duty to promote the success of the company (section 172)
3. Duty to exercise independent judgement (section 173)
4. Duty to exercise reasonable care, skill and diligence (section 174)
5. Duty to avoid conflicts of interest (section 175)
6. Duty not to accept benefits from third parties (section 176)
7. Duty to declare interest in proposed transaction or arrangement (sections 177 to 185)

Other general duties detailed by Companies House include the following:

- try to make the company a success, using your skills, experience and judgement
- follow the company's rules, shown in its Articles of Association
- make decisions for the benefit of the company, not yourself
- tell other shareholders if you might personally benefit from a transaction the company makes
- keep company records and report changes to Companies House and HM Revenue and Customs (HMRC)
- make sure the company's accounts are a 'true and fair view' of the business's finances
- file your accounts with Companies House and your Company Tax Return with HMRC
- pay Corporation Tax
- register for Self Assessment and send a personal Self Assessment tax return every year – unless it's a non-profit organisation (e.g. a charity) and you didn't get any pay or benefits, like a company car

Although you may hire an accountant and bookkeeper to manage many of these things day-to-day, you are ultimately legally responsible for them as a company director.

PERSONAL LIABILITY

This is something you really need to keep an eye on these days. Banks and other financiers often require personal guarantees, meaning you may be personally liable for debt the company can't pay.

In addition to that, you could become liable for outstanding PAYE payments should your company go into insolvency. I will go into more detail about company insolvency in the final chapter.

The legal firm Taylor Wessing's website details various other scenarios where company directors may find themselves liable, referencing the Company Directors Disqualification Act 1986 and the Trading Disclosures Regulations 2008.

As their information on personal liability mentions, a company director could find him or herself personally liable for:

a fine if the company does not comply with any of the requirements in The Companies (Trading Disclosures) Regulations 2008 and fails to make the trading disclosures required under those Regulations (Regulation 10 of The Companies (Trading Disclosures) Regulations 2008);

contracts signed by them purportedly on behalf of the company before its incorporation (section 51 of the Act);

if he acts in the management of the company while disqualified or acts on the instructions of someone whom he knows to be disqualified (section 15 of the Company Directors Disqualification Act 1986);

if he has previously been director of a company which has gone into insolvent liquidation and is then concerned in the carrying on by another company of business under a name which is the same as or similar to the name used by the insolvent company within 12 months before it went into liquidation (section 217 of the Insolvency Act 1986);

if he has been served with a contribution notice by The Pensions Regulator on the grounds that he has been party to, or knowingly assisted in, an act or failure to act one of the main purposes of which was to remove or reduce the requirement or ability of an employer to pay a debt due under section 75 of the Pensions Act 1995 on the winding up of a pension scheme;

for damages if he makes a fraudulent or negligent misrepresentation in the course of negotiating a contract between the company and the third party;

under the criminal offence of making a false statement as to the affairs of the company with the intent of deceiving shareholders or creditors of a company (section 19 of the Theft Act 1968);

under the criminal offences under the Fraud Act 2006;

for imprisonment (up to 10 years) or a fine if he is knowingly party to the company carrying on its business with intent to defraud creditors of the company or of another person or for any fraudulent purpose (section 993 of the Act);

under a contract if he fails to make it clear that he is contracting as an agent of the company and not personally;

to a third party for damages for breach of an implied warranty of authority if he concludes a contract on behalf of the company but exceeds his authority in so doing and the company is therefore able to set the contract aside; or

in relation to wrongful trading or fraudulent trading by the company under the Insolvency Act 1986.

CRIMINAL ACTIVITY

With regard to a criminal offence committed by a company, a company director is guilty of that offence if it can be proved he or she was aware of what was going on and did nothing, or was actively involved. They can also be guilty of 'neglect' even if they were not aware of what was going on, because they have a duty towards the company as a whole and should know what is being done in the company's name at all times.

SHAREHOLDERS AND DIRECTORS – WHAT'S THE DIFFERENCE BETWEEN THE TWO?

In a nutshell, shareholders own the company and directors run it. An individual can be both, or just one. It is not a given that company directors are shareholders, although this is often the case.

With creative companies particularly, it is often the case that two or three founders are both directors and shareholders, and divide their ownership equally. This can become problematic as the company grows, as company law requires that some decisions be made by directors, and some by shareholders. In the event of a dispute, all directors also being equal shareholders can muddy the waters to say the least.

It is a good idea to have an experienced advisory board in place to mediate such disputes, and to reflect specific duties of each in your Articles of Association.

WILL YOUR LIMITED COMPANY BE INCORPORATED BY SHARES OR GUARANTEE?

Most limited companies are incorporated by shares. This means that the company is divided up between the owners, who must agree among themselves what share in the company they receive and how they pay for that share. There is no minimum number of shareholders for private companies so there can, for example, be just one shareholder. Shares can be paid for with cash, or 'in kind' for work done within the company. There are also different classes of shares. A shares have voting rights within the company, so at board meetings they can have a say in the running of and structural changes within the company; B shares do not.

A company limited by guarantee is usually a charity or not-for-profit organisation. It has members rather than shareholders, and has no share capital to distribute (i.e. no money profit) because it is not run for profit purposes. It also has a board but they are often called a committee, and in terms of administration is very similar to a company limited by shares.

HOW DO SHARES AND VOTING RIGHTS WORK?

Shareholders may or may not have a right to vote on company matters in shareholder meetings. Under UK law the voting rights attached to any individual's shares depend on what is stipulated in the Articles of the company and any terms imposed in the shareholder contract when the shares were created. Most shareholders with ordinary shares do have voting rights, which carry one vote per share. This means that majority shareholders have a heavy influence on company structure and changes. However, there may be shares which have no voting rights or restricted rights (e.g. can only vote in certain circumstances) or may have additional voting rights (e.g. ten votes per share) or enhanced voting rights in particular circumstances.

For example, you may have a minority shareholder in the company who is also a non-executive director. She might have B shares, or non-voting shares, while you have A shares, or voting shares.

Because votes are attached per share rather than per shareholder, you work out whether you have a majority in a vote for any company change by counting the number of shares owned by each person with a vote attached to them, rather than by counting the shareholders themselves. So if someone owns 51 per cent of the company and everyone has one share one vote, they have the majority vote on an ordinary resolution.

In some circumstances a 'special resolution' may be required, meaning a 75 per cent vote is needed to pass it. This would be detailed in your company Articles and would be something fundamental to the company.

Once a majority has been established, you pass a resolution in writing. You only need a majority of shares voting to do this, and anyone not present can be informed in writing.

Share ownership also comes with rights to act in certain circumstances, under the Companies Act 2006. For example, with a five per cent stake in the company you can call a general meeting; with a ten per cent stake you can prevent a meeting being held on short notice if you cannot attend because of the notice. Make sure you look into these details before issuing shares. You can also stipulate rights in your company Articles, and your shareholder contract.

WHAT DO SHAREHOLDERS VOTE ON?

Shareholders vote on major company changes such as appointing or removing a director, directors' remuneration, major loans to directors, changing from a private to a public company, mergers and acquisitions, changing the company name or changing the Articles of Association.

PARTNERSHIPS

The Partnership Act goes back to 1890, and for some time partnerships were a popular business structure. They are more unusual these days because, as with sole traders, you have unlimited personal liability, so if there's a debt you can lose all your assets.

THE LIMITED LIABILITY PARTNERSHIP (LLP)

Limited Liability Partnerships, or LLPs, came into being in 2001 so they are a relatively new type of company structure. The administration process for setting one up is similar to a limited company in that it has to be incorporated under the LLP Act 2000, but there is a lot more flexibility in terms of running it, and a different tax liability. Although there must be at least two founding members, called partners, there are no statutory provisions for how an LLP should be managed; all details are outlined in the LLP agreement. There are no shares in the company, nor company directors; each partner is liable for Income Tax on his or her profit share, and must do an individual Self Assessment each financial year and pay Capital Gains Tax on any company assets sold. Partners are not generally PAYE employees of the company, although there can be salaried LLP members under certain specific rules. LLPs do not pay Corporation Tax or file company tax returns but they do file company accounts. There are many advantages in the freedom of structure an LLP affords for the creative company and if it is a small company with partners taking similar profits and doing an equal amount of work it can work very well. A major disadvantage in this structure is that there is no way of selling shares to an investor in return for capital when you want to grow the business, because shares don't exist.

NON-PROFIT COMPANY STRUCTURES

Sometimes, creative companies benefit from a non-profit structure because the work they are doing fits the bill, and having charitable status opens up funding from a vast array of trusts, foundations, individual donors and other organisations. Non-profit status also allows for various tax reliefs, and business rates relief.

If you are looking to make a profit quickly, grow your company and sell it for a decent return, this route is not for you – but do think about it if you want to do large-scale or long-running projects for the public benefit that need a constant trickle of funding. There is also the possibility of setting up subsidiary companies that are commercial and can put money back into the parent non-profit company, if you get to that stage. If you get it right you will be able to pay yourself a salary (albeit a fairly modest one) and do work you enjoy over a long period of time. Your company could be an official charity or another form of voluntary, not-for-profit organisation.

In order to set one up you must put together an independent board of trustees, with relevant skills, who are generally unpaid. It's important that trustees take their job seriously, as they may be liable for any major mistakes made by the organisation or for criminal and fraudulent activity. You must then meet certain requirements that your organisation carries out work that is for the public benefit. You can do this on the gov.uk website at: gov.uk/government/collections/charitable-purposes-and-public-benefit. There is very heavy regulation and additional company legislation around non-profit organisations that must be adhered to and it does restrict what you can do, not only in terms of content but in terms of extra admin needed to fulfil transparency and governance requirements.

Next choose a name and company structure. You can set up a Charitable Incorporated Organisation (CIO), or a Charitable

Organisation. Both these legal entities confer limited liability, as with a limited company, unless the trustees sign personal guarantees. CIO is a relatively new charitable structure, giving limited liability to the directors but also being outside of the Companies House and Companies Act structure, allowing more freedom of management. The final step is to register with the Charity Commission.

I have worked for a few non-profit creative companies myself, and always found them inspiring and enjoyable places to be. The only downside is that everyone must be extremely passionate about what they are doing in order to keep the organisation afloat, in the absence of the much easier commercial imperative (i.e. cold, hard, cash profit), and motivation in the work force can often flag. Complacency and idleness are sometimes an issue also, with company cultures often being softer and less competitive than in commercial organisations. It's important that those in the most senior roles of these organisations keep morale up, keep the company identity and cohesiveness strong, and keep caring about what they are doing.

SOCIAL ENTERPRISES

These organisations can be for-profit or not-for-profit. They are not a separate legal entity in the UK, so they use existing legal company structures and identify as social enterprises for specific corporate identity, funding and tax purposes. Broadly speaking, social enterprises are set up with specific social, educational or environmental goals in mind, and the aim of profit-making organisations is to reinvest profits in the social enterprise itself or the community or cause it was set up to serve. Because these organisations have now been around for some time, there are some funding sources tailored towards them including community development finance institutions (CDFIs) and social impact investors – for example, venture philanthropy. Social enterprises can also benefit from social investment tax relief (SITR), which has been designed to encourage individual investors to support social enterprise, in return for relief on Income Tax and deferral of Capital Gains Tax.

> ➤ Examples of a Shareholders' Contract (p.272) and Start-Up
> Company Resolution (p.287) can be found in the Appendices
> at the end of this book

INTERVIEW WITH CLIVE J HALPERIN,
PARTNER, GSC SOLICITORS LLP

Describe what you do with a business

I help businesses structure themselves, for example, working out how their shareholding and governance works, and bringing shareholders in. Then, through the life of their company, I advise on how they control and protect their IP, how they exploit it, general business advice and advice on contracts for staff, clients and suppliers.

Sometimes I'm troubleshooting behind the scenes, for example, trying to resolve issues arising in the business without necessarily interfering directly or telling the client how to run their business. Clients are much better at running their businesses than lawyers. For example, lawyers are often very risk averse and that's often a criticism. So I try and balance risk and try to help clients realise their ambitions. You can't expect every eventuality to be protected against, all business has risk. Often entrepreneurs have taken huge risks, for example, they may have dropped out of Harvard like Mark Zuckerberg and Bill Gates.

At the end of a business cycle, clients are often looking for an exit such as a sale or sometimes it's simply succession planning, or even an orderly wind-up. Then there's all the law stuff along the way such as employment, landlord and tenant, and so on.

How are most of your clients structured?

Most of the people coming to me with creative businesses structure themselves as limited companies. You tend to see Limited Liability Partnerships (LLPs) much more rarely and these days it is rare to see a traditional partnership. LLPs are often used for tax-specific reasons.

There are many advantages to being a limited company. It is an established mechanism for attracting investors and helps limit personal liability. One thing to bear in mind is that banks will often ask for personal guarantees for overdrafts for creative companies because your only asset is you. Overdrafts are on demand so banks can call you up in the morning and ask for their money back.

Shareholders can share the profit as dividends and typically, on a sale, will get their share of the value of the business. How shareholdings should be split is often a matter that is argued about – what is the respective contribution of the founders or shareholders?

Often people who approach me when setting up in business haven't thought about that. At the outset there's often not much money involved and people are relaxed about these things. But it's critical to think about how you are going to share the profits, how they will be taken out (e.g. salary or dividends) and if there is a sale how will the proceeds be shared? Often people in creative companies want to be treated equally, for example, 50/50 or a third each with three founders.

However, like a pre-nuptial agreement with a marriage, in business it makes a lot of sense to give some thought to how you should deal with a break-up or if things don't work out. It may be that you decide not to do anything about it but it's sensible to think it through.

Do you see a mix of founders?

Very few creative companies have a finance person on board when they start up. Often when people are starting up money is tight and they can't afford to invest in that kind of resource or they choose to have equipment, a website or other technology over finance support. That's understandable, but finance and budgeting for a business is so important. How much are we going to need to get through the first 12 months? What do we need in terms of working capital to get to where we want to be in a year? How are we going to live without any income? Are we going to be working part-time in another job when we're setting this up, etc., etc. Many start-ups don't succeed because they don't have enough money to see them through those initial stages.

If you're running a marketing agency you might be able to get clients in quite quickly and generate revenue. If you're producing a film or video, it's often a longer haul requiring lots of self-funding for filming, equipment hire, clearances and so on before any money can be generated.

Be careful about just starting your business on a wing and a prayer, and hope. This happens a lot in creative industries like film, music, and software and app development – they are very speculative and uncertain. That's not to say that no businesses succeed this way but it makes it much harder.

Lots of businesses are unstable in the beginning, not just creative industries. If I open a café I don't know if people will walk through my front door or if Starbucks will open up across the road or next door. With many creative companies there is no shopfront as such – other than an online presence, their main assets are their creative ability and some IP. Often it is this that becomes very valuable, such as their brand and visual identity.

I have had funders pull out quite far down the line of a programme on a whim, and I don't think that would happen with non-ideas-based, more tangible businesses.

Funders in these areas may find that easier to do because they haven't got a finished product to look at. This does happen with businesses producing something more traditional but not so often. Perhaps that risk is why many new creative businesses are looking at newer types of business models. YouTube was only founded in 2005 and yet now there are huge YouTube stars generating significant revenue. And the same goes for other channels to market of creative material such as films and programmes being commissioned by non-traditional outlets such as Netflix and Amazon Video and some Instagram channels with millions of followers. Some of these are short-lived, such as Vine, but even in a relatively short period while that service was live, there were plenty of creative people generating significant revenue.

What legal documents should be drawn up at the beginning of a company's life?

A lawyer would always advise that all of the initial agreements should be documented in a formal way to help avoid dispute and uncertainty and that's commonly called a shareholders' agreement. That would typically deal with the details of how a company should operate, and how you might deal with deadlocks between the shareholders (for example, in a 50/50 company with equal shareholders). Examples of deadlock scenarios might be: 'I want to make that film, you don't', 'I want to employ that person, you don't'. There are a number of ways of dealing with this. For example, you can give someone the final decision or you can have a mechanism where one of you can buy out the other and there is a way to separate. I have seen some terrible cases where there is deadlock and the shareholders have fallen out. In these cases the operation of the company can be frustrated by a shareholder and it can't operate properly. If the company has real value in its assets or other IP or even liabilities it's a real pain to resolve this and the court won't readily intervene to sort that out – it's often a very expensive and uncertain process to get these issues resolved. So it's really good advice to work out how you want to resolve differences up front, and document that in a binding way.

I can't emphasise this strongly enough. In these situations, people aren't always rational. Typically I will see people coming to me at the outset of the relationship and saying, 'We'll sort it out. We're both commercial people.' But sometimes what happens is people become bitter and irrational. It can be driven by jealousy, resentment or other matters. As you go through the life of a business there will be times when one partner feels he or she is contributing more to it than the others and vice versa. From time to time that's probably true. If this builds up over a period of time, people can become very resentful; this risk increases as the business becomes valuable – no one really fights over a worthless business for very long. And just like a relationship break-up, sometimes when you get company break-ups it's 'He said, she said', and you hear the list of complaints one side has about the other.

The ideal is to find a way of working out how you know things aren't working and how you deal with it.

One thing people often don't take into account when they're setting up is: who is their partner? Is it somebody very wealthy who doesn't need to work as hard or make as much of the business as you do, or is that person useful because they are able to fund it? When you want to sell out does that other person want to sell out? Maybe it's a kind of hobby for the other person because they've got a different income. Is it with your best friend? Might this ruin your friendship? There are a lot of factors to consider when choosing your business partner and starting up. But it's all really exciting and often not thought about properly. None of those is a reason not to do it, just things to be on top of.

Sometimes it's a good idea to decide up front how you measure if this is a success. Try and look forward and ask yourself, a year from now, how do we know that this has been a success? If it's not, should we separate or close it down? And if so how do we unwind it? You can always review this in a year but these are honest discussions to have with each other.

If you had two founders, both of whom were directors and shareholders, one of whom was an MD, how would that work in terms of making a final decision?

As a matter of law, the MD doesn't have any special powers in the event of a deadlock unless these are given to him in a shareholders' agreement or the company's Articles of Association, which contains rules about how a company is run. Sometimes the chairman of the company has what's called a casting vote. So if there's a tie, it's the chairman's decision. Very often with small companies, no one has worked out who the chairman is and second, if you have a 50/50 shareholding in a company, you probably don't want to give the other shareholder or somebody else that casting vote. You probably just want to have a mechanism to separate if you have irreconcilable differences. In some cases a trusted third party can be empowered to make a decision in these cases, but even then a properly advised shareholder will want a list of key decisions that can't be decided upon without his consent (for example, dilution of his shareholding). It's important though to realise that there is no one-size-fits-all. So much depends on the type of business, who is involved and what the aspirations of the shareholders are.

What about legal issues once your company has been trading for a while?

Once you have been going for a while and you're in profit, you might bring in more shareholders or investors. Often those shareholders or investors will want to have contracts which adjust the rights of the shareholders. So if you're a 50/50 shareholder at the outset and somebody else comes in, you're all going to become minority shareholders (holding less than 50 per cent). This needs to be looked at in a lot of detail to protect everyone so that, for example, you can't be kicked out on a whim. As a minority shareholder you need to make sure that you've got protection against the other shareholders ganging up on you.

Companies may also want to have some employee shareholders to incentivise people to stay in the company, often done through specific types of option schemes to make it tax-effective.

As your company gets bigger you may also have lots of other legal issues such as general contracts, HR, landlord and tenant, pensions and so on to be taken care of (now even small businesses have to have pensions). The shareholders may start to focus on their own personal requirements such as wills.

Many companies just carry on in this way until the founders retire. In other cases, there is a plan to sell at some stage in the future at a target price. Often bigger companies want to acquire creative companies. Sometimes that's done out of the blue so I get clients who call me saying 'we've received an approach'. Others clients are very systematic about it and actively seek a buyer or even a stock market flotation. If this is the goal, there are steps that can be taken to make a company more attractive and a methodology to be followed. It's a bit like selling a house – you need to decorate your house and make sure it's in good repair, then seek a buyer. This can be done yourself but often businesses appoint someone to do this for them as it's more confidential. With a business, confidentiality is often key so as not to disrupt or damage the business in the process. At the end of this, shareholders will be able to realise, in a tax-efficient way, a capital amount of money. Often that exit process requires staying on for a year or two years, particularly with creative industries, where some of the price is dependent on future performance. Often that's called an earn out.

If you want to close a company down and it's solvent, you can just wind it up and your accountant can sort it out usually. If it's insolvent, it's very important to speak to your accountant and get some expert advice because trading while insolvent can incur personal liability and result in bans as a company director and convictions.

How would you value a digital company if it was starting up? What is Intellectual Property?

A start-up doesn't usually have value but broadly IP is copyright, trademarks, design rights (i.e. physical objects in the world), patents and know-how/trade secrets. For most creative industries it's copyright (film, photos, words on a website, scripts, music and lyrics, computer software, branding logos, trademarks which form the backbone of the IP). Value, though, is often difficult to measure with creative industries. There are many stories of software and apps being sold or invested in for huge valuations even though there is no profit, sometimes no revenue and in some cases (e.g. Siri) before the product has launched.

Things to think about with IP:

- Who creates it?
- Who owns it?

This should be very carefully documented. For example, a lot of companies get people to design their website and logo but don't get a transfer of the rights to them. That means the ownership is with the people who designed them. There have been famous court cases like the Dr Martens logo where that wasn't dealt with properly. Unless you're an employee, the person that creates the IP is the person who owns it. This may includes DoPs. These issues can be covered in a freelance contract to make sure the production company owns those rights. In fashion photography the custom is that the photographer retains the rights, so you have to get the correct rights to use that in your ad campaign. A good tip is to think, if you're not going to own all the rights in every medium, how much is it going to cost you if you want to extend your usage?

A lot of creative companies are also not aware of what they can keep and negotiate on and what's market norm. For example, if using a famous song in an ad campaign, people often don't realise that, unless they limit it by time and media, the cost of it may be prohibitive.

How is skillset quantified in valuing a company?

There isn't a one-size-fits-all for valuing companies. If you've got a famous brand the brand may be valued based on, for example, historical sales or the perceived value of the future exploitation rights (e.g. merchandising for *Star Wars*). If all you've got are the people in the office, and what they are creating they don't retain because they give a buy-out to their clients, then the value of the business is probably the so-called 'goodwill' and your good clients, who have used you for a few years, continuing to use your services. Companies are often valued on a multiple of their historic profits. Company valuation is a very specialised area and there are a wide variety of factors that come into play.

Is part of your role to say what you think a company is worth?

Lawyers wouldn't typically do that as they are not really qualified to do so. They would get accountants, company valuation experts or corporate finance advisors to do that. Although ideas of value (often based on other similar transactions) can be identified in some cases, if there are several potential buyers the price can be driven up. Each deal is different because each business is different.

What are the best opportunities for monetising digital content now?

A lot of the people who are predicting what's happening now aren't going to get it right. I mentioned Vine earlier, which looked like it might be a key market but now it's being closed down. Over the last two years in music, it's gone from downloading to streaming in a huge way and that's happening in film and TV now, too. People are moving away from physically buying things – perhaps with the exception of traditional book publishing. You might have thought that the Kindle would have crashed the printed book industry the way downloads and streaming did with music but that doesn't seem to have happened. The jury is still out on how to monetise music. Taylor Swift said, 'You can't listen to my song on Spotify, you've got to buy it on iTunes.' Adele also refused to let her album *25* be streamed on Spotify. But if you're a new artist you're not going to do that. You need traction and can't limit your market. There's an emerging 'freemium model' where a lot of effort is being put into trying to migrate consumers from a free service (often ad-backed) back to a pay/subscription model. Your music has to have a lot of streams to make a lot of money.

With film there are more and more channels on satellite and cable but there are fewer viewers for each channel. If you're a filmmaker, going forward you're probably going to expect to have your film on Netflix or Amazon and perhaps even have it commissioned by them.

Other new forms of digital content monetisation are cropping up all the time. Producing clickbait and other online content is generating revenue-creating web and mobile traffic. Snapchat is really starting to take off with commercial companies.

And the way people are consuming media is changing, which provides other opportunities. Many people are now watching TV at the same time as looking at their phone and are not consuming media in the way that broadcasters and advertisers want them to. Monetising this 'second screen' effect is still being worked on. Broadcasters have got a big challenge in a fragmented market.

Virtual reality and augmented reality are going to take off in the next few years as the size, bulkiness and cost of these devices decrease. People will probably be willing to pay a premium for these types of experiences. New tech is providing lots of opportunities for content providers and creatives across all sectors. A big target for creative industries in the next three to five years will be to be involved in this sector. Already this augmented reality effect is becoming widely known. As well as Pokémon, there are apps that allow you to see furniture from a catalogue in your own room before you buy it, and with some cars you hold up your phone to the car and it will tell you what every button does without a book. All of these areas are huge sectors for creative industries ranging from animation to computer software development.

What advice would you give to creative entrepreneurs?

I would say the following:

- Set up your business structure properly
- Protect your IP and your confidential information
- Make sure you own the IP you think you own
- Document how you are going to exploit your intellectual property and skills
- Keep innovating and be adaptable because everything is moving very quickly
- Not everything is going to work first time!

HMRC COMES CALLING!

And believe me, they always do. As a business owner you must learn to deal with Her Majesty's Revenue and Customs effectively, even if you never quite learn to love them.

As part of this process you will need to hire an accountant. Make sure this person or company has experience of dealing with your kind of work, as media production is not your traditional business model. Meet different companies until you find one that feels like a good fit.

If you are a creative type, the avalanche of administration is the worst part of running any company. If I could do it over again I would spend far more time than I did finding a really good, hands-on company secretary, a solid, loyal bookkeeper, and a decent financial advisor.

When you are starting out, though, it's often you doing the hard graft until you get enough capital in the business to hire these people. In this scenario it's a case of learning on the job, and keeping on top of the admin no matter how strong the urge to stuff it all into a nice, big, ten-pence Sainsbury's carrier bag and think about it later (this I know). Dealing with VAT, PAYE, National Insurance, tax returns and the like is a lot easier when you are not in panic mode – which you will be if you wait for those warning letters to land on your mat.

REGISTERING YOUR BUSINESS FOR CORPORATION TAX AND OTHER SERVICES ONLINE

You need to register for Corporation Tax ideally as soon as you start to trade, and legally within three months. You will be penalised for late registration! Corporation Tax is a tax paid on profits by companies in the UK. So you only pay it if your company is in profit at the end of the tax year.

After incorporation, HMRC will send you a Unique Taxpayer Reference in the post, and you can register online at gov.uk.

Other things to register for as a company director include:

SELF ASSESSMENT

As a company office holder, you have to submit a Self Assessment tax return online every year. What you enter on the assessment will depend on the legal structure of your business, how you pay yourself within the business, and whether you have any additional employment or self-employment outside of the business.

VALUE ADDED TAX (VAT)

This is a tax on goods and services. You add 20 per cent for VAT on to your outgoing invoices to your clients, and your customers add VAT to their invoices to you. Whatever the balance is between these two amounts, you pay to HMRC or they pay back to you. It is a good idea to register for VAT as most of your customers and clients will be VAT-registered.

Often, even small companies will voluntarily register for VAT because their suppliers will charge it and they will therefore be paying it out and need to be able to claim some back.

Companies have to register once their annual turnover of VAT taxable income exceeds a certain amount (which in 2016/17 was £83,000).

You only need to register in the country where your business is incorporated.

PAY AS YOU EARN (PAYE)

If you plan to pay yourself a salary as an employee of the company or will have staff, you pay this way. This is a system for paying Income Tax and National Insurance to the government, from your gross salary. You can find out how much tax and National Insurance are owed by using the HMRC tax calculators, or ask your accountant to do your payroll so they are responsible for working out your tax liabilities and submitting your tax returns.

Happily, these can all now be registered for and managed online and you have your own dedicated web portal that will show you exactly where you are with each service.

TAKING MONEY OUT OF A LIMITED COMPANY

When you first start getting revenue into your company, it can be a little intoxicating. The temptation to break out the company credit card when something twinkles at you from the shelves of your favourite store, or eat out at your favourite expensive deli every day, or swan about town in a taxi in the early hours, can be rather strong. This is your company, and your money – what freedom and independence! But beware, there are strict rules around how you take money from your company.

Personal items that have nothing to do with the company should not be bought with company cash or card. That is what your salary and/or dividend payments are for. You can do what you like with your personal salary, once you have received it. If you take sums out of the company that can't be accounted for, your accountant will put it in the director's loan account, and this will be listed on your annual accounts, meaning that you owe it all back to the company.

SO HOW DO YOU PAY YOURSELF?

SALARY, EXPENSES AND BENEFITS

If you want the company to pay you an employee salary, expenses or benefits, you must register the company as an employer with HMRC through the PAYE system, and make Real Time Information (RTI) returns.

The company must deduct Income Tax and National Insurance contributions from your salary payments and pay these to HMRC on a monthly basis, along with employers' National Insurance contributions. Do not forget to do this, as HMRC will be very quick to fine you!

If you or one of your employees makes personal use of something that belongs to the business, such as a car or a house or flat, you must report it as a benefit and pay any relevant tax due.

DIVIDENDS

If you own shares in a company, a dividend is a tax-efficient way of paying yourself and other company shareholders because the tax rate is lower than for PAYE salary. A dividend is a payment a company makes to all shareholders if it has made enough profit. Traditionally the payment is made on an annual basis, although interim dividends can be paid more often if the profit projections from your management accounts allow for them. In this case they are usually paid quarterly. Legally, your company is not allowed to pay out more in dividends than its available profits from current and previous financial years. This means that you cannot pay yourself or anyone else dividends if your company is breaking even or running at a loss, whereas you can pay yourself a salary in these situations.

You must usually pay dividends to all shareholders, commensurate with their share ownership of the company, so you need to have sufficient capital to do this. You can ask other shareholders to waive their dividend fee, though, and this must be recorded in your accounts as having been consented to by all shareholders. Many small creative companies have between one and three co-directors and shareholders, in which case the process is fairly straightforward, but if you have investors who have taken a stake in the company, it becomes more complicated and you have to consider whether paying out dividends will affect your cash flow through the year. If you think it might, don't take the risk.

To pay a dividend, you first have to:

- Hold a directors' meeting to 'declare' the dividend
- Keep minutes of the meeting, even if you're the only director

There is a £5,000 allowance tax-free on dividends. After that, tax payments are as follows:

- Upper-rate taxpayers will pay tax at 38.1 per cent
- Higher-rate taxpayers will pay tax at 32.5 per cent
- Basic-rate taxpayers will pay tax at 7.5 per cent

For each dividend payment the company makes, you must write up a dividend voucher showing:

- the date
- the company name
- the names of the shareholders being paid a dividend
- the amount of the dividend
- the amount of the 'dividend tax credit'

DIVIDEND TAX CREDITS

There is a tax credit available on dividends, which is worked out separately from tax owed.

To work out the dividend tax credit, divide the dividend amount by nine.

Here's an example from HMRC:

You want to pay a dividend of £900. Divide £900 by nine, which gives you a dividend tax credit of £100. Pay £900 to the shareholder – but add the £100 tax credit and record a total of £1,000 on the dividend voucher.

You must give a copy of the voucher to recipients of the dividend and keep a copy for your company's records.

DIRECTOR'S LOANS

If you take money out of the company that is not a salary or dividend, this is called a director's loan. This is repayable to the company by you. Try not to build this up over time. It doesn't look good to potential investors, or buyers, and means you will need to settle the account some time. If you want a loan from the company, draw up a plan and have your shareholders pass it, then pay the loan back on a monthly basis.

HOW SHOULD YOU PAY YOURSELF?

As outlined in the previous chapter, your status within your company can vary.

As the founder and managing director of a limited company, you have company director status, and should also have employee status.

You will not be self-employed, as that would mean you were a sole trader rather than a limited company. This can sometimes be confusing if you have worked as a freelancer for years!

I would advise that you make sure you are an employee of your company as well as being an office holder, which is the automatic designated status from being a company director. This is because office holders do NOT have the same rights as employees. Given that you will be doing most of the grafting, and hopefully paying yourself for it out of projects, it's safe to say you are an employee, but give yourself a contract of employment just to be safe.

Make sure you are aware of the rights and benefits attached to your employment status, as they can vary.

As an employee you have the following statutory rights. This applies to you as a PAYE employee, and to your staff who are PAYE employees.

Some of these are based on EU law, so watch this space post-Brexit:

- getting the national minimum wage (this means you also need to pay yourself the national minimum wage, as an employee)
- protection against unlawful deductions from wages
- the statutory minimum level of paid holiday (good luck with that in the first two years of your start-up!)
- the statutory minimum length of rest breaks
- to not work more than 48 hours per week or to opt out of this right if you choose
- protection against unlawful discrimination
- protection for reporting wrongdoing in the workplace (whistle-blowing)
- to not be treated less favourably if you work part-time
- Statutory Sick Pay
- Statutory Maternity, Paternity, Adoption and Shared Parental Leave and Pay
- minimum notice periods if your employment will be ending
- protection against unfair dismissal
- the right to request flexible working
- time off for emergencies
- statutory redundancy pay

Most of this also applies to 'workers', who are of similar employment status to employees but more casual. The exceptions for workers are that they do not get minimum notice periods, unfair dismissal, redundancy or flexible working.

You can be simultaneously self-employed and employed, or a worker and employed – if you have different positions.

In reality, many of the people you employ will be seen as workers or employees in law, rather than as freelancers.

Generally these rights do not apply to self-employed people, but be very careful about this employment status in law. Even if you are paying someone as a self-employed 'freelancer', they could in fact be seen as a worker or employee in law and could take you to a tribunal to claim these rights if they feel they have been given the wrong employment status in your company. If they are successful in doing this, you may owe them and the government back payments.

When you are hiring staff, use the Employment Status Indicator on the HMRC website to keep yourself right, and make sure your business does not get dragged down by tribunals and fines or back payments.

Often, accountants will suggest that you pay yourself and your co-directors a low salary up to the legal tax limit, and the remainder through dividends, which are taken from profit within the company and can receive tax relief and a lower tax rate, as outlined above.

This means that you retain employee status but pay less tax.

There are some things to bear in mind with doing it this way. First, you need to take dividends out of overall company profit, so if you go over budget on projects or have losses from previous years and are not in profit you can't pay yourself this way. Creative companies have a notoriously unpredictable turnover and cash flow so just make sure it's realistic to assume you will be in profit. It's very hard to predict just how creative projects will go and they have a nasty habit of going over budget!

So you can choose to pay yourself both ways, i.e. pay a basic wage PAYE and then give yourself a dividend according to profit within the company, and many directors choose this method as it is very practical but it's also a case of getting the balance right. The dividends you can afford to pay yourself will vary so you need to be aware of that and make sure the basic wage is enough for you to meet all your outgoings, or that you have savings to fall back on.

Second, you might find it a pain when you have to take on various types of personal administration – mortgage lenders and the like – because they look for traditional PAYE employment records. I often found that it was easier for me to keep track of money by paying myself directly out of project budgets, as a PAYE employee of the company.

If you are paying yourself dividends, be aware that you also have to pay your co-shareholders a dividend, commensurate with their share ownership.

So for example: you have 50 per cent of the company and a shareholder has 50 per cent. You pay yourself a dividend of £1,000. Your other shareholder should then be paid a dividend of £1,000 as well.

Paying yourself PAYE means that you are, to all intents and purposes, an employee of the company and you will receive a monthly salary from the company. You also need to have something called a Director's Service Contract in place which details your hours and pay. Your pay can vary from month to month, as long as you keep accurate records, but again, it is useful to have a regular salary when you are, for example, buying a house. In this case you or your bookkeeper will need to do something called a Real Time Information monthly tax submission, which we will look at in detail later in this chapter.

Talk to your accountant, and HMRC if necessary, about this in detail before making any decisions.

HIRING AN ACCOUNTANT

This is one of the most important things you will do for your young company. Make sure you feel comfortable with who they are as an organisation, that you get on with your accountant personally, that he or she understands the creative industries, and that he or she will be flexible and understanding if needs be. Ask how much their basic services for your company are likely to be, and what extras might crop up. Find out what other similar organisations charge for the same services. It is likely that your company will have rocky times and your accountant will need to have the confidence and experience to guide you through and trust that you will make it to the other side, as well as help you grow when things are going well. Make sure they are on top of all the latest legislation and will look for the best value for money for you. Ask them what software they use, how they expect to receive financial information from you, whether they have a bookkeeping service, how often they expect to meet with you, what their deadlines are for financial paperwork and anything else you can think of. It is always best to go by personal recommendation from a colleague who works in the same industry, if possible. Remember, if your accountant is not working for you, you can always find another one!

FREELANCE VERSUS PAY AS YOU EARN STAFF

Any business benefits from having good long-term staff, but particularly creative ones as it takes time to build up your creative identity and it's important to have a clear brand in terms of the subject matter, tone, form and intended audience. The ideal scenario would be to have a head of development (in charge of ideas), production manager (running the show from a production logistics and budget point of view), production assistant (helping the production manager and other staff), digital manager (looking after social media and online), and shooting assistant producer (filming development tasters or creating online demos) who are there for the long haul, and grow with your company. This means having permanent PAYE or long-term freelance contract staff. With small start-ups, this is often just not possible. Money may be tight and the idea of managing several year-long salary payments out of your company budget might seem like a far-off pipe dream. In this situation, you are looking at hiring freelance staff on a project by project basis, for the length of a specific funded project and not beyond. It's not ideal, but it is perfectly doable provided you have a solid executive team who are helping shape and grow the company behind the scenes. Cohesiveness is important. If you are relying only on freelance staff who come and go the company will become fragmented very quickly, and lose its direction. One issue will be that, if project schedules overrun, your excellent freelancer may have another job lined up – and generally staff who are good can hop straight from job to job. In this case you have to hire someone to cover the overrun, and inevitably things get lost in the handover from one staff member to the next. Continuity is key for delivering excellent projects. How can you guard against this? One way is to make sure you have a good contingency amount in your project budget, so that you can figure an overrun into the schedule and keep your freelance staff member on a bit past the production run.

Another thing to bear in mind is the designated employment status of these members of staff. As mentioned before, they may not be officially self-employed in the eyes of the law – for various reasons. Make sure you check their appropriate employment status before drawing up a contract.

TAX PAYMENTS

Freelance staff should have a Schedule D number, which means that they have registered as self-employed and are responsible for paying their own tax in a Self Assessment at the end of the year. Make sure your freelance staff are aware of this.

MONTHLY REAL TIME INFORMATION (RTI) REPORTS

In October 2013 RTI was mandated for all UK businesses. This means that rather than doing your employee payroll return to HMRC at the end of the year, you submit it every month. The payroll return details have to be submitted for each PAYE employee, not freelancers who, as mentioned above, look after their own tax affairs. The details include gross salary, Income Tax, Employee National Insurance and

Employer National Insurance. Make sure you know what your tax code is as this is important for getting the amounts right.

You may have a bookkeeper or your accountant looking after this for you, and that is the ideal option because they are well versed in the ins and outs of tax legislation. Generally, it is the best money you will spend because it saves you money in the long term – as long as they are trustworthy and don't fleece you! Always ask for personal recommendations from others who run creative companies. Don't go with a cheap local one who has no experience of the creative industries as you won't get your money's worth.

If you don't want the expense of that because your payroll is small, you can do it yourself. It's also a very good way of keeping track of costs within the business. First, speak to the employee helpline at HMRC to make sure you know exactly how to go about this. Then just download the relevant software from the HMRC website, making sure it's up to date, and enter all the employee details. That may just be you and your co-director or directors at the beginning if you are choosing to be an employee rather than only receiving dividends. After setting up each employee and the general company details, you enter your tax code, the gross amount paid and the frequency of payment, i.e. monthly, and it should give you a broad idea of Income Tax, Employee National Insurance and Employer National Insurance owing. It's important to input at the same time every month, as calculations differ depending on date. You should also use the HMRC tax calculator to double-check you are paying the correct amount as the RTI calculations are not always accurate. Make sure you pay anything owing on the same day you have paid yourself and your co-workers, to avoid getting one of those nasty chasing letters from Her Majesty's Government!

RULES ON MATERNITY AND PATERNITY PAY

This is something creative businesses often get wrong, because they are solely focused on their content output and simply don't have the knowledge of or interest in employment legislation. You need to make sure that your PAYE employees, workers and freelance staff are clear about what their employment status within your company is, and what they are entitled to under that status. Getting it wrong could mean you get dragged into a costly employment tribunal.

Freelance staff who are registered self-employed are entitled to something called Maternity and Paternity Allowance. This allowance also applies if a PAYE employee has just recently started, or their average pay is less than £112 a week. This can be claimed from 26 weeks pregnant. How much allowance you're entitled to is based on how much you earn.

PAYE staff and workers are entitled to Statutory Maternity and Paternity Pay. All pregnant employees are entitled to 52 weeks' maternity leave. Maternity pay is worked out on the basis of 90 per cent of monthly salary for the first six weeks, then the statutory weekly amount for a further 33 weeks. An expectant mother needs to inform you within 15 weeks of the due date and is allowed to take their maternity leave any time from 11 weeks before the week of the due date. An expectant father needs to inform you at least 15 weeks before the week the baby is expected. Employees should tell you when the due date is, how long they plan to take off and when they want their leave to start.

Paternity pay is generally two weeks' allowance from the birth; however, legislation introduced from April 2015 gives the option of the father taking on part of his spouse or partner's paid leave (they can't both have it, alas). This can be done after the two weeks' statutory paternity period, and up until 52 weeks from the birth of the child. Although relatively few fathers have taken this on so far, it is likely to increase and indeed should be encouraged, so it's something to bear in mind. How this works depends on the length of employment, whether it is continuous employment, and salary earnings. This can take some serious working out so you need to talk to your staff about it if they are thinking about taking up this opportunity.

These are perhaps the beginnings of much more equitable schemes such as those we see in Denmark, Finland and Sweden, where both parents are given state recompense for child rearing, and/or childcare is considerably cheaper, or free.

CHILDCARE VOUCHERS

Childcare vouchers for businesses were introduced in 1989 and various schemes have run since that time. Essentially they allow up to £283 of monthly income to be tax-free. Most employers who provide childcare vouchers do so through a salary sacrifice scheme, meaning the employee agrees to reduce their salary by a certain value and receive childcare vouchers to the same value but pay no tax or National Insurance on these vouchers. You can register your company to do this through the various schemes available.

RULES ON HOLIDAY PAY

Statutory holiday pay applies to all workers, which means both freelancers and employees in your business. The current allowance for full-time workers is 5.6 weeks. Part-time staff have the same employment rights as full-time staff so, if working part-time, the allowance should be commensurate with the overall hours worked. You can work out what you owe your employee using the holiday pay calculator on the gov.uk website.

RULES ON SICK PAY

To qualify for Statutory Sick Pay employees must:

• have an employment contract with your company
• have done some work under their contract
• have been sick for four or more days in a row (including non-working days) – known as a 'period of incapacity for work'
• earn at least £112 a week
• give you the correct notice of seven days

- give you proof of their illness, for example a doctor's note, after seven days off

You start paying SSP from the fourth 'qualifying day' (a day an employee is normally required to work). The first three qualifying days are called 'waiting days'.

VAT AND TAX RETURNS

You, your financial director or your bookkeeper or accountant need to do quarterly VAT returns, which can be done on your existing online account.

Doing a return involves inputting the total cost of your sales (i.e. invoices you have submitted to clients for your services) without VAT, the total VAT charged on those sales, the total you have paid out to your suppliers without VAT and the total VAT paid on those payments. If your sales have incurred more VAT than your payments you will owe HMRC the difference and can pay it through a bank transfer; if your payments have incurred more VAT than your sales then HMRC will owe you the difference and pay it directly into your account.

You can register to do VAT returns on a quarterly basis and there is also the option of a flat fee return for businesses under a certain turnover.

COMPANY AND FINANCIAL RECORDS

Companies House and HMRC require that you keep details on file, at your registered company address, of:

- directors, shareholders and company secretaries
- the results of any shareholder votes and resolutions
- promises for the company to repay loans at a specific date in the future
- promises the company makes for payments if something goes wrong and it's the company's fault ('indemnities')

- transactions when someone buys shares in the company
- loans or mortgages secured against the company's assets

And also financial records that include:

- all money received and spent by the company
- details of assets owned by the company
- debts the company owes or is owed
- stock the company owns at the end of the financial year
- the stocktakings you used to work out the stock figure
- all goods bought and sold
- who you bought and sold them to and from (unless you run a retail business)

You also have to keep all the detailed records you use to prepare your company financial accounts, including bank statements, petty cash orders, invoices in and out, receipts, cost managers, bills, loans and tax and financial correspondence.

If you don't keep accounting records, you can be fined £3,000 by HMRC or disqualified as a company director. You need to keep these records for six years, even after you have wound a company up.

COMPANY RETURNS

Companies House requires you to do annual company returns, which simply means inputting the basic details of your company onto their database to keep their records up to date. This includes your registered address, directors and shareholder information. Failure to do this incurs a penalty so remember to do it! These returns have recently been renamed Confirmation Statements, but they are essentially the same thing. There is a small fee to do this, approximately £15, although the exact figure for Confirmation Statements still has to be confirmed.

BOOKKEEPING

It's probably a good idea to get a bookkeeper in, even if it's just on a monthly basis. It can take some of the financial burden off the shoulders of the company directors. You can use one attached to your accountant's firm, or hire a freelancer who will do lots of different companies. Again, go for one with experience of the creative industries. A lot of these will overlap with what a production manager does on projects, and the two can work together.

Generally a bookkeeper will:

- Input all sales invoices, wherever you keep these records. This could be accounting software like Sage, or Excel spreadsheets and cost managers
- Input all purchase invoices and expense receipts
- Input all sales income
- Input all purchase payments
- Reconcile the income and expenses to the bank statements (by ticking off the transactions)
- Reconcile the petty cash
- Reconcile the sales ledger and purchase ledger
- Input capital expenditure on the accounting records
- Categorise the costs in the correct place on accounting records
- Accruals and prepayments
- Depreciation journal
- Corporation Tax provision, if your company is in profit

If you use the bookkeeper a bit more, they can also do the following things, although it can be tricky when you have lots of projects going on at the same time, so generally a production manager or project manager will do a lot of this:

- Raise sales invoices
- Check purchase invoices to purchase orders

- Chase debtors for payment
- Paying suppliers and creditors such as HM Revenue & Customs
- Dealing with other financial company information and administration

COMPANY END OF YEAR ACCOUNTS
AND MANAGEMENT ACCOUNTS

Every limited company has to submit company accounts at the end of the financial year. LLPs do not do this because they use individual Self Assessment returns for partners. Company accounts need to be done by a chartered accountant.

They include a director's report, detailed summaries of your profit and loss account for the financial year, your company balance sheet, director's loan account and Corporation Tax liabilities.

Companies should also have management accounts that are updated throughout the year, and give you a realistic picture of where your company is financially – although these are not compulsory.

Your financial year will depend on when you incorporated your company at Companies House. They will set an 'accounting reference date' which tells you when your financial year ends; usually this is the last day of the month your company was set up. So if your company was set up on 7 March 2016, your first set of accounts will be due on 31 March 2017.

CORPORATION TAX

Usually your accountant will work out how much Corporation Tax is due after completing your accounts. You may not pay any for the first couple of years, if your company is not yet in profit. Even if you don't owe anything, you still need to report that you have nothing to pay on your Corporation Tax return – again, your accountant should do this as part of your end of year accounts.

BANK OVERDRAFTS AND LOANS

This can be a thorny area for the young creative company. You will probably find that you need a sizeable overdraft in your business account because clients pay erratically, according to bizarre payment schedules, or occasionally not at all. Surprisingly, large corporations can be the worst offenders with 60-day-plus payment terms, or very little budget drawdown up front and most on delivery. Without the cushion of a bank overdraft to tide you over and allow you to meet project expenses and pay your staff, you will quickly go under.

The only way to avoid using one is if you happen to have a large amount of capital sitting in your account to deal with such emergencies.

So what do you need to be aware of with company overdrafts?

1. Personal Guarantees
2. Fees
3. Interest
4. Renewal
5. Penalties

Have a meeting with a business relationship manager (if you can find one!) and ask them about all of these issues in detail. Unfortunately, most major banks that deal with small businesses have ditched the dedicated bank manager in favour of a rotating system where you get whoever is available (this changes, of course, once your turnover settles nicely into the millions). This means that there is no continuity over time and no real understanding of your individual business. Shop around for banks and find out if there are any that offer a dedicated relationship manager – this can make all the difference with a small business as that person understands when you are going through lean times, what is in the pipeline, and will give you a bit of slack. Starting from zero every time, trying to defend your business with a new person on the end of the phone or at the other side of a table at your local branch, can be a frustrating and dispiriting experience. I found that when I had the mobile number of my manager and could ask his advice I felt much more positive about cash-flow issues.

These days, things seem to be more geared towards making company directors personally liable for debt. This is presumably because of a high level of default and companies going bust, perhaps because many start-ups have no idea how to manage their finances in the first place! The concept of limited liability is, in practice, a bit misleading. Banks ask you to sign a personal guarantee against any loans or overdrafts, meaning that they can come after your assets for repayment of debt if the company has no money. They can also go after your co-directors. So any agreements with lenders should be discussed with everyone involved so that you are all aware of the risks to your house, car, holidays, school fees, family heirlooms or rich spouses. Things could get very messy indeed if these things only come out once the business is in trouble.

COMPANY AND EMPLOYMENT LAW POST-BREXIT

Some, although by no means all, of the legislation on employment and companies in the UK is directly tied in with EU law or originated in EU law so the decision by England and Wales to leave the European Union in June 2016 could have far-reaching effects on business and employment in the UK. No one really has a clue what will happen because we are at the beginning of a long and head-meltingly complex process of extrication that will last many years, but some have posited theories. It is generally thought that no big changes will take place long-term, because the UK is trying to remain a member of the Single Market and at the very least have access to it via the European Economic Area, so will have to abide by employment rules anyway. Some business regulations may be reduced, but Brexit is likely to produce serious upset in the UK economy and industry, so there will perhaps be little appetite for fundamental legislative change – even if it were possible – on behalf of the government, the business community and the public. The general consensus seems to be that no fundamental rights will be eroded but, again, that remains to be seen!

One of the main negative effects will surely be that big corporations with EU headquarters in the UK, and smaller, agile creative tech or finance companies, might go elsewhere. Places like Berlin in Germany and Dublin or Cork in the Republic of Ireland are expected to do well out of the process, although the fact that Cork was recently involved in a tax avoidance scandal with the Apple EU headquarters may not help their case. It is thought that large UK cities will lose out substantially once the exit is underway but the effect this will have on the creative start-up community is yet to be seen. Brexiteers point out that trade agreements with the larger global community outside the EU can now flourish. In reality the UK will be stuck in exit negotiations for so long, remaining a member during that time but with fewer privileges of membership, that none of these agreements is likely to come to fruition any time soon.

➤ Examples of a Budget Template (p.288) and Producer/Director Contract template (p.291) can be found in the Appendices at the end of this book. An example of a Cost Manager Template is available for download at www.kamerabooks.co.uk/ceresources

---

INTERVIEW WITH STEVE LEITH,
GRANT THORNTON ACCOUNTANTS

What is your role at Grant Thornton?

I'm an audit partner in the Media and Technology Group.

I've worked at Grant Thornton for 16 years, first working with mostly TV production companies and now alongside that I work with fast-growth technology companies.

How do Grant Thornton Media Accountants work with creative businesses?

There is sometimes confusion about different kinds of accountants, so firstly it might be helpful to mention what we don't cover. As a larger firm we don't do bookkeeping or looking after a company's (or a production's) day-to-day accounting – typically, media businesses use part-time bookkeepers or smaller firms for that. So we don't get involved in management accounting or day-to-day cash-flow reviews. The core service is if the company requires an audit or taxation support or planning (even when small companies can obtain an audit exemption, sometimes investors will want an audit so it's not always about size).

We form a relationship with the business at a very early stage and help them plan their strategy, especially around commercial deals they're thinking about. Then we contribute in helping them deal with tax relief and possible exposure.

What tax reliefs are available?

There are various tax reliefs open to the creative industries, and we deal with them across the board. An interesting one at the moment is the R&D tax credit – essentially cash-back relief from government. It can cover TV companies as well as creative technology – we've seen industries that you wouldn't expect being able to put together R&D claims. It's about whether you have a project that is in some way creating a technological advancement.

For example, we have a client in music promotion – they capture personal information coming from their website for tickets and use that data in a new way to target selling tickets in the future. In TV, the typical area will be animation or CGI and VR. The challenge with VR is the funding and distribution model – it's not the broadcaster commission model that sits as primary funding alongside international distribution deals; the problem with VR is that we have unknown distribution channels, no real monetisation model and no certainty over future cash flows. Funding is difficult for that reason so it requires cash-rich businesses in the first place. It all comes down to the major consumer tech brands and how that plays out in terms of the content world. For example, Netflix, Amazon, Apple etc. – if those guys start to fund really new media, including VR, then that might move us forward. But there's still the issue of funding content. Apple still aren't funding content in a way that will change the industry; Amazon and Netflix have done a lot recently so could move into this space as the technology becomes more ubiquitous; or there could be an entirely new platform created that stands alone. R&D tax credits at least help businesses exploring this area obtain some cash back on their investment if they qualify.

There are also tax credits or reliefs available for films, high-end television drama, children's animation, and video games – up to 20 per cent of budgets can end up being covered by HMRC. Companies would come to us early in the structuring of the programme or game. We ideally want to be involved before an agreement is signed with a broadcaster or studio so we can input on any structural points and ensure the relief is maximised.

Companies need to be careful around claiming R&D and creative tax reliefs at the same time. Often if you're already claiming one you can't claim the other. If you're doing animation or games you need to decide whether to use R&D or other creative tax reliefs. We can help do analysis regarding which one you should go for.

We also do tax structuring – how you might structure companies together. For founders we look at it from a personal as well as a corporate point of view, e.g. ensuring founder tax positions are considered in advance of an exit; or how to plan and manage expansion into international markets.

What is the valuation process for a start-up company that has IP as its main asset and makes visual content (for example, a production company, digital agency or creative tech company)? How is share valuation worked out once the company has grown and is approaching investors?

IP is key in terms of determining the valuation of a company – the tricky bit is getting to the bottom of the exploitation value of the IP. This is typically done by market research on similar products/content, size of the market, then applying discount factors within your business to take account of uncertainty, probability of exploitation potential, and the time value of money.

For example, imagine a kids' show that has aired on the BBC. In their wider exploitation strategy they will plan to be in 30 other countries and have a separate revenue stream from merchandising, licensing and international sales. If you manage to break the US market, for example, and get that kids' show on a major channel, then the potential of your merchandising revenue stream will be much higher – a valuation model must take account of such variables.

Valuing early stage, pioneering tech businesses is tricky but more and more common. These are businesses with minimal track records on generating revenues and no market competitors but they have IP – and a ton of hope value. Investors either buy that or they don't. It may have racy assumptions in, then it's just a case of making a very good sales pitch and justifying the market potential if it does take off. The assumptions can easily be shot down, but can also be supported. But at the end of the day, negotiating an investment round at a particular valuation is a bit like valuing a house ... the value is ultimately determined by what people are willing to pay for it.

We are specialists in advising on selling and buying media and technology companies. We also have a transaction advisory team, if you want to perform diligence on a company you are considering buying.

What finance roles should be in place at the beginning of a creative company's life to ensure healthy financial growth?

We come across this situation a lot, where people are at a point where it's becoming difficult to manage the financial stuff but are not yet at a size where they want to employ a finance person. There's a point at which you need to build a finance team. In the media space there are a lot of part-time bookkeepers/production accountants. Production accountants will assign themselves to a particular production rather than the company itself. There's an important distinction between production accounting and corporate accounting. At the very beginning, what you need to find is the right part-time bookkeeper and the right part-time production accountant and/or production manager. We can recommend people to do this. It can be difficult to pinpoint when in-house finance is needed, but it's probably as soon as someone feels like the reporting is becoming difficult or obscuring the ability of management to make decisions. If you're there you really should already have a finance person in-house.

What are the main things to keep on top of with HMRC – throughout the life cycle of a business?

There isn't much that is specific to creative companies in terms of basic company paperwork. All businesses have to do their annual accounts, VAT, PAYE, Corporation Tax and pensions administration. The point at which it becomes more complicated is when a creative company is using one of the tax-relief schemes available through the government.

There is a special unit within HMRC that looks after the media and creative world, dealing with creative tax-relief systems. Firms like us have very close relationships with those teams and we talk to them every day – this makes life much easier for companies that want to make the most of their tax relief.

Share option schemes are particularly relevant in the creative arena because it can take some time to raise capital and you may need people to work for less money initially. These schemes work as an incentive for potential employees by offering shares in the business. It can help to attract top talent if you can't offer much financially at first. The main one is the EMI option scheme, which has good tax relief on it and is HMRC-approved. There are some things around qualifying for EMI that you really need to get right. If you haven't done it right you can really get into hot water when your company is at the exiting point, and that is a big deal – so anything around share options you need to have a specialist involved.

Is IPO and the AIM market a realistic option for growth funding for the small to medium-sized creative company (for example, with turnover of between 100 thousand and 20 million)?

Creative companies go through phases of being fashionable and unfashionable to the City. Outside of the major media multinationals, there aren't that many media companies in the creative space on the UK stock markets at the moment. Animation is a key area, though – particularly children's animation where long-tail IP is attractive and can generate hockey-stick-type returns if things fall into place. It can be a place to go to raise money if you are an experienced management team. There are many drawbacks and obstacles to becoming and operating as a public company, though, particularly for creative leaders. Often people don't think about all the administration, investor reporting and the burden of dealing with the public markets that come with it.

How does a creative company approach potential buyers if it wants to sell up?

We sit down with companies at an early stage in the process and consider whether they are at the right point – in reality this conversation can go on for some time; timing can be everything. Our M&A team create a formal process involving an investment memorandum detailing the company's historical and forecasted financial information and then take that to buyers and create an auction process. The sale of a company is typically based on a multiple of (a) the current year financial performance and (b) the forecast for the next two to three years. What underpins the business in terms of IP and historical information is key to determining the certainty of these two metrics.

If you have generated solid programming but you don't have the underlying IP generating additional revenue streams then the credibility of your forecasts is going to be questioned. If you have returning series, have IP ownership in multiple programmes and have strong secondary sales coming through then the revenue pipeline becomes much more certain.

We look in detail at how you would be considered by potential buyers. During the sale process, buyers will be categorised according to how suitable they are for your kind of business. If there's enough interest then it's a question of creating competitive tension – the M&A team are specialists at managing that. People will table acquisition or investment offers, and then it becomes a negotiation as to whom the management team and/or owners of the business feel is the right fit in terms of (a) the financial return and (b) the cultural fit.

Because valuations are partly based on future revenue there will often be an earn out, meaning that the current team have to stay and operate the business for a period of time as part of the deal. These days earn outs are getting more and more stretched; they are around three or four years, which means you have to be happy with the buyer because you'll be working with them for that time. My advice would be to pay particular attention to the cultural side of the business as this is key in your achieving the forecasted sales and therefore the earn out that will eventually get you the return on the sale you are looking for and signing up to.

The typical fee structures for Grant Thornton are contingent, based on the valuation of the company – and there is a small, up-front fee to get everything prepared. There is no standard percentage; it is situation-dependent. Often the percentage we take will depend on how much we manage to get for the business and can involve ratchets because we are generally confident we can stretch your valuation beyond what you might expect.

Will Brexit affect how you work with creative companies?

The worries seem to be around things like access to talent and money, and importing and exporting of goods and services. In the media space, we haven't heard businesses voicing major concerns around access to talent in terms of not being in the EU. I think it would have a much bigger impact on the creative tech space, which has a much bigger reliance on hiring foreign workers in key roles. It's all a bit of an unknown.

Funding in the media space is often from self-funding (growing businesses organically and using IP to generate additional cash flows) or there's private equity involved. A major impact would be if a downturn in the economy starts to impact the ability of broadcasters and new platforms in funding content – this would impact independent, entrepreneurial companies for sure.

As a finance expert, do you have any specific advice for creative entrepreneurs based on your experience with them?

There's a common theme around growth stages of a company. You'll see companies getting to a scale where they have achieved good organic growth with a recurring revenue base and x number of employees and moderate profits – that is usually seven to ten million in revenue with profit of 500 thousand to one million. They often get stuck at that point – it's incredibly common. One of our partners once called it 'the bog'. You need to get out of the bog as quickly as possible and get to a 14–15 million revenue mark where you're then able to scale more quickly and hopefully self-fund the next stage of growth. Being stuck in the 'bog' has a lot to do with having to fund future growth before it happens. You need to start investing more heavily in development, bring in an FD and CD, and it's difficult to do that and generate returns quickly. Once companies do come through that, they're in a position to be absolutely established and it's not a big firefight every day to fund the cost base of the business. How do you get through this? By somehow funding that next stage – borrowing, or investors. A great example here is the C4 Growth Fund. They take a minority position in the company in return for cash that can help you grow at a crucial point. The BBC and Sky are doing the same so it's helping people at this key stage. The highest-profile example of this model's success is probably Left Bank Pictures – a company I supported from the very early days. They were already very successful with a highly experienced team who secured funding from the BBC for a minority shareholding in the company, from day one. This gave them the overhead base to grow the business very quickly. They never raised any more investment from that point and grew quickly, establishing returning series and valuable IP. They subsequently sold to Sony at a significant valuation.

START-UP FUNDING IN THE DIGITAL AGE

There have always been a bewildering number of funding options for the young creative company. This is even more true in the digital age, where the democratisation of everything from content creation to crowdfunding platforms can make the task of finding cash for your creation rather daunting.

The traditional forms of public funding still exist, though to a lesser extent these days, and often very much focused on tech companies – exemplified by that cluster of brightly shining start-ups in London called Silicon Roundabout.

Your friends and family remain the most popular option for seed funding.

The UK government has various schemes for creative start-ups, including Creative Industry Finance, the Business Bank, the National Enterprise Network, Creative England, the Cultural Industries Development Agency and many more.

Unfortunately, the excellent Business Accelerators scheme for ambitious start-ups has been discontinued, but may re-emerge in the future. There are more coordinated business angel platforms like Crowdcube, which pair you up with people who have the cash and are interested in investing in start-up ideas.

Business sponsorship and partnership have grown hugely over the last decade, with large corporations helping start-ups they believe in. Venture philanthropy has become an important part of the funding landscape, with high-net-worth individuals or wealthy organisations ring-fencing funding for social enterprises and community projects.

Of course, there are also the myriad crowdfunding options that now exist. This list is growing every day and includes platforms such as Kickstarter, Indiegogo, FundIt.Buzz, Funding Circle, Crowdfunder and Lend and Invest.

There are also many tech grants and loans available from organisations such as Capital Enterprise, NESTA and Wellcome.

The upside of the financial crash in 2008 is that we had to get creative, and much more democratic, with types of funding – and this has benefited the creative industries hugely.

So which of these do you choose?

This chapter is a guide to some of the best opportunities out there for the creative business or aspiring creative entrepreneur.

THE CREATIVE ECONOMY

The creative economy is a vital and growing part of the global economy. Although creative business activity has always been important economically as well as culturally, the digital age has made the finance community sit up and take notice of creatives because it has seen how massive and globally influential digital innovation can be. In fact, according to the Edge Creative Enterprise Fund and the British Business Bank:

The creative economy accounts for approximately 10% of the entire UK economy and provides 2.55 million jobs; this employment is growing four times faster than the economy as a whole.

Creative companies within this economy are in the business of acquisition, management and commercial exploitation of intellectual property, which then translates into economic value for the overall economy.

So, in summary, creative businesses are extremely important on all fronts! The amount of serious public investment schemes involving the finance sector and high-net-worth individuals reflects this fact.

YOUR BUSINESS PLAN

This is something that strikes fear into the heart of many an aspiring entrepreneur. Doesn't a business plan mean graphs and figures, projections and analysis, and standing hopefully in front of a bunch of sneery suits to pitch *Dragon's Den*-style while they reduce you to a twitching, perspiring puddle on the shiny boardroom floor? Well, yes and no. You will hopefully get to the point of pitching to a group of canny investors and convincing them to part with their cash to grow your business, but at the beginning, think of your business plan more as something that is meant to help you get to grips with the next five years of your company.

This is a touchstone for your nascent company that you can constantly refer to and refine. It is your baby, something you can get to know so well and hone to such perfection that, after a few months, you will confidently talk about facts and figures without feeling tongue-tied and inadequate. A good business plan is your friend, not something to be intimidated by. You might need the skill of finance experts to help put it together, and help you understand what the figures mean or present them in the accepted way, but the business is yours, and no one knows it like you do – or at least no one should.

Most funding organisations or investors will expect you to have a decent business plan, so you might as well get on with it.

A simple, visually engaging slide presentation with your individual company branding and some nice graphics and stills is your template. You can also use specific software templates to help put your plan together, although I have never found this necessary. The market leaders are LivePlan, Plan Magic and Business Plan Pro but there are lots out there. You can also get software tailored to non-profit and creative organisations. Make sure your language is clear and concise, and spelling and punctuation are correct.

Start with a striking title page, then a contents page. Go on to your executive summary, an overview of your company. This should be brief, not detailed, and include who you are, what you do, your place in the market, your team, your company structure and share ownership, and what your aims for the next year, or two to three years, are – depending on the funding you are looking for.

You may need to include a company valuation based on similar market competitors if you are looking for seed investment. Make sure it is a realistic valuation, preferably using the help of an experienced media lawyer. Do not overinflate any figures because most of the people and funding organisations you approach (apart from dear old Mum and Dad, possibly) will see right through them and lose interest. Valuation of creative companies, and particularly digital ones, is notoriously difficult because it is not a typical industrial business model. Similarly, with financial projections, remember that the first couple of years are likely to be slower no matter how much energy you put in or how good your connections are. It takes time for a business to gain traction and funders know this. They expect to see a realistic picture – optimistic, but not deluded.

Briefly include what you intend to use the funding for and make sure this is tailored to the priorities of those you are pitching to. Hard-nosed investors don't want to see that you are going to take a punt on a high-budget but niche passion project, and arts organisations do not want to get the sense that you have more of an eye on exit strategy than content.

You can then talk about clients and partners so far in the life of your company and then go into more detail about the executive team and staff team, their experience and roles. The remainder of your plan needs to cover press and marketing, detailed sales forecasts and market projections, your current financial position and more detail about your product.

It is definitely a good idea to pair up with finance and marketing experts on your business plan writing, if those people do not already exist in your company. Often it is possible to get help for free from public organisations or generous individuals who believe in your idea.

Think of it as the first pitching session, making others as passionate about your business as you are!

COMPANY VALUATION IN THE DIGITAL AGE

We are now in the second phase of digital transformation in the creative landscape. This means we have got past all the big, disruptive changes from analogue and hard copy to digital and are now creating things from a digital native starting point. Once we digitised all the books, music, films and information, other ways of consuming and interacting with them began to emerge. We now have the panoply of social media, an entirely different way of searching for and consuming information with Google and other search engines, our self-expression and language evolving with platforms such as Twitter and Instagram, interactive blogs, vlogs and audio-video platforms, Facetime, live music streaming, massive digital production studios, the sharing economy, peer-to-peer lending, crowdfunding and producing, self-publishing, multiscreen viewing, virtual reality experiences, automated music composition and all sorts of other emerging technologies.

These things have emerged and evolved in such a short space of time, and had such a huge effect on our everyday lives, that they could not have been predicted in any detail beforehand. This means that, to some extent, investing in a start-up digital creative company is always going to be a leap in the dark. The people and organisations that invest in the digital world don't know what changes are to come, and who the innovators and disrupters will be – they can only take a guess, based on what has gone immediately before. They can bring as much digital native talent as possible into their own organisations, and invest in as many start-ups as possible, in the hope that one or two will break through. One change in technology can have everyone else struggling to catch up. Even the valuations of big, publicly owned digital platforms like Facebook, Twitter and LinkedIn are done on a wing and a prayer, assuming that they will hang on to their captive audience and invent ever-more tailored and ingenious ways of selling us things, tracking our information and generally trying to shape our universe.

Digital natives are highly prized in today's business landscape, because large sections of the workforce as a whole are still getting to grips with what it all means, how to negotiate it and, above all, how to monetise it. The executive and management class are largely in the same boat.

The upside of this is that no one really knows what they are talking about when it comes to the future of digital, and you can capitalise on that by showing, confidently, that you and your new company are an important part of that future. There has never been a better time to innovate and convince investors that your company will be worth its weight in gold, so they should give you seed funding, or invest in or buy you – before someone else does.

FUNDING OPPORTUNITIES

This is an overview of some important and interesting opportunities out there for creative companies, but it is by no means an exhaustive list. I'm happy to say that there is so much out there in terms of new investment and funding schemes for digital that it is difficult to keep up! Some of these will disappear or change over time, too, so always check to make sure what the current status is.

THE CREATIVE FINANCE NETWORK

A first port of call when trying to work out which funding path (or paths – there are likely to be several) is right for your business. This website gives you information about seed funding, crowdfunding, business angels, venture capital trusts and business skills training.

MEWE360

A great platform for creative entrepreneurs, specifically seeking 'untapped talent' while ploughing money back into the community to give marginalised communities a voice in the business sector.

MeWe360 comprises the MeWe Foundation, which is the charity arm, and MeWe Trading CIC, which is the investment arm. The charity gives creative businesses across the UK support, training and networking opportunities; MeWe Trading CIC gives creative entrepreneurs access to funding.

You can also hire out office space in the centre of London.

They have a £1 million business incubator and venture fund for entrepreneurs in the creative industries.

SEED ENTERPRISE INVESTMENT SCHEME (SEIS)

The Seed Enterprise Investment Scheme (SEIS) is specifically for small, early stage companies that want to raise equity finance from private investors. SEIS offers tax reliefs to individual investors who purchase new shares in the company.

This scheme is a precursor to the Enterprise Investment Scheme (EIS), which offers tax reliefs to investors in higher-risk small companies. SEIS offers tax relief at a higher rate than EIS because it is designed to reassure investors who are taking a chance on a very early stage company that has very little or no trading and profit history.

SEIS applies for shares issued on or after 6 April 2012.

Tax relief for investors is available on Income Tax (50 per cent of the cost of shares, maximum £100k) and Capital Gains Tax.

To be eligible for SEIS the company must meet certain conditions:

- Fewer than 25 employees
- No more than £200,000 in gross assets
- No previous investment from a venture capital trust
- Be in an EIS scheme (Enterprise Investment Scheme)
- Can't receive more than £150,000 total from SEIS
- Trading for less than two years on the date shares are issued
- Must not be controlled by another company
- Must not be a member of a partnership
- Be UK resident or permanently established in the UK
- Exist only to carry on a trade that qualifies for SEIS

Within three years of the date of share issue, all the monies raised by that issue must be spent for the purposes of the qualifying business activity. For example, it can't be used for buying shares in another company, or paying dividends back to shareholders, but can be used for research and development of the qualifying trade.

Most trades qualify for SEIS, as long as they are commercial, for-profit businesses. A few do not, although they are not likely to be relevant to the creative industries apart from the caveat that receipt of royalties or licence fees is prohibited.

CREATIVE TAX-RELIEF SCHEMES

Creative industries tax reliefs currently available are:

Film Tax Relief

This is for British feature films which are intended for theatrical release. You can get Film Tax Relief at 25 per cent of qualifying film production expenditure (this means budget spend that meets the requirements for qualifying as a British film), regardless of overall budget. Films can be official co-productions with other countries and spend within the UK or must pass the cultural test, which comprises various elements including British cast and crew, set in UK/locations in the UK, British writer/producer/director, English language and UK subject matter and themes. Each section gives you points, and you must accrue 18–35 points to pass the test.

To apply there must be one production company registered with Companies House before filming begins.

Television, Animation and Children's Television Programme Tax Reliefs

These are for high-end productions covering drama, comedy and documentary, with larger budgets and a minimum running time of 30 minutes, intended for broadcast on TV and/or the internet. Relief is available on either 80 per cent of total core expenditure, or actual UK core expenditure – whichever is lower. Similar rules apply for qualification as a British production with a UK production company and the cultural test, and 10 per cent of core expenditure must be within the UK.

Animations and children's programming must pass the animation cultural test and children's television cultural test OR qualify as an official co-production with other territories.

Video Games Tax Relief

As with the film, TV and animation tax reliefs, the company making the video game, or one of the co-producing companies, must be incorporated in the UK. Relief is available on either 80 per cent of total core expenditure, or actual UK or European Economic Area core expenditure – whichever is lower. It must qualify as British under the video games cultural test, and the game must be intended for release into the market. The core expenditure required is 25 per cent of overall expenditure and it can take place in the UK OR the European Economic Area.

With all of these schemes, there is no cap on the amount that can be claimed.

....

A CAUTIONARY TALE – CHRIS ATKINS AND CHRISTINA SLATER

In July 2016 a shocking story emerged that serves as a cautionary tale about using these schemes, particularly when there is no cap on the amount that can be claimed. Chris Atkins and Christina Slater, two experienced documentary producers, found themselves jailed for defrauding HMRC through film tax-relief schemes when producing their 2009 documentary film *Starsuckers*, a biting critique of media corporations and celebrity culture. They were convicted on two counts of conspiracy to cheat the public revenue and one of fraud, after a long and exhaustive investigation by HMRC discovered that they had claimed tax back fraudulently for the film's investors by inflating invoice figures. Chris Atkins was jailed for five years and Christina Slater for four. The time and resources put into this investigation show that HMRC are serious about creative industry tax fraud, so don't be tempted into cooking the books no matter how desperate you are to finish your project or how important you think the message of your film might be for the general public. We can only live in hope that similar time and resources are being put into tackling tax avoidance by global corporations in the UK, and closing loopholes that can be legally exploited by them.

RESEARCH AND DEVELOPMENT (R&D) RELIEF

This is used most by creative tech and gaming companies but, because so many creative companies are developing platforms now, there may be an R&D component to your project or company that you can claim tax relief for. There are different schemes according to size of company, so make sure you get a media accountant to advise you on what route to take and also make sure that it doesn't conflict with other government grants or tax-relief schemes you might be running. HMRC have a dedicated department for dealing with creative tax-relief schemes; however, my advice would be to let a good media accountant sort out the details with them rather than taking on that level of complexity yourself. With such a specialised area, it will save you money in the long run.

THE BRITISH BUSINESS BANK

Officially up and running since 2014, the British Business Bank was created in order to facilitate funding and investment for small and medium-sized enterprises (SMEs) across the UK. It was felt that, after the financial crash of 2008, official lenders such as banks were loathe to part with cash and so a separate government institution was needed to get businesses going again.

The British Business Bank is supporting £2.4 billion of finance to tens of thousands of smaller businesses, and it participates in a further £3.3 billion of funding for small to medium-sized companies. It doesn't invest directly in companies, but has over 80 partner organisations that will directly invest, or provide loans.

Their website is a mine of information for businesses from start-up to growth, including a comprehensive Business Finance Guide, and they have lots of programmes including start-up loans, growth loans, dedicated investment funds for the North of England and the Midlands, and Enterprise Capital Funds. They have helped lots of creative companies, particularly digital creatives, and are definitely worth checking out.

CREATIVE INDUSTRIES COUNCIL

The CIC is a platform for all the creative industries and links up to finance and investors via the Creative Finance Network. It is a good resource for funding information across the creative industries.

CREATIVE INDUSTRY FINANCE

This is an initiative that started in September 2014 and operates across England. We used the East London Business Centre, which is part of Creative Industry Finance, for a business loan and found the process not only painless but very supportive, especially for very small businesses.

It has four lending partners: the Arts Impact Fund, Big Issue Invest, Responsible Finance and Ratesetter.

You can do a quick eligibility test online at www.creativeindustryfinance.org.uk to find out if they will potentially lend to your business. If you are eligible, you then go in for a meeting. At the beginning of the application process you are assigned a one-to-one business advisor, and they evaluate your business and give you advice on the specific areas you might be weak in. That could be presentation, advertising, cash flow, staffing or managing clients. You then complete a series of steps in order to get ready to pitch to a funding panel.

INNOVATE UK

Innovate UK ran competitions for grants to creative, digital and design businesses in 2015/16, with total funding exceeding £30 million. It continues to run grant schemes for emerging and enabling technologies. The Smart funding scheme provides grants for start-ups and SMEs to help them develop their innovations – from proof-of-market through to proof-of-concept and on to prototype development. It provides grants of up to £250,000 per project.

HORIZON 2020

An interesting one for digital creatives working in medical research and healthcare, Horizon 2020 is a European funding programme for businesses and researchers and is to invest more than €600 million across seven new initiatives launched in September 2016. One of these focuses on digital health.

CREATIVE ENGLAND

This is a far-reaching fund that covers everything from film to games to interactive healthcare in the whole of England.

They also have an Equity Investment Scheme available for digital creative companies outside of London.

Schemes running at the time of writing include: short film production, feature film development, film enterprise, and for games the Greenshoots games development fund and Hardware, Software and Services grants as well as business loans and the aforementioned Equity Investment Scheme.

CREATIVE SCOTLAND

Creative Scotland have various funding schemes running up to 2018 including Regular Funding, which provides three-year funding to creative organisations; Open Project Funding for individuals and organisations; and Targeted Funding, aimed at digital arts, music, film, young people and disabled artists. There are also many interesting funding initiatives as part of their Funds Delivered By Partners schemes.

CREATIVE EUROPE

There are a variety of opportunities here, including the Media Programme, aimed at creative companies producing film, TV and video, animation, games and literary translation work throughout the EU. There are quite strict criteria for many of the schemes, however, and in some cases it might be more suited to growth funding than start-up funding – for example, many require previous distribution of content and 12+ months of trading. It's worth a look in your general business plan as there is a lot of funding to be had.

EUROPEAN DOCUMENTARY NETWORK (EDN)

This is an international community for documentary filmmakers with excellent information on funding and co-production. Once you join you have access to the EDN Financing Guide, a comprehensive global overview of broadcasters, funds and distributors in 30 European countries.

THE EU CULTURAL GUARANTEE FUND

Launched in June 2016, the Cultural Guarantee Fund was set up to help creative SMEs in Europe access finance and is part of the Creative Europe programme running 2014–20. The European Commission has earmarked £93 million to provide guarantees to financial intermediaries, meaning banks and other investors, to encourage them to offer financing to the creative industries. The Creative Europe website states:

> Overall, the facility should help to leverage over €600 million in additional lending. The Guarantee Facility responds directly to the current needs of the cultural and creative sectors. SMEs have found it challenging to access loans due to the nature of their

business, a lack of tangible assets or an uncertainty of demand ... In addition, the facility is intended to help the financial sector to improve its understanding of the cultural and creative sectors.

UK creatives will be eligible for 2016–17 funding and loans. After that, who knows ...

INVEST NORTHERN IRELAND

This organisation has several funding, loan and skills-support options available for the creative industries, including: Propel, a scheme of salary support grants; Innovation Vouchers, funding up to £5,000; Co-Fund NI, which is co-investment in deals between £240,000 and £450,000; and the Growth Loan Fund, providing business loans of between £50,000 and £500,000.

A new technology development centre has also been opened in Belfast, called the Tech Hub, with funding from Invest NI and Chelsea Apps Factory.

ARTS COUNCIL NI

This organisation ran a very successful Creative Industries Innovation Fund between 2011 and 2015, so look out for further schemes aimed at the creative industries.

DIGITAL UNION

This is a network aimed at creative companies in the North East of England.

NESTA

NESTA have several dedicated funds and mentoring schemes for the creative industries. These include the Digital Innovation Fund for the Arts in Wales, the Digital Research and Development Fund for the Arts, the Creative Business Mentor Network, and Destination Local.

They are also supporting crowdfunding platforms via their Innovation in Giving fund, having been given a £10 million award from the Cabinet Office.

WELLCOME TRUST

Wellcome have lots of imagination and deep pockets. We have worked with them a few times and the projects have always been cutting-edge and interesting. Their remit is the intersection between art and biomedical science, but though it might sound narrow in practice, this area is extremely broad. The creative industries can get funding from a number of Wellcome initiatives including the People and Society Awards, the Arts Awards and the Broadcast, Game and Film Awards. They cover drama and fiction, documentary, games, performance, video installation, live events, animation and everything in between.

TIPPING POINT FILM FUND

This fund draws on public support through crowdfunding to fund cinematic documentaries and campaigns, from inception to distribution – exactly the way charities fund campaigns. You can apply to have your film taken on by the fund.

THE FLEDGLING FUND

This fund is aimed at visual storytelling that has a social impact. They have a rolling grants programme and also a Special Initiative on Emerging Forms of Documentary Storytelling, aimed at photography, virtual reality, interactive and other cross-platform projects.

THE BFI

The BFI fund film projects and companies. They support creative industry business development through their Creative Clusters Challenge Fund, Film Enterprise Fund (in partnership with Creative England), Digitisation Fund, and the Film Skills Fund (in partnership with Skillset).

Diversity is key to their project funding. The Production and Development Fund and the Diversity Fund will support projects that reflect the diversity of the UK in subject matter, in front of and behind the camera.

BRITDOC

This is another must-go-to organisation for the socially conscious creative. Started by Jess Search, an ex-Channel 4 commissioner, to encourage independent documentaries that do not necessarily meet a broadcast remit, Britdoc has blossomed into an international touchstone for documentary filmmakers who want to change the world. Currently Britdoc runs a number of funds, including the Bertha fund for journalism and campaigning, the Circle funding group of philanthropists looking to finance documentary, and the Genesis fund for experimental forms in documentary.

FILM LONDON

Film London run the Micrówave scheme for feature films, London Calling scheme for shorts, and FLAMIN scheme for Artists' films. Applications must meet the criteria for being based on or featuring London, check the website for more details.

VENTURE CAPITAL, VENTURE PHILANTHROPY AND UNIVERSITY INNOVATION FUNDS

NATIONAL ACCELERATOR AND INCUBATOR PROGRAMMES

Unfortunately, the excellent government-backed national Growth-Accelerator scheme, launched in 2012, has now been discontinued, but many privately run accelerator and incubator programmes remain in the UK's largest cities, particularly for digital start-ups and growing digital companies.

Along with countless biotechnology and engineering firms, large media, tech and communications organisations such as Guardian

Media Group, Telefonica and Microsoft now have their own accelerator and incubator programmes, as does Barclays Bank. One of the largest digital schemes is Codebase, in Edinburgh.

Approximately 40 per cent of these schemes are privately run and, historically, 25 per cent of national schemes have been run by universities and business schools such as Oxford University Innovation, Kings Venture Accelerator at King's College London, Accelerate Cambridge at Cambridge University, the Imperial Incubator at Imperial College, and Edinburgh Research and Innovation at Edinburgh University. These usually capitalise on cutting-edge research originated within a group of partner universities. You can make contact with these organisations UK-wide via the Knowledge Transfer Network.

Accelerators and incubators both offer opportunities for fast growth to companies and entrepreneurs accepted onto them, and create a much better chance of getting interest from venture capital firms further down the line.

The two models work in different ways. Accelerators are focused on the rapid growth of existing companies by offering intensive business mentoring, expert advice and practical support worth several thousand pounds, in return for a small percentage of the equity. Some invest capital, others take an option to buy an equity stake in the future. The goal is to make companies investor-ready, and then help to pitch to investors.

Incubators are more geared towards interesting ideas and technologies that can be patented and/or turned into a company. Essentially they are 'hothousing' schemes that help create and then shape a company using co-working spaces. Many incubators offer seed funding, too, with investments ranging from £10,000 to very occasional six-figure sums.

Which one you choose will depend on the type of company you are, and how much control you would like to have over running your company. Obviously if you have already been going for a short time and have brought some good clients on board, you are in a stronger position when approaching one of these programmes for help.

According to a 2014 report by Telefonica, 'The Rise of the UK Accelerator and Incubator Ecosystem', the survival rate after the first two years of companies created or grown in this way is thought to be approximately 92 per cent, much better than the average start-up survival rate of approximately 72 per cent.

Many start-ups have already been snapped up by big digital beasts such as Apple, Google and Facebook. Apple acquired Semetric, a music analytics company that created the MusicMetric tool, to enhance Apple's new music-streaming service Beats. Google bought several UK companies specialising in artificial intelligence including Dark Blue Labs, a data analysis tech company and Vision Factory, which develops visual recognition systems.

Some of the most interesting and productive accelerator and incubator programmes in the UK include:

Seedcamp
Founded in 2007 in London by a group of 30 European investors, Seedcamp operates as a micro-seed investment and mentoring programme.

Bethnal Green Ventures
An accelerator three-month programme for start-ups that want to create sustainable social innovations.

dotforge
Part of the Tech4Good group of accelerator programmes, dotforge is based in Sheffield. All of the Dotforge Impact start-ups are sparked by a desire to solve a social problem which is a catalyst for tech innovation.

BBC Worldwide Labs
This is a programme that supports innovative digital media companies and includes six start-ups each year to become part of the BBC ecosystem.

Firestartr
Firestartr helps start-ups by providing seed-stage capital to accelerate success.

Founder Institute

The Founder Institute offers a four-month entrepreneur training and start-up launch programme focusing on practical business-building skills, assignments and training courses.

Red Bull Amplifier

This is a project designed to find and help the growth of the most promising new music start-ups through a creative partnership.

Innovation Warehouse

London's community for entrepreneurs, offering support in mentoring, training sessions, investment (angel network), co-working, and everything that supports the high-growth business.

Pearson Catalyst for Education

A three-month programme that supports start-ups focused on learning-by-developing pilot programmes and providing resources from experts and industry leaders.

Microsoft Ventures

It's a three-month programme created to help early stage start-ups that work in cloud, mobile and internet. The programme provides training, top-quality mentorship and free tools.

Digital Greenwich

The accelerator programme gives business support to digital SMEs who are working on innovative products in health, transport, energy and digital home.

The Young Foundation

The accelerator, a four-month programme that supports start-ups in health, education and housing, provides expert tutoring, business support and social investment.

Entrepreneurs for the Future

For digital entrepreneurs living and working in the West Midlands.

C4DI

Based in Hull, this has focused on priority areas such as engineering, renewables, tourism and social/healthcare.

....

CASE STUDY: GUARDIAN MEDIA GROUP AND FOUNDERS FACTORY

Media organisations such as the Guardian Media Group, owners of the *Guardian* and *Observer* newspapers among others, have been canny and forward-thinking in their assimilation of digital trends and development of cutting-edge digital talent. In 2015 they backed Founders Factory, a multisector, corporate-backed accelerator and incubator founded by serial entrepreneurs Brent Hoberman, Henry Lane Fox and Jim Meyerle. GMG and Founders Factory have now launched the second phase of their initiative to find the next big innovation in media.

Opening in October 2016, five companies per year will be accepted for the digital media accelerator programme and will have privileged access to the Guardian Media Group and other corporate backers including L'Oréal and publishers Holtzbrinck Macmillan. As well as exposure to big investors and expert business advice the companies will get hands-on support from digital experts at Founders Factory to develop their digital media enterprise.

Last year's accelerator participants have enjoyed considerable market success already, and according to the Founders Factory website, they include:

Vidsy

A self-serve platform for brands to commission and distribute video content from a community of 1,500 filmmakers. Founders Factory supported Vidsy's transition from an agency model to a marketplace (launching in September), and in six months revenue has quadrupled. The company is now working with a number of international FMCG brands, including Founders Factory partners the *Guardian* and L'Oréal.

People.io
Giving people ownership of their data, to enable the next evolution of human connectivity. The first product is a platform that enables a person to license their data and attention. The company is credited with changing the perception of how brands use consumer data, and since its launch people.io has received cross-industry investment from a number of Europe's most successful entrepreneurs, including Thomas Höegh and Nick Robertson (ASOS).

....

KNOWLEDGE TRANSFER NETWORK

Innovate UK's Knowledge Transfer Network (KTN) is a forum for businesses, entrepreneurs, academics and investors to network and collaborate across the UK. The KTN includes a dedicated creative, digital and design community.

ARTS ALLIANCE

This is a London-based venture capital organisation targeted towards film and digital. They invest in seed, early stage and later-stage creative companies.

SAATCHINVEST

An early stage technology investment company, investing anywhere from £50,000– £400,000 seed and early stages.

TRANSMIT START-UPS

This organisation specialises in creative and digital start-up loans for England and Scotland.

CREATIVE CAPITAL FUND

This is a £6.5 million fund targeted to the creative industries in London. All current funds are now invested but the fund will open again in the future.

AXM VENTURE CAPITAL LTD/NORTH WEST CREATIVE FUND

Similar to the Creative Capital Fund, but in the North West of England.

ANGEL INVESTMENT NETWORK

This is a platform similar to the crowdfunding Crowdcube website, which has thousands of investors registered and looking for businesses to park their money in. You can register as an entrepreneur, submit a proposal and business plan, and if you are accepted you get paired up with interested investors. There are various fees for various levels of accessibility.

TECH CITY

Aimed at UK digital businesses from start-up to growth, Tech City has lots of programmes tailored to the different stages of your digital company. The Digital Business Academy is a free set of 11 courses about how to start and run a digital company, created and run by a partnership of UCL, Cambridge University JBS, Founder Centric and Valuable Content. A good starting point for the digital entrepreneur.

GAMES LONDON

A joint initiative between Film London and Ukie, a trade body for the UK games industry, with £1.2 million investment funds for games projects.

CHINESE INVESTMENT FUND FOR CREATIVE TECH

This is a new fund for European tech start-ups. Get in early to access some of the £500 million pot of cash!

THE FORD FOUNDATION

Just Films covers social impact documentary and ran from 2010 to 2015. It was due to reappear in 2016-17.

THE LONDON CO-INVESTMENT FUND
AND CAPITAL ENTERPRISE

The London Co-Investment Fund is founded and managed by Funding London and Capital Enterprise. It has raised £25 million from the Mayor of London's Growing Places Fund to co-invest in seed rounds between £250,000 and £1 million, led by selected co-investment partners.

They are looking to invest in high-growth tech, science and digital start-ups in London: http://www.thecreativeindustries.co.uk/media/322389/creative-industries-routes-to-finance.pdf

CORPORATE PARTNERSHIPS

Businesses provided about £150 million in direct support, sponsorship and partnerships with the cultural sector in 2011–12, according to the Department for Culture, Media and Sport.

The easiest way to get a corporate sponsor involved in the first instance is to have a one-off event, exhibition, show or digital project around these things, and ask for a corporate donation. There are specific rules around corporate donation for creative industries that you must investigate first, and you have to choose the donor wisely. Companies usually get Corporation Tax relief on the amount they have donated. Make sure it is a corporation that would be naturally aligned to your brand and content, or would want to be associated with it, and vice versa. Corporations often have ring-fenced marketing budgets that can put money towards creative enterprises that will enhance their own brand and fulfil their Corporate Social Responsibility (CSR) remit. Be aware that you will have to treat your corporate sponsors well – whatever related perks are available, make sure you indulge them. That might be free tickets, hospitality, a private screening or performance, a public introduction, or something else appropriate to the project.

If you can get a sponsor involved in a longer-term project or start-up idea, then so much the better. Longer-term brand association can lead to genuine collaboration on content and company structure and growth, and lots of pro bono expert advice.

The decision within a large corporation to support or sponsor an organisation is generally made by senior directors, marketing departments, CSR specialists, or by sponsorship agencies acting on the corporation's behalf. Make sure that you and any staff dealing with your sponsor organisation maintain a good relationship at all times – limit the number of people allowed to deal with them so that you can be across the communication and smooth over any issues quickly and effectively.

Corporate sponsors are usually looking for significant marketing, brand and accreditation benefits from their sponsorship or partnership with your company. Make sure these are crystal-clear before signing any agreements and getting your eager paws on the money. You don't want your start-up looking like a branch of Barclays.

CROWDFUNDING PLATFORMS

Most of us have probably received that email from friends, family or colleagues by now – the one where someone you know has a creative project on Kickstarter, Indiegogo, FundIt.Buzz or Crowdfunder that they want funded. Usually you will see a short pitching video (of variable quality, but getting better and better!) and then a list of 'perks' – benefits that the small investor receives for putting in anything between £20 and £5,000 towards getting the project off the ground. Often, if you have invested, this is accompanied by an increasingly irritating weekly, monthly or even daily 'newsletter' informing you of how the whole thing is progressing in your name.

For the first several years, crowdfunding was mostly run along these lines, called a rewards-based system. It was geared towards smaller projects, or seed funding up to a maximum of £40,000, and small investors did not expect a financial return. In 2014, the market for rewards-based crowdfunding was estimated at £26 million in the UK.

More recently things have evolved and now the market is huge, and complex.

Bigger, more serious platforms have arrived on the scene and are specifically geared towards business start-ups. These are called equity crowdfunding or peer-to-peer lending platforms. These require a serious business plan to apply.

KICKSTARTER

Although the platform Kickstarter has launched thousands of new companies and raised hundreds of millions it's not always good news when you have a creative project. Setting yourself a non-flexible limit for fundraising can mean a whole lot of heartache, and no cash at the end – so think hard about the approach you take on here!

Kickstarter is great for creative tech products where a tangible prototype or demo can be showcased. A case in point is the next generation of virtual reality headsets from Opto VR, which has done well enough to begin production.

....

CASE STUDY: *FIERCE: THE MOVIE*, CALIBRATE FILMS

Zoe Davis runs digital content company Calibrate Films, and currently has several projects in development and production including *Fierce: The Movie*, a feature documentary about the international drag scene. The project started with Kickstarter and then moved across to Indiegogo.

During the process Zoe realised that without a team of highly organised people working alongside her, it was near impossible to succeed on Kickstarter. She no longer recommends crowdfunding to colleagues. Zoe says:

> *It can be a lot of hard work for very little return, unless you are highly organised, and I'm now responsible to fulfil all the pledges that were made. On Kickstarter you can only keep the money if you make your target, and we were under. On Indiegogo you still get to keep the funds, but you can't necessarily deliver what is promised (a full film) because you have not raised the funds to complete it, so you still have*

to look for further funding if you are to fulfil your promises to your contributors. This can mean that the stress carries on well past the campaign, because you are under a lot of pressure. However, I've taken this to be a good thing; because I am accountable to my contributors, this keeps me going.

Zoe thinks that the Kickstarter revenue model of not receiving funds unless you reach your target is actually more honest because, realistically, you can only genuinely fulfil the promises and make the film if you have raised the funds to do so – in the end she could have raised the same amount by working freelance for a month, rather than taking on a very intense crowdfunder.

The crowdfunder put a lot of pressure on Zoe and her team, financially and emotionally. Zoe says:

It is very emotionally draining to beg for money from friends, and you're constantly reminding yourself not to become disheartened when people don't respond as enthusiastically as you might expect. You've put your heart and soul into the project, but for many people you're just another person asking for donations.

Zoe is now finishing the documentary using other funding routes and has had a very positive response on social media.

....

NEXTPIX CROWDFUNDING GRANT

A good supplement to your Kickstarter or Indiegogo campaigns, Nextpix/Firstpix will fund films with a first- or second-time director and a budget under $250,000, which have part or all of their budget crowdfunded. The film should have a positive humanitarian message. They give a grant of £5,000.

CROWDCUBE

Crowdcube is one of the market leaders in business crowdfunding. It mixes professional investors with members of the public who have a bit of cash to spare and want to take a punt on a start-up or help a business to grow with a view to exit. The application process is, reassuringly, more rigorous than with other crowdfunding platforms and not everyone gets through. With almost 250,000 investors signed on and approximately £137 million raised, it's certainly worth a look for ambitious creative start-ups, or after the first couple of years of running a successful business.

CREATIVE INDUSTRY CASE STUDY

Games Grabr is a social network platform for gamers – a place where devotees can share, buy and play games. Pitched as 'like Pinterest for gamers' by MD Tony Pearce, it has so far attracted 221 investors and £454,734 in funding.

FUNDING CIRCLE

The tagline here is 'Stop Waiting on Banks' – which will be music to the ears of creative entrepreneurs as banks are notoriously cautious when it comes to supporting the creative industries. In a relatively short space of time, Funding Circle has become widely used and is focused on small businesses. Investors include public bodies such as the UK government, local councils, universities and financial organisations. More than £1 billion ($1.5 billion) has been lent to 12,000 businesses in the UK, USA, Germany, Spain and the Netherlands.

Their website quotes the founder of Peak Design, a US-based company, who explains why their more rational, flexible approach helps start-ups:

Traditional lenders are just too slow. Banks are mail, Funding Circle is email. That's all there is to it. Eliminating that wait time meant more money in my pocket. Two weeks versus six months is the difference between launching a new product or not.

NESTA CROWDFUNDING MATCH FUND

This is a pilot match fund, created by NESTA and backed by Arts Council England, Lottery Fund and the Department for Culture, Media and Sport. It is focused on arts and heritage and hopes to kick-start a new trend in match funding for the arts and public sector, rather than relying on the current, much more rigid grants system. There is £125,000 in funding available for the pilot scheme, and it works for individual projects as follows:

- A top-up model where 25 per cent of match funding is released once a project has achieved 75 per cent of its funding target

- A bridge model when projects crowdfund up to 25 per cent and then 'bridge' funding is released which brings them to 50 per cent. The funding is then conditional on the project getting the final 50 per cent.

ANGEL LIST

This platform allows start-ups to get investment from seasoned angel investors, as well as posting jobs and finding collaborators online.

The model is that venture capital organisations and angel investor individuals form a syndicate, agree to co-invest with each other, then find companies to invest in.

For the last year alone, there are some impressive stats: $149 million invested in start-ups, 398 start-ups funded, and 3,047 active investors.

The list of crowdfunding platforms grows daily for rewards-based, equity and peer-to-peer lending. Some other platforms geared towards creatives include:

- Ideastap
- Lend and Invest
- Zopa

INTERVIEW: LUKE LANG,
CROWDCUBE CO-FOUNDER

What is Crowdcube?

Founded in 2011 by South West-based entrepreneurs Darren Westlake and Luke Lang, Crowdcube is the UK's first and leading equity crowdfunding platform.

Crowdcube enables everyday investors to invest alongside professionals, angels and venture capital firms, making investing in great British businesses accessible, affordable and rewarding. For ambitious businesses, from a range of sectors, Crowdcube is a platform to raise finance with the added benefit of being backed by the crowd.

With a rapidly growing community of over 300,000 members, over £185 million has been invested through Crowdcube, funding more than 440 raises for start-up, early and growth-stage businesses. Funded businesses include Monzo (previously Mondo), the mobile challenger bank, which raised £1 million in just 96 seconds, Sugru, the world's first mouldable glue, which raised £3.4 million, and the world-famous Eden Project, which raised £1.5 million.

How does it differ from other crowdfunding platforms?

Crowdcube was the world's first equity crowdfunding platform; now, five years on, we've grown to be the largest, having amassed a crowd of over 300,000 people, who have invested more than £185 million in over 400 businesses. Crowdcube enables investors to invest and hold a direct shareholding in the business, rather than via a nominee, resulting in investors having a direct link with the businesses they want to support. There are no fees for investing on Crowdcube, either up front or on any returns, and for businesses, our fees only apply if the raise on Crowdcube completes.

What is the process for getting your company on to Crowdcube?

For a business to be approved to pitch on Crowdcube they will need a business plan, financial forecasts for the next three years and a compelling video pitch that clearly explains the investment proposition. Investors also want to be inspired and excited, so it's important that the pitch doesn't lack passion or enthusiasm for the business. Essentially there are three key elements to get across in a pitch for investment – the idea, how it could impact the market and how investors could see a return on their investment.

Before listing on Crowdcube our experienced legal, financial and compliance team will conduct thorough due diligence on the company, its legal structure, financials and directors using leading third party providers such as Creditsafe, Experian and Onfido. We also verify evidence supporting any claims being made by the business such as market size, contracts and partnerships to ensure the information provided is accurate.

The Crowdcube team will guide businesses through this process every step of the way from preparing and approving the pitch, promoting it to Crowdcube's investor community and handling all the administration and payments to finalise the investment round.

Have you worked with the creative industries (film and video, creative tech, digital start-ups)?

Yes. For example, Seadog Productions, which was founded by Monty Halls, one of the UK's best-known adventure presenters, writers and broadcasters. Seadog Productions, which aims to produce world-class television and video content, raised £415,000 from 345 investors on Crowdcube in 2015.

Another great example is 12th Battalion Productions, which is producing a full holographic, feature-length production. The company raised £139,000 from 38 investors in February 2016.

In terms of digital start-ups, there are plenty of businesses to choose from. For example, JustPark, which is taking parking into the digital era, raised £3.5 million on Crowdcube thanks to investment from over 2,700 people. Another example is goHenry, a digital banking solution that aims to make children smarter at managing money, which raised just shy of £4 million, and Run an Empire, the strategy-running game for mobile that's based in the real world, which raised £123,000 from 120 investors in 2015.

Are investors interested in film and video projects or do they prefer digital marketing or technology companies?

There isn't a typical profile for businesses that are suited to crowdfunding. We've helped a broad spectrum of businesses raise finance, from start-ups looking to raise tens of thousands to get their businesses off the ground, to more established brands such as the Eden Project and River Cottage, which have raised over a million on Crowdcube in a matter of hours, to fund the business's growth. Many businesses are drawn to crowdfunding to access a diverse pool of investors looking for interesting investor opportunities – from film and video projects, digital or tech companies, right the way through to breweries and banks.

What would be your advice to a budding creative entrepreneur who wants to use Crowdcube as part of their start-up plan?

Crowdcube's advice for businesses seeking investment through crowdfunding would be to start with a compelling pitch that provides a clear overview of the proposition. It's important to cover what makes the business unique, the potential market opportunity and the strategy for growth. People are also inspired to invest if the proposition is something they're already interested in or if it's just too compelling or interesting to ignore, so if the business ticks one or both of those boxes it's off to a good start. It's also important to remember that no investor wants to take on more risk than they have to, so the more tangible developments a business can demonstrate, such as sales, contract wins or partnerships, the better. Lastly, investors will want to know how the investment will be used and, essentially, how and when they could see a return. All of this needs to be supported with a sound business plan and financial forecasts.

How far has Crowdcube come since its inception, and where will it go in the future?

Equity crowdfunding came into being just five years ago when Crowdcube was first established. Since then, Crowdcube has continued on its mission to make investment easy and rewarding for anyone, anywhere with over £185 million having successfully been invested in over 430 raises, more than any other platform in the UK. Crowdfunding has well and truly come of age and, with Crowdcube members reaching over 300,000, it's clear investors are eager to back great British businesses.

Far from being a last resort, Crowdcube is now fast becoming the first choice for businesses raising finance, from ambitious start-ups right the way through to growth-stage businesses, many of which have venture capital backing such as Monzo, JustPark and Revolut.

Crowdfunding investors are also starting to see early signs of success with over £5 million having been repaid to investors on Crowdcube through the sale of Camden Town Brewery, E-Car Club and Wool and the Gang, as well as through bond interest repayments.

Going forward, Crowdcube will continue to inspire investment. To do that we're working with bigger brands to bring a wider range of investment opportunities to the crowd and, with plans to launch new products in the near future, we're continuing to grow from our innovative roots at a rapid pace.

CREATIVE FUNDING AND BREXIT

The announcement that England and Wales had voted the UK out of the EU struck fear into many people working in the creative industries. Anyone I spoke to about it felt the same way as me: bereft. This is because we have all benefited hugely from EU culture, massive funding, co-production treaties, and from the creative cross-fertilisation that comes from our ability to live and work anywhere in Europe. The idea that we would suddenly be separated from our European colleagues, having been part of the same family for such a long time, is heartbreaking and makes us want to run for the hills (provided those hills are in Berlin, Dublin or Copenhagen).

We now have questions about our creative relationships and funding in the US thrown into the mix, with the election of Donald Trump – currently an unknown quantity.

Between 2007 and 2012, the Creative Europe programme, through its MEDIA fund, gave £37 million to creative businesses in the UK and spent £39 million on promoting British films to the rest of Europe.

The EU's £93 million Cultural and Creative Sectors Guarantee Fund, as outlined earlier in this chapter, has only just launched and will give creative businesses in the UK unprecedented access to finance throughout the EU – while it is part of the EU.

Creative businesses have access to over 500 million potential customers throughout the EU and can employ talent from any EU member state without a work permit, and work across Europe without visas – flexibility that has been essential to filming in locations all over Europe.

Brexit could mean we lose all of this. It could also mean we get hit by tariffs on sale of our content to EU members, although some film co-production treaties may be able to continue as they are agreed by the Council of Europe rather than the EU.

There have been voices within the film industry warning against the proposed Digital Single Market Strategy (DSM) of the EU. The DSM seeks to end geo-blocking of content across Europe, and stop territorial copyright in digital content. Rebecca O'Brien, MD of Sixteen Films, who has produced 15 of Ken Loach's films, is 100 per cent pro-EU in general but says in an article for the *Guardian*:

The Digital Single Market Strategy (DSM) ... threatens to make it impossible for distribution companies to secure rights to films on a territory-by-territory basis. Ultimately, all films made available on any online platform would have to be made available across the whole of the EU at once. By ignoring the complexities of the European model for film financing and distribution, this prescriptive vision in fact threatens to make Europe's fragile film industry unsustainable, and ultimately to short-change the very European consumers it purports to empower.

Surely, though, it is preferable that creatives in the UK are sitting around the table when it comes to discussions about things like the DSM, and can influence decisions, rather than complaining from the sidelines.

There are optimistic voices in the industry, too. Highly experienced media accountant Bobby Lane, head of outsourcing and business development at Shelley Stock Hutter LLP Chartered Accountants, says:

I believe there are more opportunities for creative businesses than there were before Brexit. There is a huge pool of talent in UK creative industries and international businesses will still want to tap into these resources. Previously, if you were putting a proposal together for, say, £10,000, that might have seemed expensive to an international client, but now it is far cheaper due to the weaker pound. With the short-term reduction and weakening of the pound, UK creative businesses are even more appealing as suppliers as well as acquisition targets. People are investing in creative businesses for their skills and what they have to offer – they still have the same skills and are now cheaper to engage with so what's not to like?!

However, if you are a creative business dealing with international companies, given the massive currency fluctuations over the past few months, it will be very important to seek advice and identify ways of reducing your currency exposure or risk.

It is now more than ever vital that creative firms stay close to their business advisors as we are still waiting to see the effects of Brexit. Good professional advisors should be able to guide them through the uncharted waters and advise what they should be doing as the rules change and develop.

INTERVIEW WITH CHARLIE PRICE,
DIGITAL TECH START-UP MINI SCREEN PICTURES

What does Mini Screen Pictures do?

Mini Screen specialises in making entertainment programmes for mobiles and tablets. More specifically, helping broadcasters to maximise the value they can get from their content through social media channels in order to create real value for their franchises and their campaigns.

The problem currently is that, when broadcasters and brands are creating this bonus content for drawing people into the subject matter, there is a lot of fragmentation in the market. There are lots of 2nd screen apps but they have a short shelf life; no one wants to keep lots of apps on their phone, and also when people are on their phone and watching TV at the same time, they're probably not really interested in what's on TV, or they're engaging with their mobile during an ad break. So there's a misconception about what 2nd screen is for and that's something we want to challenge.

Brands know that content cuts across more than any other kind of advertising, and with a billion users on YouTube every month, brands feel like they have to be on there. But the truth is, discoverability is bad for everyone – even the biggest brands. The music-streaming service Deezer has three million users worldwide, half of whom are subscribers. They have approximately 100,000 YouTube subscribers, and their content gets sporadic views – about 10,000 views a month.

So discoverability and fragmentation are issues that everyone has and that we want to address by creating this platform.

We are filling the gap for a bespoke platform that can offer high-end content that also feels entertaining to them but is to YouTube what LinkedIn is to Facebook; it's a more tailored professional approach, high-end TV spec content that really utilises the mobile platform. The mobile platform is underused – the cross-platform mantra is watch what you want however you want whenever you want, but the mobile platform is considered an afterthought and most of the content you watch on there is either suited to another device or another medium. So it's narratively and technologically unsuited.

What made you decide to create a tech start-up?

I started Mini Screen Pictures because I hated commuting and I knew that, back in 2012, everyone had a TV in their pocket (BBC iPlayer had just started enabling downloads at that time), but that there was really no content out there that was bespoke for and exclusive to that person who was on the go. That was my starting point. In many ways nothing has really changed with 2nd screen since then, although there have been lots of efforts.

I think there's a whole world of people who would love to engage with content on the move. We have other interesting ways of monetising the content as well. Ad blocking is a problem, too. Those pop-up ads are irritating. I don't want to see a picture of a pair of shoes I've already bought.

So the difference with your platform is that the brand is integrated within it?

That's right. We redefine engagement. The way measurable engagement currently works is that you send an ad out, you can see that people have watched that ad, but we say if someone downloads the app, watches the show, then can click on links and actually buy relevant stuff, i.e. fashion or booking hols from a travel show, that is 100 per cent engagement and can literally affect the ROI for brands investing in this content.

What does the platform look like?

When you go into the Mini Screen app you see the most recent content and it's very mobile-centric, i.e. large images full of interesting TV shows. It's basically what you would see on TV except everything has got the name of a brand. We're not shoving brands down people's throats because they are going to the app because they are interested in the content, and if they are interested in the content that means they don't mind that it's branded. It might be short-form or long-form with TV spec. It's either a live broadcast through our platform or available on demand. Imagine you have something like *Later with Jools Holland* sponsored by Deezer. You then go to that show; it says it starts at this time, which is when you're commuting home. Then you get introduced to loads of new music, which is what you already like. You can share the content and also moments from it, i.e. capturing screenshots and sharing it really easily without having to leave the platform (this can't currently be done).

Also hotspots that you could click on and go and buy tickets for that band's next concert or download a single or download Deezer's app. All while remaining in the Mini Screen app world.

I don't believe that anyone loves but they do like and appreciate certain brands' values, and admire certain brands. Also they are linked to TV shows that you do actually love and have an emotional connection with. It's a positive association for both parties.

As the app grows and we get more content we can syphon off different things for different genres like sport, music, etc.

Is the interface like anything existing?

Yes, we were inspired by Soundcloud, which is very pictorial before you even start viewing content, i.e. the icons are very big. There's a list-style approach. We want to make it as easy as possible to engage with. A lot of the on-demand platforms like Inlayer, Amazon Prime, Netflix, etc. are struggling to make sure all their content is viewable because they have so much content they have to put out there and so their icons are so small. You don't feel bombarded by the content.

How did you put the company together?

I was working in film and TV development back in 2012 and wasn't getting enough freelance work. I came across a project that was making a continuing drama, i.e. something like *EastEnders* for smartphones and tablets. It was all very amateurishly done and didn't have a business model but it was a Eureka moment for me. I had a conversation with someone from Kudos when I was in an interview to get on their books as a script reader and he said, 'I'm sure someone will make a lot of money from this platform in the future' and I'm thinking, 'That could be me.' So I then worked on getting out of London and living the entrepreneurial dream of moving back in with my dad and trying to set up the company. The company was incorporated back in 2012 and I was looking for a shape at that time to make 2nd screen content narratively and technologically better. I read up on how to run a company, I got some info from the Prince's Trust, but a tech media company wasn't a good fit for them. I wanted to use my knowledge in development to get some scripts in but I came to the conclusion that the only way to do this was to do it properly, which would be expensive, so I then had to raise the money and I started networking and getting advice.

How did you find the people that you talked to initially?

It was very serendipitous – I found people on LinkedIn who were doing this, i.e. media consultants people doing mobile video hosting. A friend of mine, Christian Harris, who's now head of Deezer in the UK, was doing something with his own company called Gorillabox video hosting. I didn't know the first thing about building the platform but I knew I needed to learn so I found him, and he was very supportive. I remember going to a Creative England event and meeting a lady called Claire Barry who ran the Oxford TV and Media Finance Network, and she told me to come to that, which is when I met more people from a finance background. A lot of them didn't get it. At that point things were so broad that the pitch was hard. People were saying, 'Where's the content?' I realised we needed some example content to reduce the perceived risk of the business. I started trying to get start-up micro loans to make stuff that proved the concept so I could then go and raise more money on a seed round for 2014.

What happened next?

2014 was the worst year for me. I was trying to raise £150,000. I'd got a start-up loan from the Start-up Loans Company to make proof-of-concept material, and they had a delivery partner called Translink Start-ups. Obviously a completely new tech idea where there were no comparable businesses is a hard pitch. I tried to get a wireframe of the app done, some teaser content, and it did the job roughly, but it didn't strengthen the case as much as it should have. But you have to learn as you go along. I'm not sure if this time spent was a good or a bad thing – I did learn from it.

So we then tried to move on to SEIS. This is when you discover how difficult it can be to get in front of investors who are really willing to invest in media.

At that point it was still just me and a business plan because I thought I wouldn't be able to get anyone decent into the company unless I could pay them. I didn't have anyone at that point who was willing to work on it either full- or part-time for sweat equity (working for shares only). So 2014 was a rough year. I started working with an independent financial advisor to try and get access to high-net-worth individuals, and we came so close a few times. I almost had £75,000 from one investor but he took 2.5 months to deliberate after our meeting and finally put his money into a gourmet burger start-up because he could understand the risk versus rewards of that basic market and couldn't understand the 'daily challenges' that I would come up against with Mini Screen.

So by 2015 we changed tack. I had a good rapport with my IFA who had worked hard to get some money in for me and we decided to get something through accelerator programmes. That didn't work. So mid-2015 I decided to make a last-ditch attempt because this had been going on for too long and I wasn't making any money from it – to get a CTO on board for sweat equity. So I spent a couple of months searching for a software developer to build the app as that's what I needed first. I can't make content unless I have a business; I don't have a business unless I have an app. I was very lucky to finally go to a monthly meet-up called TechWednesday in Birmingham and came across Dave Evans who had been involved in developing the earliest versions of video-playing tech and was also a successful entrepreneur. He eventually said, 'OK, let's do it.' After so long of trying to get to MVP (minimum viable product), which is the earliest stage at which you can get into market, that first barrier was finally lowered and we started to make progress quite quickly. We also discovered and solved lots of problems along the way.

The stage we're at now is market fit, getting our first clients on board and building that brand identity. So we built the app, started testing it, then I started looking to get the third co-founder on board, to manage the production side. I was managing the client relationships on a day-to-day basis and Dave was looking after the tech side. I needed someone to manage the production process for the content. I got back in touch with Claire Barry and she put me in touch with Producers' Forum and Media Parents. Then I put an ad out there and the applications started coming in and everyone was very experienced across broadcast, so much more than I expected. Everyone was at the exec producer level. I had about 40 applications. I talked to everyone, mostly to find out from them what was attractive about Mini Screen. There were then about ten people that I interviewed.

After all that time formulating an idea, living with my dad, not having any money, starting to be more and more uncomfortable with being in my overdraft all the time, to suddenly be in a situation where you've got an app that's developing, you're starting to get in front of the right clients and you're getting validation from people who have worked in the broadcasting world for decades and have a lot of experience, advice and value to add was amazing. So I ended up landing on Zoe who was able to situate the company in Birmingham because I needed the flexibility, so I went for someone who didn't necessarily have the most experience but had the most flexibility. So Zoe came on board and I had my co-founding team. I then started reapproaching people like Ascension Ventures, who I'd met up with a year earlier and who had said, 'We like it but you're too early stage

– come back when you've got a team and a product.' I'm now just waiting to hear back from them. I'm meeting loads of agencies and clients now who want to do more with their social media content. We'll soon be approaching broadcasters to use the platform for their digital content.

What were the terms with Dave?

Initially I wanted to get someone on board after I'd had investment and could pay them, and I was prepared to give them equity. But in the end we had a letter of agreement that said 'I will give you an equity stake in the company' so there would be a low wage and a decent amount of equity and co-founder status. We had a very loose gentlemen's agreement and got work underway. He would do what needed to be done in his own time. Obviously if someone's going to work on something for nothing they've got to really love what you're doing, but it's also more valuable to investors because they want people that have shown commitment. Dave's now been working for nothing for the past six months and Zoe's been on board for the past few months. Zoe still has freelance work and we fit around that; if Dave has something that comes up then I'll have to fit around that. I can't have first call on their time. The way I want to run the company is getting autonomy and delegation right, and that is about people having skills that complement each other but don't overlap, because when skillsets overlap you get internal competition because they're doing the same job and there's no real differentiator in how they work. We keep communication lines open. Dave coming on board was a watershed moment. We don't have a shareholders' agreement formulated yet because it costs money to do that, which we don't yet have. I am a big fan of vibes and trusting people because I believe that if you do that it pays you back a lot more. If I ever went back on my word, they wouldn't get involved, so there's no point in being shady about it. There was one point where there was a miscommunication about share valuation pre- and post-investment with Dave, just something that got lost in translation, and I made it my priority in that moment to sit down and get it sorted out so everything was resolved in the most transparent and up-front way. In a couple of hours what could have been a bit of a crisis was resolved perfectly amicably.

What do you think makes you a good CEO?

I think leadership is something I'm good at. There were experiences in my life that have made me good at leading people. I remember starting boarding at a school called St Johns in Windsor, when I was six years old. I was crying because I missed home. The headmaster came in and said, 'OK, don't worry, what sweets do you like?' I said Skittles. He said 'OK'. He then looked around the classroom and asked everyone else what sweets they liked. They all told him and he said he'd be back in 20 minutes. He came back and gave me the Skittles, which cheered me up for a bit, and gave everyone else sweets, too, so they didn't feel there was preferential treatment. It showed compassion. That was my first lesson in leadership. I've never had a problem talking to people who are older and wiser than me and using their advice and experience. I think that's a very powerful way to create a decent company culture. I have read books as well – on start-up culture. You have to give people responsibility and autonomy and trust them to respond well to you and perform well for the company. In a bigger company you have a manager who acts as the conductor to an orchestra. Everyone plays their part. There's not really any room for people to speak up, it's very rigid. The way that start-ups function is like a jazz combo group. You have a small number of musicians, a loose foundation for how things are going to go, but within that there is the scope and perspective for people to express themselves in their own individual way. Pixar have the Brain Trust. I don't think that happens in enough creative companies.

INTERVIEW WITH JOHN SPINDLER,
CEO OF CAPITAL ENTERPRISE, CO-FOUNDER
THE LONDON CO-INVESTMENT FUND

What is Ideas London?

An innovation space funded by Cisco and University College London for early stage tech start-ups.

What are the differences between creative tech and other creative industries?

I feel that the creative business model and the business model for tech are actually very different – the people look like each other and are educated to a similar stage but have different focuses and priorities.

Most creatives are there to produce a piece of work that demonstrates their creative talent.

Tech is about finding what customers want, and finding a product that solves a particular problem for that client. So it's an iterative, ongoing process where the creativity is in the problem solving and not necessarily in the end product. So it's been interesting to see how in London the dominant access to the finance industry enjoyed by the creative sector is now being superseded by the tech sector, with the creative sector being squeezed out.

In most creative businesses, the number-one guiding principle is to create something that will get critical acclaim, that will get recognition – and in marketing terms, to create a brand which will allow them to get more work. Only once they get established at that, which for most creatives is mid-career, five to ten years in, do they start to look at it from the perspective of a business, i.e. have I got anything here that can live outside my personality and creative talent and is repeatable, replicable and scaleable.

The big difference with tech came in the mid-noughties and in London in 2010/11, when companies decided not to be focused on just selling labour on a project for a third party, but to develop their own products and then sell those products until the company has an independent life from the owner and the product is scaleable. To make money you need to sell it to millions.

What's happened in tech is that they've taken some of the best creative talents and put them into tech businesses. With my investor hat on for people who want to get to incubators and accelerators, we have a phrase which is 'tech enabled business model'. The purpose is things that change the nature of how you deliver value to your customers. We are interested in people who, via doing a YouTube channel, change the very nature of the thing they are producing and selling.

Which creative tech platforms are you working with now?

Several, including We Are Colony and Filmdoo, which are all around the on-demand distribution and creation model in content. We probably haven't realised yet just how revolutionary Netflix is and how it has changed the nature of how people consume and interact with content.

What is happening in the creative tech arena right now?

The FANGS – Facebook, Amazon, Netflix, Google –are still acting like start-ups, investing in moonshot innovation, telling all their staff to keep thinking about the innovative. They manage to keep entrepreneur capitalism as their model, rather than making money off existing assets, which is called rentier capitalism. Most creative ventures are still using the rentier capitalism model, i.e. I produce a product, I protect it and then I rent it out – in an age where entrepreneur capitalism means getting an ongoing relationship with the buyer and the client. Innovative businesses today are asking how they can use the premium model of hooking the client, establishing a long-term relationship and then having a walled-garden approach where they can extract value from them over a long period of time. Also we are moving to subscription models. The *Guardian* group have got cash flow for another 18 months – they will surely have to introduce a subscription fee.

We were ahead of the game in the UK with the BBC iPlayer, but that is an example of how difficult it is when you are trying to do innovation but also preserve an existing business model, which was free broadcast over the air. The BBC should have opened iPlayer up to everyone, including independents. They shouldn't even be thinking about commissioning content. Netflix uses an algorithm to gauge what the customer wants, and buys that. The biggest problem facing the creative sector at the moment is the impending death of the advertising model, which will affect how things are consumed that are currently free. This is due to ad blocking, the spread of content, the inability to corner an audience, the plethora of distribution channels, and partly also our resistance to advertising. It's interesting that TV has come back because the big brands can cut through there.

We have lots of start-ups come to us and say they need to get early traction and at some stage they need to work out what paid acquisition routes work, and most of them come back and say the best is still Facebook. Facebook is very cost effective above any other platform. The difficulty you've got trying to come up with new platforms trying to find an audience to track and sell things to is that you're not fighting old media now, you're fighting the giants' new media.

If you look at apps, it is a designer medium. The most expensive person to employ now is the head of product, i.e. the kind of person that can design quickly and creatively in response to data.

Another example is data-driven design. In the commissioning space this is like the Netflix model, i.e. use an algorithm to work out what the data says then create a product out of that or curate content in reaction to that. But it's a fine balance because you can't be too reactive; you have to have faith that your design will work rather than constantly changing it.

In games it has been difficult to cut through the noise – there seems to be less mid-market in games. It's the one per cent that become enormous hits and everyone else loses money. The same games stay at the top of the charts. Indie game developers have found it much more difficult to make money than seemed likely a few years back. The attention economy – a few years ago it was thought there would be 30 to 50 apps you would use every week. As it turns out, there's about eight There's just too much noise; it's too hard to make an informed choice.

One of the dominant use cases for mobiles is no longer ads but chat, and there is loads of chat commerce. Chat commerce works in that you plug in to social media and you use an influencer model. If you have a big following and you plug a product in your social media stream you will either get a discount for yourself or you can pass the discount on to your friends. This has worked particularly well with wealthy women. A start-up doing this has become big in nine months. It's so much stronger if a friend says to you, 'I've got tickets for x at a 20 per cent discount,' than it is to use a banner ad.

Then there is Machine Learning AI – for example, Dukedeck. Dukedeck generated music using AI, which is outside copyright fees. There is another start-up doing the same for visuals, i.e. if you want to produce visuals for a website or poster you can get one designed using publicly available images that can be used outside copyright. Machine Learning AI will target things that are one-off and expensive, and one of those things is using creative talent (so it's designed to put creatives out of a job). In 50 years it will be only the premium market that uses humans for these things.

The desire of consumers not to have to pay for content is very strong, and the creative sector is still struggling with this. People will pay for labour and services but they won't pay for content. They will pay to see you perform in your band; they just won't pay for the music – or if they do pay they will want to rent it for a low amount.

Can you name a couple of example clients?

Tech Savers and Sound Labs, producing interactive toys. The Eet Group.

We've also looked at a company which was opening up the supply chain and getting rid of the middle man, to enable designers to do a small production run of clothes at a much cheaper rate. The model used tech to remotely programme the knitting machines that produce the cotton and the patterns, allowing a designer to design a shirt, send it automatically to the knitting machine in Bangladesh, produce the clothes without hand-programming the machine, and send you back the shirts, reducing the cost of that production by one half or two thirds. This frees up the designer to be more creative and not have to always go with big brands like Topshop. They had lots of investors around them and they tried to go with another consortium of VCs and angels so we lost out. I thought they were classic disruptive tech, but for some reason it's not happening yet.

How do you get involved in companies/what are the different stages?

In Capital Enterprise we have 75 members, including spaces for the creative sector and universities including London College of Fashion and Ravensbourne. I support them to create programmes and get funding so they can offer their services to the creative sector, including private sector and government funding. That's the bulk of the work I do.

The only category where we do the direct service is around investment, that is the London Co-Investment Fund. We decided that it would be good if companies had an aggregator to advise them, tidy up their proposals and introduce them to investors. We do that at all stages. At least 50 per cent of the clients we see would have been referred by one of our members, i.e. LCF or an incubator/accelerator.

We are the first people that look through your business proposal with the eyes of an investor rather than the eyes of a producer, partner, advisor or customer. We then give you feedback and support to meet the not necessarily logical criteria of an investor who is putting his/her own money or that of their institution in a business with a view to selling their shares for a profit. Sometimes you can come to us very early and we might say you are six months away, you need to get your team together/do your first product, etc.

To give a bit of context, only one per cent of businesses in the States receive venture capital; in the UK it is around 0.4 per cent. If success is either floating on the Stock Exchange or being bought up, 75 per cent of businesses that float or get bought never take VC support. So you are much more likely to be a scaleable business that someone will eventually buy if you do take external support or equity capital. You have to then go for growth.

Last year there were around 1,400 companies in the whole of the UK that received some form of investment from angels and between 300 and 400 that received funding from VCs. The irony is that those kinds of companies generate 30 per cent of all the new jobs in the UK. The majority will fail, and fail more than once. Most of us have not been brought up to fail fail fail and then succeed. Often the key is not to mitigate your chances of failure but to increase the chance that you could lift off.

Business plans are not as important as you think. I need to know: will external finance make a difference, and if so, how; will you at some stage be able to make a return for that investor and if so, how?

So there are different stages and different proof points you need to go through.

Faith pitches: you've got an army of people together who believe in you, and I know that there are very few facts. It's a perfect act of rhetoric where you try to make me part with my money. We do this little trick; we say to pitchers: imagine there's a long lost uncle who has left you £250,000 but the rules are you can't invest in your own business. You have two choices. You can either invest in one of the other start-ups you've met here, or invest in a one-bedroom flat in the Haringey ladder that has doubled its value every year for the past six years. Who here is putting their money in the flat, and who will invest in another company here? Sit down if you would invest in property. Most of them sit down.

With a faith pitch it's the team – what's your experience and credibility. If you're inexperienced then you will have to show me more. First thing to do is build your team and refine your offer.

What is your opportunity hypothesis, how well do you know your customer, the choices they make every day? How well do you know your competitors? You have to be able to come to me with a simple hypothesis that says we will solve this problem for this client and by doing so we can build a company that is scaleable. Every hypothesis has to have a test. Then I will ask: what's the test? What do you need my money for, to test the hypothesis? And in doing so, what do I get, what do you get?

Further down the line it's looking at the product: does it work, does it deliver value, does it stand out? Your market traction – what evidence do you have that customers love you? And then your business model – how do you make money? Sometimes we draw out little maps of every step before the customer has to pay. Once we had 18 steps in that map – can you see the problem with that? Eighteen things that could go wrong. What you want is: I do that, they pay.

Then the type of market, so some investors will only go for companies that can go really big – there's no point in a ten million exit at best because they wouldn't make any money for their infrastructure costs.

Then we look at momentum, which means who else has invested in you? Give me something that gives me confidence that smarter people than me are using you, investing in you.

The later stage it is, the more money you are looking for, the more evidence I need.

Once we get involved we will spend some time doing due diligence on you.

Do you invest yourselves?

Yes, we do.

You give us a pitch deck, info on your team to check out, a demo of the product, and we look at our own data on that space. Then we make a decision based on a traffic light system. Red is either it's too early or it's not for us – which is the majority. Then we might suggest an accelerator. Amber is we like the team and the space is interesting, the product is OK but the pitch deck is awful. This is a problem because the pitch deck gives us clarity and focus, and without those half the game is lost. We did DD on 1,086 companies last year; we invested in 27 of them and we got another 90 investment from elsewhere. So out of that 1,086 there were about 250 that were greens, another 250 that were ambers and the rest reds. There's a one in five chance roughly that we can get you to investment.

People think it's all about the sizzle but it's not; it's about the steak.

What would your advice be to a creative tech start-up or one that's trying to work with creatives?

Keep on learning, keep your mind open. The skills you have now are probably inadequate for what you will need in ten years' time. Make yourself the expert in your field. To all creatives: stop falling in love with your own artistic talent, your own creative vision, and try to think more like a tech business.

Don't fall in love with your own product, fall in love with the problem. That's a quote from Brad Feld.

➤ **An example of a blank Investment Agreement (p.294) can be found in the Appendices at the end of this book**

PREMISES, BUDGETS
AND CASH FLOWING

One of the first things to think about with your new creative company is office space. Do you need it? This depends on several things: how many people are in your company, how many projects you are starting with and whether they involve clients coming to see you. Is it viable for you and your other staff to work from home and are you comfortable with that idea? Is it important that you have a 'front of house' or is most of your business done by email, phone and online? Most importantly, can you afford it?

Choosing premises can be a tricky business. You might be wowed by that shiny tech start-up/creative agency hub building down the road, the one with the ping-pong tables, yoga and massage classes, chill-out room and beer-stocked fridge – but check how much it is really going to cost you over the course of your time there. Many of these hubs have hidden costs that just keep rising year on year or sometimes month by month and they are often in up-and-coming areas where rents can suddenly shoot up. Make sure you check out a variety of options, not just the ones that make you feel cutting-edge but also the smaller, dingier, more modest variety that might suit your purposes, and budget, a lot better.

If you choose to work at home, there are lots of things to consider in terms of space, distractions, motivation, managing other staff working from their homes and agreed flexible working hours.

Before you make any final decisions on premises, do your one-year, three-year and five-year company cash flow. If this is something you are not familiar with, there are examples included and a list of organisations that will help you, for free.

I can't emphasise enough how important it is to understand your cash flow as a small creative business. Creative companies are not your run-of-the-mill business model and are often hair-raisingly unpredictable in terms of turnover and cash flow. Clients can sometimes be fickle, reluctant to pay on time or at all, renege on agreements or neglect to sign contracts leaving you high and dry unless you have a cushion of money to keep you going through the lean periods.

It is also extremely important to budget your individual projects realistically, and ideally to have a good production manager to keep on top of it all for you. If funds don't allow this yet, educate yourself and/or your business partner on all the ins and outs of budgets and cash flows.

OPEN-PLAN, PRIVATE OR FLEXIBLE SPACES?

Before we look at the options for premises, a word about how to structure your working space. This could be a very important decision for the well-being of your staff, and therefore the health of your company. For a long time open-plan offices were extremely popular everywhere and for creative companies – at least in my experience – they seemed to be the norm. Large institutions such as the BBC and many production companies regularly used large, open-plan spaces and often 'hot-desking' – where no one has a dedicated working space and you just grab whatever is free at the time.

Recent research from a national survey of workers in Denmark, Surrey and Exeter universities, and various others, shows that this could be bad news for your company. According to these studies, large, open-plan office environments can lead to increased stress, aggression, isolation and exhaustion for employees, slash productivity across the workplace, lower morale and job security and increase the risk of spreading infection.

On the few occasions I worked in a hot-desking culture, I always found it frustrating. There was endless faffing about trying to find a space in the morning, which delayed starting; it affected work progress because there was no continuity or permanent place for storage; I was always switching machines; it was harder to form relationships with colleagues; there was never a reliable private space available for meetings. I had no sense of ownership over my environment and therefore my place of work did not feel welcoming or secure.

Forward-looking tech companies such as Google, Pixar and Microsoft have adopted a flexible approach to work spaces, with recent research in mind. Susan Cain's book *Quiet* describes how Pixar Animation Studios offers:

> *a mix of solo workspaces, quiet zones, casual meeting areas, cafes, reading rooms, computer hubs and even 'streets' where people can chat casually with each other without interrupting others' workflow … employees are encouraged to make their individual offices, cubicles, desks and work areas their own and decorate them as they wish. Similarly, at Microsoft, many employees enjoy their own private offices, yet they come with sliding doors, movable walls, and other features that allow occupants to decide when they want to collaborate and when they need private time to think.*

As mentioned before, Google headquarters in Dublin, Ireland have a 'nested' approach to work spaces, with closed rooms of between six and eight people as well as more open areas.

All food for thought when planning your company's working environment!

OPTION 1: YOUR OWN PREMISES

When I started out with my business I did so at the much mythologised 'kitchen table' at my flat in Hackney, East London. I also spent a ridiculous amount of time at the local Turkish café having meetings and spending too much money on mochas and spinach and feta pancakes, but it was still a hell of a lot cheaper than paying for an office space. It was a year before I had enough going on to justify renting a space, and then it was just two desks in a converted basement flat in Dalston. I was renting from another film production company run by a couple who had once lived there and now rented the space out to three different 'micro' businesses. The others had small rooms of their own at the back, a film composer and an IT consultant. We shared a kitchen/dining area and bathroom, and it all worked pretty well, most of the time – unless I happened to organise a production meeting at the same time as the others in which case things got a little tense and overcrowded! Communication was key and when it broke down things were difficult, but while my business was small this was rarely a problem.

Within the year, when I had a few productions going and we were all running out of chairs and bumping into each other, I moved into the film composer's back room where I was able to have four desks. The following year, when I started asking to rent out additional desks in the space outside, it became clear that it was time to graduate to my own office.

It was exciting to have a big, shiny space just for my company but I made a few mistakes with my first foray into proper premises. First, I chose aesthetics over practicality. We moved into a beautiful art deco building with a breathtaking, newly designed atrium, recently redeveloped into a live/work space for creatives. It had a concierge desk, art gallery, restaurants and cafés on the ground floor, lots of funky, inspiring start-ups and established creatives on the first and second floors, and flats and meeting rooms above. Post was distributed to the offices via several lifts. It was in the creative hub of East London and felt like the centre of everything. Because the space was still in the process of being redeveloped in places (red flag number one) the offices were relatively inexpensive although there was an additional 'service charge' (red flag number two), which could be increased after the first quarter. The next two years were a nightmare. The spaces had been designed without proper ventilation and there were no windows. The lifts continually broke down. Post and parcels never quite reached their destination. A pipe from the flat above leaked onto our edit suite. The complicated key-swipe system meant we were always being locked out, or the front door was being left open by mistake. The internet didn't work properly. Building work on the top floor meant that our room would be flooded with drilling sounds and literally shake during client meetings, edits and voiceovers. During one of the many glittering art-world launch events downstairs, thieves broke in to several spaces and stole equipment. The water went on and off. There were three changes of management in the short time we were there. And inevitably, the service charge just kept going up and up.

Luckily I had hired a property solicitor to deal with the premises contract and negotiated a two-year break clause in the five-year lease. When the two years were up, we scarpered – but not before a highly stressful negotiation with the new management team when they tried (unsuccessfully) to claw back our large deposit.

I learned several lessons from the experience. It was great to have a swish, cutting-edge office space for our big corporate clients on the rare occasions they visited, but that was the only real advantage to being in the building. Other clients never really came except for the odd meeting, which could have taken place in a café anywhere. Essentially, we were not a client-facing business and so the look and feel of our offices should have been lower down on our list of priorities when finding our own premises.

When I found our next premises my priorites were rather different. As well as value for money I was looking for a solid, established landlord organisation with continuity and a good reputation; a space that was functional and comfortable for production and team purposes but not necessarily for all client meetings; an available separate meeting room; a building manager I could contact by phone any time I needed to; good transport links and close to a station; good health and safety in place; good security; no service charge or a fixed service charge and allocated post boxes for offices. In the end I found all that, albeit in a slightly shabbier building!

OPTION 2: SHARED PREMISES

Many creative companies share an office space and might expand or contract as needed within that space, if possible. There are lots of advantages to this. You don't have the stress of a large rental amount going out every month and having to deal with all the admin yourself. You can take a bit of space when you need it and shrink when you don't. You have the buzz and company of another business in the background. However, there are some disadvantages and it very much depends on the structure of the space. If it's open-plan and you have lots of client and pitching meetings in-house you might want to feel that you have your own space rather than having a rival company sitting in the background and listening in! There is less autonomy about what to do with the space you're occupying, as the owner/subletter inevitably has a say and you might feel restricted – or you might just not get on with them. The best option is to sublet a private office within a bigger space so that you have the best of both worlds and can use additional desks if you need them but structure your own space the way you want it.

OPTION 3: 'PAY AS YOU GO' OFFICES AND WORKING HUBS

A very practical solution depending on how your projects work is to have short-term office lets for the life of a project/s only.

There are lots of short-term-lease office spaces that you can rent for three months to a year, for the life of a project or projects, then leave when you're in a phase of development and don't want to spend a large amount on overheads.

Alternatively there are hubs you can use on an ad hoc basis for meetings, etc. but these work less well if you have to do a lot of phone bashing and a concentrated burst of production.

Some good places to go in the UK and globally are:

- TechHub, global, UK offices in London and Swansea – £375 per year flexible membership, £475 per month unlimited access
- ImpactHub – global, UK offices in London – £475 per month
- Baltic Creative, Liverpool – smallest units £300 per month
- OpenSpace, Manchester – from £147 per month
- Techcube, Edinburgh – £10 per day to £100 per month
- Fruitworks, Canterbury – £60–£200 per month
- The Melting Pot, Edinburgh – pay as you go option or £370 for full membership
- Central Working, London and Manchester – £99 for club membership, £499 for resident membership
- Rainmaking Loft, London – £395 per month
- Rentadesk, London – £195 per month hot-desk, £295 per month private desk
- Co-Work, London – £450 per desk per month
- 90 Mainyard, London – £90–£200 per month

Office Insurance and Production Insurance

You need to make sure your office contents are insured, and that you have appropriate production insurance in place to cover things like damage, travel, illness and public liability for creative projects. This can all be done under one insurance policy, and it's generally best to get an annual insurance policy so that you are covered whatever you are doing within the company.

Key Man Insurance

This is a specific insurance covering key members of your executive team. It means that, if you or your co-director are ill or otherwise unable to work for a period of time, an amount will be paid out to cover losses and an interim replacement if appropriate.

OPTION 4: FLEXIBLE WORKING AND WORKING FROM HOME

Flexible and home working are now buzz words in the working world. Larger corporations have come under pressure through a very welcome change in attitudes that prioritises work/life balance and accommodates the complexity in our lives. Shorter days so you can pick up the kids, four-day weeks, starting earlier and leaving earlier – these are all becoming more normal. Another development, which is a bit more controversial, is the move to home working. Many companies swear by this and others are suspicious of it. Marissa Meyer famously reversed the home-working policy at Yahoo, and received a serious backlash from her industry peers and the media for doing so.

To me, the idea of nine to five (or, as is more often the case in creative industries, ten till six or nine till six) is now a bit antiquated. The best way is to work out how to get the most out of talented staff and make sure that they feel their needs have been considered, too. As long as the work gets done when it needs to be done, there can always be a certain amount of flexibility. I have always employed part-time staff and worked around children or other work/life commitments, for the right person. I believe in an open, flexible working environment where the best talent is nurtured and the importance of enjoying life outside of work is acknowledged. Flexible hours, home working, allowing collaborations outside my company, and trusting staff to get the job done their way are all important to me as a boss. It doesn't work out with everyone, of course – but I've found that for the majority it does.

As well as production managers, researchers and production assistants, I have frequently hired executive producers and development executives part-time because, with these positions, having continuity and the right person for the job is more important than slaving away until midnight. Often this would be the same person, someone with high-level experience in both production and development, so they could swiftly move from pitching a project to overseeing it if I was overstretched or could be flexible about taking up the slack on other projects. They took responsibility for getting the job done in the time they could manage, in constant communication with me and with clients. People at this level often have complicated professional and personal lives, portfolio careers, kids and parents to look after. If issues with childcare or any other life challenges came up, we talked about it and worked out something practical. I always cash flowed for this as part of my long-term company spend, and worked around each individual's availability when drafting their freelance contract while also being realistic about the demands of projects. It was a planning exercise, but it worked. Contracts varied from short, around three to six months, to longer term with these senior staff free to work with other companies on the proviso that everything was transparent and non-disclosure agreements in place. A non-disclosure agreement basically says that any ideas that are being worked on within the company stay within the company and are only pitched through the company.

With home working I have found that, like anything else, its effectiveness depends on the employee. The more senior the person, generally, the better it works. Often junior staff are less sure of themselves and their roles and need constant guidance, the company of others and the motivation of an office environment, or at least a group environment.

With mid-senior staff it can be tricky to gauge. I have found production managers to be particularly variable, and as they are so crucial to a project running on time and on budget, you do need to be careful! My advice would be to work alongside employees in the office for some time first, and get to know them before deciding when and how often to allow home working. If you feel anxious about what is getting done and are constantly having to follow up with the person by phone and email to reassure yourself, then it is not working and you have to stop doing it immediately. Remember that you are paying this person and relying on them to help you keep your business viable; you can't afford to take chances. It can be a difficult conversation to have when you want to go back on the home-working arrangement, but you have to get on with it – be honest but diplomatic. Say you are finding it difficult to keep track, and would prefer your staff working alongside you for a while.

Obviously if you do not have premises then home working is the only option, but perhaps you can have certain key members of staff working at your home, at least for a time, to allow some cohesion and momentum in the projects you are working on. If and when a project starts to feel fragmented and lacking in energy, it's time to get the team together so they can bounce off each other and feel the satisfaction of collaboration. Human beings need the affirmation of others to feel useful and motivated. I have found that it's less the distraction of social media that's an issue (that can happen anywhere!) than the isolation, which means staff start losing their way and feel they don't have a stake in your company or the project they're working on. So organise something that makes you feel like a team on a regular basis. Perhaps that could mean going to a café or your living room for a team meeting, a few times a week. Think about what would work best for the needs of your projects and your staff, and schedule it all in advance.

You can also create a workflow document with members of staff to help you all stay on track with home working – and talk about how it is going at regular team meetings that you will always need to have. Are people finding it easy or difficult getting on with things in a home environment? Is being in the middle of domestic chaos distracting them? Sometimes it can be difficult to be in a work headspace when you're tripping over the cat, or boxes of toys, or the wash basket and dishes need to be done. In this case, if you are not in a position to offer an office space, could the person go to a local café to work, and you provide (limited) coffee money out of petty cash? It might be worth it if it means getting things done. I have always found it a bit easier to work with the buzz of anonymous activity around me – and judging by the scores of people frowning behind laptops at my local deli, I'm not alone!

A lot of the planning you do around working styles and schedules will depend on the personalities of the individuals involved, how they work in a team and how they work alone – so there isn't a general template. You need to be chief psychologist in your organisation, and work out what will bring out the best in different members of your team.

Recently I made an attempt to re-enter the job market after eight years of working solely in my own company, looking for a two- or three-day-a-week job. As a sole parent I wanted a temporary break from the responsibilities of running a company and running a small person; I had a desire to work as part of a team again, and be inspired by new ideas; and most importantly, I wanted to work part-time so that I could be present in my child's life for the early years.

I was shocked at how difficult it was to find part-time work at a senior level. The (very few) part-time jobs that existed were for more junior positions that I was overqualified for, and when a senior one popped up once in a blue moon it was usually for factual entertainment, a genre I have not worked in for years. I found myself applying for full-time jobs and then trying, fruitlessly, to negotiate part-time hours; or applying for jobs outside the industry I had worked in for 15 years. When I brought up the possibility of job shares, compressed hours or part-time, I often got blank stares and a sense of panic/confusion – this was not possible in production, apparently. And certainly not talked about up front. I felt like I had broken some kind of taboo.

What was going on? Was it just me? I spoke to colleagues and realised that no, it wasn't just me – the production industry has not yet progressed with the times when it comes to flexible working.

Things are so fluid in our digital age that we have to adapt and embrace new ways of working.

Job Shares

Job shares are another option that has become increasingly popular. Although I never had the opportunity to use them, if I was starting over it would be something I would build into job descriptions for the right role. A new initiative called Share My Telly Job (http://www.sharemytellyjob.com/) is trying to make headway with job shares in TV.

Job sharing is much easier in established professions like the Civil Service, with a huge integrated network. Some creative industries have been better than others at embracing the brave new world of 'Hire Me My Way'. Though many small, agile companies can and do hire staff on a part-time and individually tailored basis, the bigger beasts of film and TV are very bad at even acknowledging the possibility.

Timewise is a rapidly growing organisation that aims to create many more quality part-time and flexible jobs, and a job market fit for the twenty-first century.

....

CASE STUDY: TIMEWISE

Timewise co-founder and joint CEO Emma Stewart used to work in TV documentaries at a senior level and then, having had kids, found she couldn't get a senior job. She and Karen Mattison, co-founder and joint CEO, then realised they knew many women trapped in jobs they were overqualified for. They set up Timewise to try and build a quality flexible jobs market. The website was originally aimed at women, but is now for men also. Emma says:

> Legislation on flexible working has changed and flexible working as an issue has landed. Currently it is still seen as a perk, but we're changing attitudes in organisations. We are encouraging them to be open to a conversation about how people work, at interview stage. Less than one in ten good-quality jobs mention flexibility at the point of hire and yet half the working population is looking for flexible working.

They have launched the Hire Me My Way campaign, with a goal to make a million good-quality jobs flexible by 2020. Currently, 8.7 per cent of quality jobs are flexible. This is based on 3.5 million jobs over the £20,000 salary level. So far, employers have responded positively. Timewise have been giving them the insight to understand that they need to let candidates know they are already working flexibly, rather than keeping it a secret. Employers assume that job applicants know they are open to flexibility without mentioning it specifically in the job ad, but that is not the case. Virgin Money has now said to prospective applicants: 'we'll match your salary and we'll match your flexibility'.

Early adopters have been professional services – larger businesses that really need to retain and attract female talent. Innocent Drinks have also come on board. They are talking to smaller digital and tech companies, but say creative industries can be a tough nut to crack because the volume of work is challenging. Emma says: 'Nowhere has cracked this – Sweden is doing a six-hour-day trial at the moment, but they have the infrastructure to support it.' Success depends on various factors:

> *Firstly, change starts at the top. Leadership must buy into this. Then you have to let people in the organisation know, and let candidates know, that you are open – that's cultural change. Helping people and teams to think about how jobs are designed, at job spec stage, to embed flexibility. Lastly, communicate – put the flexibility statement on the job ad.*

CASH FLOWS

It's always a bit easier to have a bookkeeper come in, perhaps once a month, to make sure all is well with your company books.

It is good practice to keep an ongoing management accounts document throughout the year, so that when it comes to your end of year company accounts they are a lot less onerous.

However, you may not want the expenditure in the first year or so and in any case you must be completely on top of incomings and outgoings in your company irrespective of whether a bookkeeper is helping with this.

The first thing to get your head around is the art of cash flowing. This requires an Excel spreadsheet detailing what is coming in and going out of your company over the next six months, year, three years or five years. It helps you to manage payments to staff, all projects and all overheads and administrative costs according to how much is coming in to the company and when. It stops you from incurring penalties from going over bank overdraft facilities and attracting bad will or threatening letters from suppliers and staff who don't get paid on time. It allows you to survive, eat, pay your rent or mortgage while running your business. It's essential, particularly in the first years when you are less likely to have a nice, fluffy financial cushion during hard times.

Money coming in includes all funding and revenue streams including:

- Projects being commissioned
- Loans from banks
- Loans from public or private sources including friends and family
- Public funding from institutions
- Private funding from any individuals and foundations
- Royalties from distribution of content
- Income from subletting or renting of space or equipment
- Income from giving presentations and talks as a representative of the company
- Any other source of income for the company
- VAT received back
- Tax rebates

Money going out includes:

- Direct project costs
- Staff salaries
- Office rent and service charges
- Insurance
- Travel
- Research and development
- Phone and internet
- Computer expenses
- Subscriptions
- Electricity, gas and water

- Website costs
- Bank charges
- Income Tax and National Insurance costs
- Entertaining, i.e. buying lunch or dinner, hosting an event
- Bank charges
- Printing costs
- Postage and courier costs
- Foreign currency gains/losses, i.e. exchange rate when receiving or paying funds to an international client or supplier
- Any other outgoings in the company
- VAT

Different cash flows serve different purposes. A shorter-term, six-month-to-a-year cash flow tells you what is happening right now in the company and gives you the confidence that you can continue trading because you have enough confirmed business coming in over that time. A three-year to five-year blocks out what you expect and want to happen in the company, based on growth so far and prospective future business. It is often essential in order to secure growth loans and funding or private investment.

PROJECT CASH FLOWS

Often with a creative project, the budget you have agreed with your client will be paid to you according to a specific payment schedule and on specific payment terms. You need to factor this in to your cash flows to make sure that you are not going to be caught out not having enough money in the coffers to cover project and staff costs while waiting for your client to pay you.

It can take time to understand how essential cash flowing and budgeting is and what all the numbers mean. I have certainly never been a fan of budgets and numbers but I have grown to respect them and have relied on cash flows to keep me going over the years.

PREMISES, BUDGETS AND CASH FLOWING

BUSINESS RATES

This is another cost that you need to be mindful of if renting premises for your company. Business rates are annual payments for businesses using premises in the area, set by local councils, and can be quite steep. Happily, there is a government exemption scheme for small companies but you may not always meet the criteria so you need to check the square footage of your premises, and your turnover, to make sure that you will not be paying thousands of pounds out of your annual budget for business rates. Do your research on this before deciding on an area for premises. Once you are settled in you still have to apply for the exemption, so make sure you or your production manager or co-directors do this as soon as possible.

BUDGETS

You will also have many different projects and company budgets over time. Budgets are a comprehensive breakdown of where money will go and usually cover above-the-line costs (across the whole project or company staff working on that project) and staff and below-the-line costs and staff (i.e. production costs and freelance crew hired for that project only) separately.

Usually a budget is one of the first things you will need once you have successfully pitched a project to a client or won business from them some other way.

You should always be across budgets as the business owner, even if they are being drafted and run by production or project managers. Have them report to you on a regular basis with a cost manager to show where spend is going, if you are over or under budget or your project is financially on track.

Generally there is a fee that goes back to your company, called a 'production fee', of between ten and twelve per cent of the overall budget. However, as digital production becomes more competitive and budgets ever lower, I have noticed that some digital agencies in particular waive this fee.

PART **TWO**

HIT THE GROUND **RUNNING**

PUBLICITY AND ADVERTISING

There are many hundreds of production companies and creative agencies in the UK; indeed there are hundreds in London alone and scores in every other major city.

HOW DO YOU GET YOURSELF OUT THERE?

As with content production, there are positives and negatives to the digital age in terms of publicity and advertising. On the one hand, the world is your oyster. If you are a digital native, living, contributing and socialising mostly on social networks, you can reach almost every corner of the globe without much effort. The question is, what do you say and how do you say it effectively? In the digital space terms like pay per click, search engine optimisation, advanced data analytics and keyword generation are bandied about everywhere. It feels like you need a degree in digital marketing just to work out how to get people to notice you.

This comes back to the question of USP. In a massive sea of voices, opinions and visuals, you need to hold on to your core identity and not be swept along with the crowd. Attaching yourself to causes and organisations that care about the things you care about is a good start. Being bold in your opinions and endorsements and ruthless but engaging with your self-promotion on platforms like Facebook, Twitter, LinkedIn, Tumblr, Vimeo, YouTube, Instagram or Kickstarter is important to get your brand known online. A blog using free or inexpensive platforms like Wordpress or Weebly is also a good foundation from which to build your following. Being a content curator as well as a content producer means that people follow you for both your judgement and your talent.

You can start to contribute to the industry community by writing articles for industry groups on online platforms such as LinkedIn, Talent Manager, Media Parents, The Drum, Digital Arts and in magazines such as *Broadcast* and *Wired* as well as promoting your content there. You can also get involved in industry events, by becoming a festival sponsor. This is one of the most effective ways of getting your name known and meeting potential collaborators.

Even in the digital age, face-to-face networking is still an extremely effective means of making contact and there is no shortage of opportunities for the start-up company or the more established business, if you make it part of your work schedule to attend these events rather than seeing them as an inconvenience or an extracurricular activity. How much you enjoy networking depends very much on your personality type. Although sociable, I am on the introverted side of the spectrum and have always struggled with large groups of people I don't know, which has made me a reluctant face-to-face networker over the years. When I have attended networking events, I have often been pleasantly surprised, although I usually need some alone time afterwards!

YOUR ONLINE PRESENCE

Whatever platform you are using, it is important that you create a brand and that you are faithful to it. What constitutes your brand goes back to the USP question – who are you as a company? What is your culture, what are your priorities and aspirations? How do you want to come across, who is your audience, who would you like to connect to or be associated with? This will be heavily influenced by the directors and executives in your company – how many of you there are, what your individual personalities are, what your responsibilities within the company are, who your mentors have been. I built a brand over time because of creative choices that followed my interests, and a unifying brand has organically emerged. Although I have helped to create content on a variety of platforms – TV, digital, live events, cinema, business to business, schools and universities – it has generally had a focus on the following things: young people, education, human rights, women, innovation, new talent. These are areas I am naturally drawn to. No doubt if I was naturally drawn to shiny floor entertainment and celebrity I would have more money in the bank, but creative pursuits are subjective and, to an extent, you need to follow your heart.

So when using Facebook, Twitter, LinkedIn, Instagram or any other social network as a brand, you need to police the content to make sure it is commensurate with how you want to be seen. Rants and hilarious drunken posts are definitely best kept within your private social sphere; you never know when such things will come back to bite you.

Have a look around at people who are doing what you aspire to do. How do they present themselves and their company? Often there will be a main website and then breakout pages for specific creative projects, films, campaigns, product demos, etc. Often they will link to other pages and organisations that inspire them or that they are partnered up with and/or sponsored by, and official platforms that give the stamp of authenticity to their work such as IMDb or distribution outlets. You can also enter into distribution deals on a pay per click (PPC) basis with digital platforms or agencies. Generally there will be pages for company info, team, work (sometimes divided into genre and past/current work), projects in development, contact details. You may also have links to your Vimeo, YouTube and other channels, and should have a very clear shareable button for people to put your content out there across social media, including Tumblr, Instagram, Pinterest, Facebook, Twitter and LinkedIn. If you can get enough traffic to your page, and make it easy and immediate for them to share, viewers will do a large part of your marketing for you.

It does help if your team are up there with photos and clear titles and biogs. It helps the viewer connect. Generally, straightforward, friendly looking head or mid-shots are best. Some creative companies favour photos from childhood, action shots, production stills, animations and line drawings – or head shots that do something quirky when you pass your cursor over them. Whatever does it for you (just make sure it also appeals to your brand image and audience).

Showcasing your work, whatever medium you work in, is essential. Don't be too wordy on your website – lots of text doesn't look great. Use a lot of visuals – photos, graphics, animations and videos.

MOBILE AND TABLET FUNCTIONALITY

If you are starting from scratch with your online presence, then this needs to be built in at the very beginning – or if you are improving on your current presence it must be an integral part of your plan. If there is inhibited functionality of your website on smartphones, you are losing out on potential business and consumer interaction as these devices are now so ubiquitous and popular. This doesn't mean you need to have a site that is as cutting-edge as the beautifully interactive Google Glass Experiment, or have complex differences between device designs. It just means, when building your website, that you should make sure you use a developer who is knowledgeable about how to make all your content engaging and interactive on different devices. In essence, make sure your website is optimised for mobile and tablet. You can check out the efficacy of your current site with a handy little tool from Google, called the Google Mobile Friendly Test. If people can relate to you across their desktops, laptops, tablets and smartphones they will interact with you and share your content a hell of a lot more.

SOCIAL INFLUENCERS AND BLOGGING

Many companies and campaigns use 'social influencers' to get their message across. This could be a celebrity, someone very well known within a specific industry, or an online influencer with millions of followers. Some of the biggest YouTube stars, like Swedish gamer PewDewPie (over 40 million followers), British star Stampy Garret (eight million) or MyLifeAsEva (five million), can do a better job than anyone else of endorsing your product. Talent managers now have a large roster of YouTube stars to hire out to brands, with many becoming official spokespersons for specific brands, such as Gigi Gorgeous for Crest toothpaste. Think about whether this could be of use to you. Do you know anyone who has a massive online following? Can they be an ambassador for you? Which celebrities or well-known figures in business have you worked with? Can they officially endorse you?

A lot of marketing today is working out how to get people to physically interact with a brand, outside of the online world. Live music is an emotional connection. Merchandising produces a physical object. Real-time experiences like Secret Cinema have been hugely successful. People will pay a premium for the authenticity of live events, because these experiences are unique.

Blogging is something we are now all familiar with but the territory is changing, with hobby bloggers being replaced by professional bloggers who can be hired to get your name and content out there. So you can either choose to blog yourself, if you have plenty of followers or are linked to people who do, or use a professional blogger to target your reach a bit more. The digital age has brought a lot more fluidity in terms of content writers; nowadays it isn't only professional journalists or trained copywriters who write for public consumption. The role of journalists and bloggers is becoming increasingly blurred as corporations choose digital natives over trained journos who have had to adapt to online writing styles. This is difficult if you are a seasoned journalist trying to make a living having grown up before the digital age kicked in, but potentially good for you if you are good with words and digital technology as you do not have to pay a professional or depend on curators and critics for all your publicity coverage.

VIRTUAL REALITY AND AUGMENTED REALITY

In the near future, virtual reality looks likely to transform entertainment, film, gaming, communication and many other things that make up our world. For those of you who know of it but have not yet experienced it, VR is defined thus by Google:

> the computer-generated simulation of a three-dimensional image or environment that can be interacted with in a seemingly real or physical way by a person using special electronic equipment, such as a helmet with a screen inside or gloves fitted with sensors.

Our next generation of mobile phones will soon have functionality built specifically for viewing virtual reality content. Facebook has put serious money into its VR subsidiary company, Oculus, to produce 360 Video content. Concerts, sports events and other entertainment will be offered with the full VR experience package and sophisticated hologram technology.

Opto VR have produced a low-cost VR headset with integrated sound, branded as 'virtual reality for the living room'. Aiming to produce the first 500 headsets using seed funding from Kickstarter, Opto is the first portable VR headset, where audio has been an integral part from the beginning of the design process. The speakers sit within the headset, therefore users don't need to add their own headphones. Opto supports any smartphone with a screen size between 4 and 5.1 inches. The headsets are priced at a mere £75, and as of August 2016 they have started production on the first batch.

Already on the market are several headset options. On the more expensive side are Oculus Rift, HTC Vive and Sony Playstation VR, and Samsung Gear VR and Google Daydream View are accessibly cheap.

Filmmakers of all genres are getting excited about 360-degree cameras and companies specialising in the '360 immersive experience' are popping up everywhere. TV series will be watched and interacted with through VR headsets, particularly effective for big natural history programmes where you can, for example, experience the jungle along with the presenter. Sky are making a big investment in virtual reality TV. The broadcaster released a virtual reality app, Sky VR, and 12 free short VR films in late 2016. Gaming, already using VR in many cases, will be taken to another level. Conferences and meetings will be held using VR. Progress will be exponential, as is the case with disruptive technologies, and costs for all the various uses of VR will quickly come down.

Artificial intelligence has been part of the creative scene for many years and there are some interesting new applications in the creative industries. British start-up Jukedeck has created a neat piece of technology for composing music using artificial intelligence, which is threatening to usurp film and video composers. Users can choose a mood, style, tempo and length for their track, then the AI creates one tailored to their project. Users get five songs a month for free before paying $7 per track, although it costs $150 if they want the copyright.

Keeping ahead of the curve in creative industries means understanding how this technology will shape our interactions with the world and each other, and thinking about how we can bring it into our work before those who are funding us have worked out what they want. Production companies such as NextVR are looking to be the Netflix of virtual reality and have millions in funding to get them there; this space offers so much potential to producers of creative content now and in the future.

USING DIGITAL PR AGENCIES OR EXPERTS

There are lots of online marketing agencies out there. These are specialists in getting your company profile seen online. These companies have staff titles such as 'creative architect', 'digital shaper' and 'relationship crafter'. They pitch themselves as masters in the occult world of digital navigation, marketing and personalised advertising, knowing the language, data analytics and tools needed to be heard and seen above everyone else and get viewers to 'convert' to buyers of your product. They specialise in pay per click

(PPC) technology, where a client company places an ad on a website and pays the host a fee each time the ad is clicked on, and search engine optimisation (SEO), which means increasing the amount of traffic directed to your website by, for example, placing you at the top of search engine results.

How useful this is depends very much on what your product is. Are you launching a campaign that would benefit from a serious online presence, producing business promos and trying to attract big corporate clients, launching a new app or tech company, or breaking through with an innovative new gaming platform? Then perhaps you should be thinking about using some of your budget to bring a specialist in for digital marketing. It depends on the financial resources at your disposal and your brand identity. Alternatively, you can use a bit of cash up front to train yourself up in the dark arts of digital marketing, reducing costs in the long term. Given the increasing demand for 'digital native' skills in every sphere, it's probably a good idea to polish up your skills regularly anyway.

IN PERSON NETWORKING

This will always be the most useful way to connect in business, no matter how sophisticated virtual interaction becomes. Even when virtual reality has become so mainstream that events are coordinated through multiple VR headsets, it will never beat the real thing. As those of us who have tried online dating know all too well, it's possible to feel you have connected deeply with someone by social media and have zero chemistry in person. Our brains and the memories laid down within them are linked to emotional experience, so people who make an impression in the flesh are much more likely to stay with us and those relationships are more likely to move forward in the real world. For those really important connections, I always make sure to meet the person face to face.

So what are the options for in person networking?

PRIVATE MEMBERS CLUBS

Quite a bit of the business I have brought in through the years has been through less formal or structured networking, for example as a member of the Frontline Club or the Hospital Club in London. I have also visited clubs as a guest with friends who are not creative industry-related themselves and found business clients who want to tell their stories through video. Private members clubs can be very useful in this regard, if you use them often enough to meet the same people again and again, but be discerning if you are going to end up spending a lot of time there. I found that some of the more popular media private members clubs did not feel right for me, having spent a lot of time in them as a freelancer and with friends who were members – and they were often very expensive. Find out who among your contacts is a member of a club and invite yourself along for an evening to check out the vibe, before committing to an annual fee! Often these clubs are by referral only, i.e. you have to be put forward by an existing member, but this is not always the case. There are clubs in every major city so just do some research online to find out what there is available in your area. These clubs are also extremely useful if you don't have a dedicated office space as a place to meet clients. Prospective clients, particularly larger ones, often feel reassured that you are a serious partner if they meet you in salubrious surroundings, so if you bag them, that can be worth the fee alone.

Most major cities have a few members clubs that work this way so do some homework online and get plugged in to your local community.

BUSINESS COMMUNITIES

Organisations such as the Federation of Small Businesses (FSB) and the Institute of Directors (IoD) can be very useful to the budding creative company. They offer legal and financial advice to members and also hold a variety of monthly networking events nationwide, and panels about forthcoming company legislation changes. Because these organisations are for all SMEs, you also have the opportunity to meet entrepreneurs from industries very different to your own. The advantage you have in these situations is that you are perceived to be one of the most interesting people in the room and everyone wants to talk to you – creative industries always seem more glamorous and exciting than any other industry to the people outside them! So you can exploit this interest to make contacts outside your immediate sphere that might be very helpful for your business in the years to come.

There are also many membership organisations tailored to the creative industries such as the Creative Industries Federation, the Directors, Producers and Writers Guilds, the Producers Alliance for Film and Television (PACT), the Broadcasting, Entertainment, Cinematograph and Theatre Union (BECTU) and Innovate UK. Some of these cater to digital and creative tech although there are fewer than with broadcasting, cinema, music and theatre. Places like Passing Clouds in London have a nice, offbeat feel for meeting like-minded people and showing your work, and Frontline Club is great for campaigning work.

INDUSTRY EVENTS AND NETWORKING OPPORTUNITIES

Whatever creative industry you are in, there will always be a plethora of networking events and opportunities available – you just have to look for them online. Find the bars where creatives in the industry area you want to work in gather and make them your regular haunt. Even better, start a networking night yourself! It's as easy as creating a Facebook page, finding a venue with some seats on a Friday night and sending out invites to like-minded people. You never know where it might lead.

FESTIVALS

Festivals are a really excellent way to network if you do them right. Start small and work your way through, as the larger ones can be overwhelming for the novice.

There are literally thousands of festivals for the creative industries, from film and TV to music, art, digital and games. A good place to find global creative festivals is www.withoutabox.com.

It always helps if you have a project exhibiting at a festival, because you are then automatically 'on the inside' and will be shepherded around by those in the know and introduced to the right people. However, it's by no means necessary because, at festivals, people are generally feeling more relaxed and sociable. Not everyone, and you will see harried VIPs scuttling around trying to avoid conversations, but generally speaking. Best rule of thumb: approach people in a relaxed and interested way; don't get hammered and subject them to a barrage of spittle, sweat and beer breath as you panic-pitch in the bar, the lift or toilet.

As a member of the advisory board and producer at Sheffield Docfest, I have been involved with many inspiring events – from the Specialist Factual New Talent Pitch for expert presenters that we created and ran with the festival and Discovery Channel, to the Wellcome Trust Pitch and 2016's panel, Female Trailblazers and New Genderation.

Some good festivals for TV, film and video:

- Sheffield Docfest
- London Film Festival
- Sundance
- IDFA
- Berlin Film Festival
- Cannes
- New York Film and TV Festival
- Edinburgh TV Festival

For digital innovation:

- FutureFest
- QFest
- NODE
- FutureEverything
- MUTEK Barcelona
- Transmediale
- onedotzero

For games:

- Independent Games Festival
- Resonate
- Dare
- Insomnia
- EGX
- Game Space
- Pixel Heaven
- The State of Play

....

CASE STUDY: SHEFFIELD DOCFEST

There are various ways creative companies can get involved with Sheffield Docfest. Putting a company representative forward to talk on a panel session covering a pertinent topic is one. Each year the talks and sessions programme includes a range of speakers from production, distribution and marketing companies discussing their latest projects as well as industry developments.

Many companies/creatives will help produce a session, giving them an opportunity to shape the session's topic and content and giving them free access to the festival and networking opportunities with over 3,500 industry delegates. Some companies will sponsor a session which allows for branding opportunities across the festival's print, publications and website.

There is a whole section of the festival, called Alternate Realities, dedicated to artificial intelligence, virtual and augmented reality, curated by Mark Atkin. Crossover Labs is another opportunity for digital tech and filmmakers to collaborate on forward-looking projects.

Digital creatives and innovation will be of particular interest to the festival in 2017. Events manager Nigel Fischer says: 'The festival is always looking to involve emerging digital platforms and companies working in this area and discuss possible collaborations.'

....

TIPS FOR INTROVERTS

Some of us love getting out there, pressing the flesh, getting our energy from other people. I'm not one of them. Something I've discovered is that, while I really enjoy the company of others, I get my energy from time alone to recharge and contemplate. Also, I enjoy small groups and one-on-one better than large crowds. So all the parties, networking events, festivals, conferences, etc. that come with the territory of running a creative company can sometimes be a drain on the energy needed to push ahead, rather than a spur to collaboration as they are intended to be.

The tendency to be introverted or extroverted can be situation and company dependent, and it is on a fluid spectrum so don't be too quick to box yourself into a category, but it does help to be realistic about how you interact and what brings out your confidence or inhibition.

Over the years I have learned to respect the calm inner voice that says 'it's time to go' but also not listen to the panicked inner voice that says 'get me out of here!'. The former is telling me that it's time to recharge, the latter is not giving the event a chance because of social discomfort – which can ultimately mean losing out.

So force yourself to stay for an hour, at least – and remember that there are several people there in exactly the same boat as you, however confident they appear. Human beings vary in the way they negotiate these situations but you can be sure that at any large networking event there are many introverted as well as extroverted people present, and if they can stick it out for a bit, then so can you.

I was at a swanky event years ago with a friend and was bemoaning my awkwardness to him afterwards when he said, 'How do you think I felt? – I was the only brown face in the room.' It really made me think, and put my own difficulties into perspective. Sometimes we're so inside our own heads that we don't think about the internal experience of other people.

Often it's the first conversation that is the most awkward and difficult to kick off, and after this people join your group so that it flows more easily. You eventually find that you are enjoying yourself, and time has flown as much as the wine! If no one is approaching you to start that first conversation, you must do it yourself; just remember that if it doesn't go well you will probably never encounter this person again so it matters very little – and if it goes well you may have found a partner, collaborator or funder for your work.

As the best-selling book *Quiet* by self-confessed introvert Susan Cain attests, extrovert is not always best. Remember that the qualities of thoughtfulness, perspective, listening ability, authenticity and focused attention are attractive in these situations, too. They are also essential to running a business well. Mixing extroverts and introverts according to their strengths within organisations makes very good business sense – just look at Apple, founded by introvert Steve Wosniak and extrovert Steve Jobs, now the most successful company on the planet.

PITCHING FOR BUSINESS

Now that you have worked out your identity as a company and content provider, you can confidently go forth and pitch.

To whom do you pitch? The possibilities are endless and for that reason you need to be smart and discerning. Do not waste your time trying to get business from a broadcaster, business, charity or institution, brand, online platform or public fund if it does not fit your company profile and ambitions. Pitching to the wrong people and being constantly stalled, ignored or rejected is demoralising and demotivating.

Having said that, you will often be stalled, ignored and rejected by those who perfectly fit your company profile and ambitions, too. This is frustrating and confusing but, crucially, with persistence you will get there in the end and the relationship is much more likely to be a fruitful one. Do not take being ignored personally. The people with the purse strings and the commissioning power in any organisation are overwhelmed by people just like you trying to get their voices heard and their wonderful ideas realised and often it is not enough for one person to like your idea; their boss has to like it, too. In addition to talent, shameless persistence and the hide of a rhino are your best assets here.

So what are the options? This chapter goes through the many and varied avenues for pitching your factual idea in the UK, from a TV programme to a campaign viral, cross-platform project or live event, business promo or artist film and video piece.

THE BRAND-NEW WORLD OF CONTENT

The digital revolution has brought many changes, not least the way content is commissioned, consumed and distributed.

When I started working in TV and film in 2001, there was a very different and much more conservative landscape. Creative content was boxed into convenient categories with clear lines between cinema, TV, animation, graphic design, radio, print journalism, broadcast journalism, corporate video, advertising, music video, live theatre, artists' moving image and live performance. Each box came with its own platform, be that exhibition in cinemas, terrestrial broadcast on TV, projections in a conference room or live venue, graphics on a computer screen, live action in a theatre or street performance space, or video installation in an art gallery. Each box also came with its own funders and gatekeepers. Films for cinematic release were funded mostly by film studios, private investors, small amounts of public funds, tax-relief schemes and TV broadcasters based on a pitched script or treatment, crew and cast list. TV was funded by a rarefied breed of commissioning editors, the top of the TV tree, sitting up in their swanky offices within large broadcasting corporations guarding their purse strings and perusing written scripts and proposals. Corporate video, as it was called then, was a poor cousin to other content and was paid for by corporations to show mostly at events and sometimes on their websites. Ads and music videos were paid for by brands and record companies and made mostly by large, cutting-edge agencies for terrestrial broadcast. Artist film and video was funded primarily through public funds, galleries and private investors. Product placement was something you only saw in US blockbusters and HBO productions and brand-sponsored content was limited to indents for soap operas. There was a sense of separation between all these things, an internal hierarchy to them, and considerable training and expertise was needed for most of them. Teams needed to make content were much larger and therefore there were many more specialised jobs available. Although kit was already beginning to get a lot cheaper, it was nowhere near as cheap as it is now and this was also a prohibiting factor in producing content and meant that trained specialists and hired equipment were needed a lot more. Budgets were bigger and the volume of content considerably less.

Today, all of this has changed. Digital switchover for TV broadcast only happened in the UK in 2012 but the landscape has changed irrevocably since then. So what has happened?

Well, there is the emergence of digital platforms like Netflix, Vice, Amazon, Hulu, iTunes, Google Play and the rest. These platforms are the ultimate digital disrupters and have thrown the market into disarray, but also raised the bar for content creation. Then there has been the proliferation of video across all social networks and on platforms like YouTube, Vimeo and Dailymotion for several years, as well as the use of branded content across the board, constant increases in global and domestic digital channels, high-end business promos, campaign videos and virals, the widespread use of animation, sophisticated graphics and CGI across all content, digitisation of cinematic films and TV archive, and the widespread democratisation of the filmmaking process brought about by much lower technology costs. Among other things.

As a result of this audiences have moved online, particularly younger ones. In fact, age demographics, both in terms of audience and content creation, are very important when looking at the digital revolution. Millennials, loosely defined as those born between the 1980s and 2000, are leading the way in all things digital. On the younger end of that generation, some viewers will have never known anything but digital – no terrestrial, cable or satellite viewing, or traditional TV sets for them – and interactivity and user-generated content is as natural as breathing.

According to an Ofcom report, *Public Service Broadcasting in the Internet Age: Ofcom's Third Review of Public Service Broadcasting*:

> *Live television remains hugely important, but catch-up TV and content premiered online is increasingly significant to audiences, especially younger ones. In fact today, only 50% of 16–24s'*

viewing, and 61% of 25–34s', is watched when it's actually broadcast. Viewing of live TV news by young people also dropped, by 29%, between 2008 and 2014.

There is now a blurring of all categories. Everyone wants to use video content to spread their message, be that big business, small social enterprise, non-profit sector, academia, science and technology, entertainment, retail, arts or creative enterprises. Not so long ago people told their stories in the written word, even on websites – sometimes accompanied by still images. Now almost everyone uses moving image to get their narrative across. Websites now use video as a matter of course, no matter what the industry. There is now no need to pay a big, expensive facilities house for camera and editing equipment, and a large crew of people with specialist skills to create content, because the technology has become so cheap and widespread that people can learn it themselves.

The proliferation of Internet Protocol Television (IPTV) set-top boxes, through which TV services are delivered using the internet and integrated with other digital platforms such as social media and gaming, has been a game changer for viewing patterns, content creation and content distribution.

Of course, there will always be specialisms and highly trained people within any sector, and not everyone can make a CGI blockbuster, fixed-rig TV programme or do special effects, high-end graphics or virtual reality. Good writers will always be top of the tree creatively because of an innate talent that can be improved on but can't really be learned and the best creatives and producers will generally get the pick of the best projects. But in general, content is much easier to produce and much higher in volume because of it.

This volume has in turn led to a further blurring of the lines in terms of what different creative companies do. When digital agencies first emerged, they mostly concentrated on website and graphics design, ecommerce (selling things online), digital marketing and gaming. Now they do all these things plus film and video production, high-end animation, big social campaigns, branded content for broadcasters and business to business, education projects, music, 360 immersive projects, games and much more. Many funders are turning to small, agile digital agencies to make short-form digital content where once they would have asked traditional production companies, because they can do high turnover, high volume, low cost and have all the complex techie talent in-house.

Traditionally, production companies did TV, radio and film production. Now they overlap hugely with digital agencies because so much of the content they produce is digital. Digital has moved from being an 'add on' to broadcast programmes or films to being the main event. Production companies are now expected to deliver very sophisticated online projects in addition to, as part of, or instead of films or programmes that might be broadcast on TV or radio or exhibited in cinemas. Nowadays many production companies also do campaigning, entertainment or educational web projects alongside their films.

The two have become interdependent and the lines dividing creative content have disappeared with the advent of digital.

The market has become saturated and digital distribution companies are now legion. Standing out and creating your own following, with the help of appropriate platforms that enhance your brand, is now key – it's a patchwork that you put together in a collaborative process, often with non-exclusive distribution deals.

A huge increase in production company consolidation over the last decade – this means large groups buying up smaller independent companies – has changed the landscape further with content being much less varied and more 'on brand' for the parent company. Global TV entertainment formats such as *X Factor*, *The Voice*, *Strictly Come Dancing*, *The Great British Bake Off* and the like have become multimedia juggernauts that just keep on going (although in the case of *Bake Off*, Channel 4's outbidding of the BBC for ownership of the format has had unintended consequences with major talent leaving the show). Consolidation has taken place partly in an attempt to keep swimming against the massive tide of global content and competition that the digital revolution has brought about. In such a market, it is very difficult for the small independent production company or 'indie' to survive, but many do still manage it.

WHAT DO CREATIVE CONTENT COMPANIES DO?

Of course, the output of the creative industries is hugely varied. For the purposes of this book I have concentrated on film, TV and digital visual content production but many broader issues also apply to music, art and publishing.

Across the board, production companies and digital agencies cover these areas:

- Cinematic film production
- TV production
- Digital film and video production
- Branded digital video content
- Educational video content
- Ads
- Music videos
- Gaming
- Ecommerce
- Digital marketing
- Digital campaigning
- Website design and build
- Distribution platforms
- Written digital content

And the platforms they do it on are as follows:

- TV – domestic and international channels and networks, and their companion digital platforms
- Digital – free online viewing, pay per view, subscription, mobile, games, apps, IPTV set-top boxes
- Theatrical – cinema release
- Festivals – worldwide and domestic festival screenings

- NGO/charities
- Education – universities, trusts, schools, digital arts and community projects
- Corporate
- Branded content (TV or digital)
- Live events/outside broadcasts
- Art galleries, installations – video artists

Some channels, like our main public service channels, the BBC, ITV, Channel 4 and Channel 5, are free to air. Others, like Sky, Virgin or Netflix, are subscription-based and some are pay per view, or a mixture of subscription and pay per view. Many subscription channels like Sky, Netflix and HBO are now introducing 'over-the-top' or OTT offerings, separate from their subscription-based ones, through various digital streams and service providers. Increasingly, TV channels like BBC3 and BBC Education are moving entirely online.

Most broadcast networks or studios will commission companies to make programmes for them and give them the budget or co-produce with another channel or fund to make up the budget, although some are acquisition-only, meaning that they will only buy in finished content.

Forbes magazine claimed 2015 was the 'tipping point' for digital video distribution because many major distributors and content owners introduced over-the-top (OTT) video services, which are direct to consumer and not tied to a pay-TV subscription on a particular channel or network. For example, Sky introduced platform Now TV; HBO created HBO Now; satellite provider Dish introduced Sling TV. Netflix, leading the way in OTT as in so many things, teamed up with multiple service providers that have their own pay-TV content, and many pay-TV providers are making entirely new content available on advanced connected set-tops in order to guide those consumers onto their subscription-based channel. Set-top boxes are becoming ever-more advanced home entertainment stations with models such as the Amino Live combining pay-TV, OTT, user-generated content, gaming, social media and apps.

FUNDING STRUCTURES

There are several ways of funding your creative content nowadays. The traditional models of commissioning, acquisition and pre-sales are still popular in the world of TV, but have now been mixed with more innovative models of distribution, ad-funded content, subscription, payrolls, product placement and brand sponsorship. The rise of subscription video-on-demand service Netflix is having a huge impact on funding structures, too. Now available in 190 countries, Netflix commissions and licenses content on a global level, rather than a regional one as has traditionally been the case with film and TV. This means that the days of international pre-sales to different countries by content creators and owners may be numbered, as if they want a Netflix deal, other territories will be cancelled out.

Let's look at these different options in a bit more detail.

COMMISSIONING

This means the funder pays at least a proportion of your budget up front for your creative project, whatever that is, and ultimately funds the whole thing. For example, if you pitch an idea to a broadcaster, they might give you £100,000 to make a one-hour documentary programme that will go out on TV and online. That money will be divided into a number of payments, for example, four. This is called 'budget drawdown'.

Many creative projects will run this way, with budget drawdown set out according to a production schedule that is agreed by both parties in a contract.

There might be 30 per cent paid on signature of contract, 30 per cent on beginning of principal photography (when you start filming), 30 per cent on beginning of post-production and 10 per cent on delivery of the finished product. Although things have become a bit more brutal in some digital commissioning spaces, where there might be only 10–20 per cent up front and the rest on delivery.

You will either retain some rights in this project, or it will be a 'buy-out', meaning that the client you make it for owns it outright. This is something that should be established at the outset and included in your contract.

Going back to what we covered about project budgets and company cash flows, you must be aware with business arrangements like this that you need to have the cash flow that allows you to continue and finish your project without going bankrupt and failing to pay your staff!

ACQUISITION

This means a funder pays for the finished product, usually a lower amount than if they had commissioned you to make it for them, so you have covered the costs of the project in some other way and are then selling on the finished product.

In this case you will usually retain some ownership, or another party will have funded it and retain some along with you. If you have funded the project yourself you will retain rights, or if another party has co-funded with you these rights will be shared. You will have organised this at the beginning of your project in a separate business contract.

Issues of cash flow do not apply here, as this is revenue that is coming in after a creative project is finished.

Today's market is saturated with distribution companies, which means that magnetising digital content is harder than it has ever been but also many deals are no longer exclusive, working on a pay-per-view basis (see below).

For example, a broadcaster might pay you £20,000 for your film and retain broadcast rights in the UK for a period of seven years. They may take some streaming rights also. You and/or your co-funders would retain other territories.

CO-PRODUCING AND PRE-SALES

Often different funders will collaborate together to make up the budget for a creative project. So an online drama about mental health might be funded by a development grant from the BFI, three broadcasters, the Wellcome Trust and a crowdfunding campaign. The rights in that project will be split across these co-funding partners according to what is useful to each individual organisation. Pre-sales is a process whereby buyers from different global territories give you money up front towards your production budget, in return for the promise of rights when the content is completed. Many larger films and programmes are funded this way. Those rights could be TV, streaming, theatrical or other ancillary rights. You might bring a professional distribution company on board to help you do this, but whether that is worth doing depends on the size, scale and reach of your content because they take a cut of the money raised.

DISTRIBUTION DEALS

As mentioned above, you can pitch a creative content project in development to a distributor or sales agent, and they may help you to sell it, for a cut of the funds raised. You can also approach acquisition departments at your chosen channels and funders directly yourself.

You can go straight to platforms such as Vimeo, YouTube and Dailymotion.

Alternatively, you can distribute your finished product using a reputable sales distribution company that is appropriate to your market and they will take a cut of those sales. The selling of your product will involve contacting buyers directly, including it in their global catalogue, taking care of tech specs for streaming, pitching at international markets, and including your film in their publicity and advertising spend to raise its profile. Often it can be a frustrating process for the originator as it is hard to know how much your product is being pushed by these intermediaries, and I have found that a bigger distributor will prioritise their big-name titles.

In the digital space, with platforms such as iTunes, Hulu, Amazon, Netflix and Xbox, these intermediaries are often called aggregators.

Of course, all of this comes at a price. While traditional distributors often cut a deal around the 20 per cent mark, aggregators can ask for anything between 15 per cent and 50 per cent of revenue split from distribution on digital platforms.

The digital distributor Distribber is designed to be a more democratic way of getting your content onto digital platforms, without all the hidden fees and opaque processes associated with many other intermediaries. It is a good option for lower-budget content but can be difficult if the stakes are higher, and therefore a more subtle negotiation is needed, because it is a more automated and less individual service. They don't ask for a cut of revenue, but you pay a one-off fee to use their service. Fees vary depending on the platforms, territories and length but go up to approximately $1,600. If your content is not taken on by any of the platforms, you get refunded less a $120 processing fee. You can find all details of fees, as well as a breakdown of revenue split for showing on different platforms, on their website, distribber.com. Titles such as drama-documentary *The Age of Stupid* have been very successfully distributed this way but the downside is that you don't have an individual constantly negotiating on your behalf to get the very best deal possible.

In reality you may sometimes need a very experienced producer or sales agent you trust, to do these complicated deals and ensure the acquisition or pre-sales fee is commensurate with the rights you are giving away.

DISTRIBUTION RIGHTS

The issue of rights and distribution is an important one in the digital age.

Traditionally, independent content creators licensed out their work to various territories for a commissioning fee. Clients owned only that territory or set of territories and the creators owned the rest. For example, a broadcaster might commission a film for UK broadcasting rights for seven years.

Globalisation and digitisation of content mixed with the regional nature of most traditional commissioning structures means that producer rights are being recalibrated all the time and creative companies are losing out to big networks.

Companies will want to retain as many rights as possible in their content so that they can sell it on, often a very important source of ongoing revenue for a company – but that is becoming more and more difficult.

Many broadcasting corporations, studios, online platforms and other clients now only do full 'buy-outs' for commissioned content, so that they can exploit all rights globally. Competition is now so fierce that they have to hold on to as many revenue streams as they can. As mentioned before, VoD giants such as Netflix now have such immense global reach that a deal with them – either distribution or commission – cancels out other territories.

In addition, theatrical releases are being hit by the VoD market as simultaneous release in cinemas and online, called 'day and date release', becomes more popular.

This is usually negotiated by the executive producer and the kind of deal may depend on their level of experience in the industry and negotiating skills, although these days buy-outs are often non-negotiable.

Online sharing and pirating is another issue that can compromise your content and being able to monetise it. If it is available for free, you are not getting any revenue from downloads.

Geo-blockers and paywalls are used to block and protect content, and online platforms will take content down if it is rights-protected, but they are not always well enforced.

....

➤ **An example of a blank Pre-Sales Agreement (p.298) can be found in the Appendices at the end of this book**

....

MONETISING ONLINE VIDEO

The digital video space has changed a lot since YouTube launched in 2005, opening the floodgates for user-generated content with its cute cats n' kids videos. Classier video-on-demand services like Netflix, HBO Now, Hulu, iTunes Video, Now TV and Amazon quickly took over the market and YouTube now have a rental paywall for some video content. UGC is still shared on social media, but viewers of online video now expect much more sophisticated fare.

That said, there are still lots of ways to monetise your online content in parallel to these big distributors. Vimeo on Demand, Amazon Direct Video, Dailymotion and YouTube are just some of the digital video platforms out there that can still be monetised. Some, like YouTube and Vimeo, are easy to navigate but if you want to be ambitious and cover lots of bases you can use a specialist online distributor such as Quiver Digital or Create Space to access platforms, and platforms such as Distrify will give you high-quality streaming at low cost, too.

Revenue is split between the platform and the creator, at varying rates depending on the platform, and there are a few different ways of monetising your online video content.

You can choose to do pay-per-view advertising, pay-per-click advertising, in-video product placement, or a paywall for renting or buying your video. You can also receive Bitcoin donations.

Pay per view means that the ad is visible on your video for at least one second and you are paid by the client per thousand views of your video; pay per click means that you are paid only when the viewer clicks on the ad. With product placement it depends on the brand – for example, you may be asked to mention or feature the product in the first ten seconds of the video. Paywalls can be set up on your videos using paywall software like Paypal or iBill. YouTube now has a rental paywall feature that can be enabled on video.

To enable payments from advertisers on YouTube you create an account and turn on account monetisation. This connects you to something called AdSense, a vehicle by which you get paid a small sum by brands for featuring their ads on your YouTube videos. You create an AdSense account for payment, and in so doing you agree to the set revenue split, which is 45 per cent to Google and 55 per cent to you (quite a big chunk to Google, given that Vimeo take only ten per cent, but then Vimeo has a considerably smaller audience). Google build up credit in your account until it reaches $100, then pay it into your bank account. You are liable for tax on those earnings.

Then it's up to you to direct traffic to your website, through any and all means necessary, to get the money rolling in.

Of course, that's easier said than done. In 2013 the average income for YouTube content creators was $7.60 per every thousand views. So you'd need to be up there with Gangnam Style (2.6 billion views and counting) to be a multimillionaire.

Vimeo on Demand is a nice way to get your content out there because the built-in, customisable design means you can create and maintain your own brand identity, and it has a smaller but more discerning viewership.

The revenue split is also considerably more generous with 90 per cent going to the creator and ten per cent to Vimeo. This is only available on Vimeo Pro, which costs approximately £160 per year, so that is a cost, but a very low one.

You can set the price of your video, and the territories you want to sell it in. You can sell directly from your own website, too, as this is a non-exclusive distribution deal. Videos can be streamed across mobile and tablet, set-top box and computer at full HD.

The biggest problem for selling your content is still volume of traffic. Vimeo do not curate, so again, it is up to you to direct traffic to your page and increase your revenue, although they do have a feature called 'Staff Picks', which, if they choose it, will highlight your video for a period of time and may up your sales.

PRODUCT PLACEMENT AND BRANDS

Always a tricky area with creative content because it involves a degree of 'selling out'; quite literally, product placement means that you feature branded content in your video. Brands will offer either cash or in-kind goods in exchange for this. Product placement has been used in feature films, online video and international content for a long time, but was only legalised for broadcast content in the UK in 2011. UK-produced broadcast programmes that feature it have to comply with broadcast regulator Ofcom's rules; for example, products such as cigarettes, alcohol and prescription medicines can't be featured and product placement can't be featured in children's content, current affairs or religious content at all.

Another more recent way of working with brands is 'brand integration', where a story you produce revolves around a brand. According to content strategist website Contently, brands are becoming a new kind of studio – with several high-quality, high-concept shorts and features using brand integration. Google funded a movie called *The Internship* starring Vince Vaughn and Owen Wilson, which, admittedly, bombed at the box office – but it seems that this may be the shape of things to come.

In *The New Hollywood – Why Brands Are Making Movies*, Tessa Wegart claims:

> *In 2015, Americans spent more time each day with digital video than they did social media, and studies have shown that 80 percent of millennials reference videos when they're making purchasing decisions. Rather than focusing on short, agency spots to run on rented TV air time, many brands are opting for a different approach: creating in-house media teams to produce high-quality short films. Most importantly, they're releasing those films on their own digital channels.*

Recent examples cited are the Johnnie Walker-funded *The Gentleman's Wager II*, an 11-minute movie starring Jude Law, and *Two Bellmen*, a film by Marriots agency.

Obviously the creative freedom involved in these collaborations is pretty limited. Many content creators see this kind of collaboration as an exercise in soul-selling, but if you can view it as simply working on an advertising project, and not compromising your baby, there is no doubt that the cash is there for the taking.

PRE-ROLL OR POST-ROLL ADVERTISING

Pre-roll or post-roll advertising is when a short, 5- to 30-second advertisement (depending on the length of the video) runs either before or after your video. It can take the form of a commercial or graphic slide, with or without voiceover.

BRAND SPONSORSHIP

Often brands, trusts or foundations are happy to fund or part fund videos and TV programmes showcasing a theme, social issue/cause, or point of view that suits their identity. Many broadcasters and digital platforms now have a brand sponsorship department, and work with content creators to broker deals.

BITCOIN DONATIONS

Bitcoin is a new currency that was created in 2009 by an unknown person using the alias Satoshi Nakamoto. Transactions are made using peer-to-peer technology with no intermediaries, so no banks; there are no transaction fees and you can remain anonymous. Bitcoins are not tied to any country or subject to regulation, so international payments are easier and cheaper, and no one owns it. Some web-hosting services and online retailers will accept them and the list is growing.

You can ask for Bitcoin donations from viewers who like your video – many people are collecting Bitcoins in the hope that they will increase in value over time.

OUTBRAIN

You know those irritating but hard-to-resist 'top ten' lists that pop up on your screen constantly? It's these guys. As 'content amplifiers', they float these tempting little nuggets of trivia before you so that you will then be directed to content created by their many clients.

Anyone can sign up to Outbrain to promote their videos, campaigns, blogs, brands, books and every other kind of digital content. As detailed on the Outbrain website, the process is fairly simple:

> You set your daily budget (as low as $10/day) and pay only for the clicks you get with our flexible, cost per click (CPC) model.

> We will keep recommending your content until you have used up your daily budget.

> The higher the CTR, the more we will recommend your content as it is obviously interesting to audiences across the web!

THE YOUTUBE AND INSTAGRAM STARS

Everyone knows about the big YouTube stars these days, even if it's only young audiences that avidly watch them. Parents are often flummoxed by their popularity as they appear to be doing very ordinary things like playing video games or bringing out their high-street shopping haul for inspection. Some perform dazzling feats like dancing and playing the violin simultaneously, others do satirical news shows or movie-star-based make-up tutorials.

These are the new mega celebrities and they bow to no one – in fact traditional brands, music publishers, entertainment agents and broadcasters are actively chasing them.

These kids are a very modern example of do-it-yourself digital stardom, with their massive viewerships and serious earning power. In fact, they seem to turn the time-honoured tradition of media moguls moulding and exploiting naive young performers on its head. But look closely – the YouTubers make cash from a variety of sources including hosting pay-per-click and pay-per-view ads, endorsing products and online subscriptions – and many now have managing agents, or are tethered to big corporations, too.

There is a huge variation in quality, style and subject matter among the YouTubers, and some are harnessing their popularity for noble ends and keeping their own vision clear despite flattering attention from every direction. Joseph Garret is a case in point.

CASE STUDY – JOSEPH 'STAMPY' GARRET

Joseph 'Stampy' Garret is a UK-based YouTube success story, and a very inspiring one for the budding digital entrepreneur who would like to use the digital world to educate as well as entertain. His YouTube show is based around playing the game 'Minecraft' (hugely popular with children worldwide) and teaching viewers about science and maths through creating worlds and narratives within the game.

Disney-owned Maker Studios recently approached Stampy to create a show with them, called 'Wonderquest', which Stampy has described as 'Like a Saturday morning cartoon'. Wonderquest is filmed within the Minecraft game, rather than being live action or animation – and although it is scripted there is a lot of fluidity and spontaneity with the narrative and characters because that's the nature of the game. So this is an entirely new digital-within-digital format of kids' programme, and no doubt there will be many more to come as the digital space continues to innovate. No one working at Disney was doing what Stampy was doing, no matter how young their staff, so they had to seek him out – and this will keep happening with the YouTube innovators and media giants. It will be interesting to see how much those young, cutting-edge stars can stay true to themselves with multibillion-dollar studios breathing down their necks!

THE CURRENT BROADCAST LANDSCAPE

By broadcast I mean traditional television channels and their digital offerings, as well as digital video-on-demand channels that commission, co-produce or acquire content from companies.

There are now hundreds of digital channels and platforms to choose from internationally, and scores of domestic channels, too.

The many hundreds of channels featured on freeview are free to air and include the main UK BBC network, ITV network, Channel 4 and Channel 5 and many major news networks including Al Jazeera and CNN. Some networks such as Sky, Discovery and Virgin are subscription-based and some are pay per view.

Many subscription channels like Sky, Netflix and HBO are now introducing 'over-the-top' or OTT offerings, separate from their subscription-based ones, through various digital streams and service providers.

Some previous TV channels in the UK like BBC3 and BBC Education have moved entirely online, and no doubt others will follow.

Large corporations dominate the marketplace because they can have global reach, but there are also many local channels that have emerged in the last few years.

Commercial pressure to produce content that will work in the global marketplace is huge and TV corporations like Sky, Discovery, BBC and Channel 4 all feel that pressure.

Most broadcasters will commission companies and individual content creators although many are now acquisition or co-production/pre-sales only because they don't have big enough budgets to commission fully on their own.

Back in 2004 the broadcast regulator Ofcom introduced specific 'terms of trade' stating that 25 per cent of broadcast content in the UK should be made by the independent production sector, opening the door for hundreds of independent production companies (or 'indies') that had previously been excluded from making broadcast content.

Large broadcasters in the UK such as the BBC and ITV have in-house production teams that produce the majority of their content, but they also have a duty to work with the independent production sector. Channel 4 works with independent companies only, and has now become an investor in production companies through its Growth Fund.

Public Service Broadcasting, or PSB, is still an obligation for a lot of broadcast content in the UK and guarantees a degree of quality that the UK is globally respected for. PSB means content that is broadcast for public benefit, rather than purely commercial purposes, and it covers various kinds of content such as news and current affairs, factual, arts and religious programming. This remit has also ensured that marginalised groups and regions, and smaller, less commercial companies, get at least some air time. As stated in Ofcom's third PSB review in 2015:

> (PSB) is legislated for by Parliament, which requires high-quality content, made for as wide a range of audiences as possible, and for public benefit rather than purely commercial ends. PSB's mission is essentially the same as Lord Reith's original BBC dictum 'to inform, educate and entertain'. Crucially, it should be available to all.

In return for delivering, PSB broadcasters get access to spectrum – the radio waves that broadcast their services and, in the BBC's case, licence fee revenue from the paying public.

However, the dominance of digital is threatening PSB. Digital TV needs less spectrum, and if channels go completely online, they will not need it at all. The BBC licence fee is under threat as the corporation works out how to properly monetise online content. Commercial pressure from globalised content is overshadowing domestic concerns about PSB quality and funding for PSB is dwindling.

Even given the irrepressible rise of digital platforms like Netflix, Amazon and Vice, at the moment the majority of broadcast content is still commissioned by traditional broadcasters and commissioning editors and produced by in-house teams like the BBC and ITV Studios, and the independent production sector.

Broadcast networks and commissioners are absolutely obsessed with viewer demographics. Millennials (roughly defined as those born between 1980 and 2000) are notoriously hard to pin down and measure in terms of their content-consumption habits, and so they are a demographic that many content providers obsess about, and endlessly try to impress. There is a sense of panic in many traditional broadcasters that, unless they can nail this younger viewership, they are doomed in the digital age. This panic is exacerbated by a sense of confusion among many commissioning editors when it comes to handling the digital landscape, because many of them did not grow up watching content that way. If they are over 35, like me, they watched scheduled programmes on terrestrial TV channels at the time of broadcast, or recorded them on VHS or DVD machines. I have sat in on countless commissioning meetings with broadcasters where they are desperately trying to attract the fickle millennial demographic at the expense of their older, more loyal and still numerous viewership. The truth is there are very few traditional broadcasters that are really successful at doing this, but content providers such as the Huffington Post, Vice Media and AJ+ from Al Jazeera have been more successful at cornering the young, adult-orientated, online viral market, and BBC3 and All4 have done so to some extent, too.

A huge increase in consolidation over the last decade (large media companies buying up smaller ones) has not really led to a larger share of output being taken by independent companies, but it has significantly affected the content that is created.

WHERE DOES YOUR BROADCAST CONTENT GO?

The digital landscape is vast, varied and constantly evolving. As well as the aforementioned multiple online video platforms, all major broadcasters now have online platforms, some of which commission original online content as well as streaming existing TV content online.

For example, Channel 4 in the UK now has All4 Shorts, original short-form content for their online platform All4. International news and current affairs network Al Jazeera has AJ+ which commissions purely online. Al Jazeera, like Vice News, gets some of the best access to current affairs stories around the world by using local content creators and growing organically within countries. Al Jazeera is one of the few established and highly respected news networks that makes long-form observational documentaries looking in depth at world issues, as well as shorter-form pieces.

The BBC and ITV iPlayers are extremely popular for viewing, although as yet only BBC3 and BBC Education commission for online only.

Traditional print media have got in on the act, too, with video commissioning departments at most major newspapers and current affairs magazines such as the *Guardian*, the *Sun*, the *New Statesman* and *The Economist*.

The Economist is doing particularly interesting work in the documentary shorts area with international stories across current affairs, social issues, politics, science and tech. Recent series include *The Disruptors*, about industries undergoing change; *Futureworks*, about the industries of the future; *The World If*, looking at possible global scenarios; and *Global Compass*, international current affairs films. Some of the shorts are sponsored by organisations such as Salesforce, Virgin Unite and Ernst & Young (although they are now known as EY).

The *Guardian* is also upping its video content game, under the stewardship of Charlie Phillips who heads up their documentaries commissioning. *Guardian* documentaries cover domestic and international stories in short-form and longer-form, up to 30 minutes. For the latest series of 12 films, released monthly in late 2016, they have partnered with the Bertha Foundation, which concentrates on social and economic justice and human rights. The films will cover international stories and raise awareness about people and movements making a difference in the world.

THE BIG BEASTS OF DIGITAL

VICE MEDIA

One of the most interesting and popular digital media organisations of the last ten years is Vice Media. With its origins in a modest alternative lifestyle magazine founded in Montreal, Canada in 1994, Vice expanded into digital video in 2006 and never looked back.

Vice built a reputation for gung-ho, youth-orientated current affairs content with an irreverent tone, shoestring budgets, incredible access and – initially at least – slightly ropey production values. Vice News is now one of the most name-checked documentary platforms in commissioning meetings with factual commissioners, as it has managed to win over that holy grail of the modern media era: a millennial audience. Helped along these days by the hiring of Kevin Sutcliffe, formerly head of news and current affairs at Channel 4, Vice News has gained some fairly breathtaking access across the globe over the last few years, including direct access to North Korea's Kim Jong-un via his Western bestie, US basketball player Dennis Rodman; inside Islamic State-occupied Raqqa, travelling alongside IS militants, a first for any network; and bedding in with cannibalistic Liberian warlords.

Films are presented by a ragtag bunch of young correspondents, indie filmmakers, local journalists, inexperienced staff members, or by Vice co-founders Shane Smith and Suroosh Alvi. Budgets are low, and the devil-may-care attitude of the network has landed it in hot water several times, most recently with the arrest of two journalists in Turkey on false terror charges and another in the US at a Trump rally – although it could be said that this goes with the territory, as current affairs journalists for Al Jazeera, Channel 4 and other networks know to their cost.

Now part owned by A&E networks and merged with Canada's Rogers Communications, Vice just keeps growing. In November 2015, Vice and A&E Networks made an unexpected foray into traditional TV, announcing Viceland, a cable network that would feature Vice-produced content for a millennial audience, something that no doubt left its TV rivals dazed and confused. More recently, Vice took a stake in UK production company Pulse Films.

Commissioning, development and creation of programming for the VICELAND UK TV Channel and Vice Films in the UK is headed up by Al Brown.

You can pitch to Vice via various email addresses detailed on their website, although they are very frank about the fact that, like all networks, they are inundated with ideas and will not get back to you if they are not interested. A better approach is to ask for a meeting with one of their commissioning editors so that they can get to know you and your company before developing ideas for them.

All of the big broadcasters already commission; however, Netflix and Amazon have now been in the commissioning space for a few years, and are creating their own high-end content using the independent production sector.

NETFLIX

Netflix are big news in global digital content. The video-on-demand platform now operates in 190 countries and, according to its website, has 83 million members. Having been around for a few years they have now massively expanded their in-house production arm, and are hiring freelancers in large numbers to make content for them in-house, as well as commissioning new work from independent filmmakers and continuing with the acquisitions that made their name.

2016 was the year Netflix ramped up their production rate and our screens are suddenly filling with original drama, documentary and movies alongside their acquired content. Breakout dramas like *House of Cards*, *Narcos*, *Stranger Things* and big documentary series like *Making a Murderer* will be followed by a whole raft of new originals like UK-produced drama *The Crown*, and even an eight-part series with YouTube comedy star Miranda Sings. By the end of 2016, Netflix had almost doubled its quota of original series, from 16 to 31, and had released ten feature films.

Netflix is predicted to be the second-largest producer and funder of content anywhere in 2016 – with an estimated $5 billion spent on new productions. They keep their cards close to their chest and are rather coy about budgets and fees, as are those who work with them, but in the absence of specific numbers it is safe to say they have serious money to spend and seem genuinely interested in diversity of output across all genres. Big original dramas may be up to seven figures, and original documentary series are often said to be in the six-figure to high-six-figure sum range, too. Acquisition and pre-sales are significantly smaller and will vary according to the genre, experience and profile of the producers, directors and cast but the fees are relatively large in the marketplace, because Netflix take the rights, meaning that you generally can't sell elsewhere or exhibit your film theatrically.

The sheer scale of their viewership and subscription-fee revenue means that they are more cash-rich than anyone else and have the freedom to experiment in a way the more traditional broadcasters can only dream of doing. Traditional broadcasters like the BBC and C4 are funded by a mixture of state funding, licence-fee revenue, advertising, global content distribution and now private investment, but in many cases they are starting to lag behind their digital upstart rivals.

Suddenly other producers are running to catch up with, emulate, or simply join Netflix. Many welcome the arrival of a big player with deep pockets and an interest in diversity of content rather than churning out blockbusters and entertainment; others feel threatened by or suspicious of this particular big beast. There has been much anxiety among broadcast rivals about how to keep up, and discussion about introducing a paywall for digital content that is currently free to air, for example on BBC iPlayer. According to *Variety*, the exclusive streaming of feature film *Beasts of No Nation*, starring Idris Elba, at the same time as its theatrical release caused many cinemas to boycott the film in protest.

The Netflix name is coming up across the film and TV industry with original commissions, big acquisitions and co-productions, and on industry panels at festivals and other events as they raise their profile ever higher. Whatever the range of opinions, it has to be said that Netflix have a genuine commitment to high-quality, long-form documentary as well as their high-budget dramas and movies, so content creators should definitely be engaging with them. As I write this, mega budget drama *The Crown*, produced by British production company Left Bank Pictures, is getting rave reviews. I was recently glued to brilliant US period chiller *Stranger Things* and will now be glued to the next series of dystopian British drama series *Black Mirror*, which previously aired on Channel 4.

The platform has been good news for documentary makers particularly, as very few other big VoD market players are so engaged with the independent documentary genre. It has brought serious arts and current affairs films like *The Square*, an Oscar-nominated documentary about Tahrir Square in Cairo during the Arab Spring, and *What Happened*, *Nina Simone*, a biopic about the singer Nina Simone, to a mass audience, and commissioned a variety of new series including *Captive*, a documentary series about global hostage-taking, from Simon and Jonathan Chinn's indie Lightbox.

As mentioned before, Netflix does not talk numbers – either in terms of deals, fees or viewership figures – and this can be frustrating for everyone involved in the production of content for them. The lack of transparency means it is currently difficult to get a clear picture of the Netflix audience and its viewing patterns, and how to place your own content in terms of pricing and reach, which can put you on the back foot in approaching intermediaries to negotiate on your behalf.

Getting Your Finished Film on Netflix

Getting a distribution deal with Netflix often means they take the rights, so it should be planned carefully. It is often (although not always) a good idea for feature documentaries, because they tend to do less well at the box office, and for less-well-known filmmakers in general who want to reach a really wide audience. It is also a good idea for lower-budget features as you recoup a good amount of a small budget. Another benefit of a big player like Netflix is that they have a big publicity and advertising budget to push your film.

If you think your film might make a lot of money back on selling to global territories, though, it may be wise to resist the temptation to distribute with Netflix.

The first step to showing on Netflix is to get on their database, which generally has to be done via an experienced producer, distributor or sales agent with good contacts and experience in the Netflix community. It's not something you can easily do yourself, unless of course you have such contacts. If it proves tricky to find a willing partner, you can take the option of paying indie distribution company Distribber to help get your film on the database. As mentioned earlier in this chapter, they charge a one-off fee, but don't take any rights.

Once you have cleared this hurdle, it is advisable to get an experienced intermediary on board in any case, such as a seasoned producer or sales agent, to help you broker the deal. Netflix are in an extremely strong market position and they will negotiate hard on any deal.

Getting a Direct Commission or Pre-sales with Netflix

Again, it all comes down to contacts. Netflix do not accept unsolicited pitches, from anyone. From the horse's mouth:

> We do not accept or review unsolicited materials or ideas. For that reason, we will not consider any materials or ideas we receive that were not specifically requested by Netflix or submitted via an aggregator or established agent through the appropriate channels.

In other words – go back to that producer or aggregator to make contact for a meeting. Netflix has acquisition and commissioning departments in various territories, and they take meetings with individuals or intermediaries with whom they already have a relationship, or who have the kind of track record they are likely to be interested in. The upside is that Netflix has been so prolific in the commissioning and production of original content recently that such people should not be too hard to find. They are usually now present at all markets and festivals for pitching forums, too, so the key to meeting them face-to-face is to get into those forums.

Netflix is cornering the pre-sales market with its huge global VoD reach. One hundred and ninety countries and counting is a lot of territory, and it is changing the way films are financed. The increasing use of 'day and date' release for cinema and digital streaming is also hitting theatrical exhibition hard because many viewers will choose to watch on one of the digital platforms rather than going to the cinema. In short, you may be pitching to Netflix alone for pre-sales in the future!

Both Netflix and Amazon have to guarantee that at least 20 per cent of video content in their catalogue is from Europe, according to new EU broadcasting rules – so a long and fruitful production relationship with UK producers is on the cards.

Some Netflix names to look out for at industry markets, festivals and conferences:

- Ted Sarandos – Head of Content, Netflix
- Jason Spinarn Koff – Director, Original Documentary Programming
- Jihan Robinson – Manager, Content Acquisition, Netflix
- Chris Whiteley – VP Business Development, EMEA Netflix
- Lisa Nishimura – Netflix VP of Original Documentary Programming

....

NETFLIX CASE STUDY: *THE DIVIDE*

a Film by Katherine Round. Dartmouth Films in Association with Disobedient Films (Previously Literally Films)

The Divide is an ambitious, independently produced documentary film about global inequality that will hit you hard and make you think. Before the advent of digital crowdfunding platforms, such an important film would have been a very tough one to kick off. It was financed through a mixture of crowdfunding (three campaigns totalling around £120,000), foundation grants, a MEDIA grant and some pre-sales.

Filmmaker Katherine Round, director and producer of *The Divide*, and the co-founder of Disobedient Films, which is pioneering new forms of storytelling in the factual sphere, says:

> On completion we were faced with the additional costs of clearance for music and archive to enable us to distribute the film worldwide, in cinemas as well as broadcast and online platforms. We raised enough to cover the costs for UK cinema release, which helped the film enormously, but were left with a £50k shortfall for worldwide rights on additional platforms. We worked with 101 Films to broker a deal with Netflix, the big advantage being an up-front fee that would enable us to cover enough of the clearance costs to make worldwide distribution possible.

The deal covered UK and US territories only (to leave options for other broadcasters in wider territories), and also allowed a simultaneous release on iTunes, Google Play, Amazon and HMV. Without the acquisition fee from Netflix, they wouldn't have been able to release the film beyond UK cinemas and festivals, so it has been a landmark development for the project.

Katherine says: 'It's exciting to see developments like the Netflix model, which enable creative, boundary-pushing documentaries to find an audience.

AMAZON STUDIOS

Amazon video content is spread across Amazon Prime and Amazon Instant Video. They are keen to reach out to UK and international producers across genres, and have a $1 billion pot for original content globally from 2015–17.

Amazon take an outwardly democratic approach to the pitching process. They have a creative 'open door policy', which means anyone can upload a taster video, a concept video or a pitch document for a creative project. Amazon Studio has already greenlit a series that came in through this online platform: *Gortimer Gibbon's Life on Normal Street*, a kids' series that's now on season two. If interested, Amazon will contact you to offer a fee for an option on your idea, and talk to you about the role you might have. After creating a pilot, Amazon use the public as a focus group – 'crowd testing' the content to decide what should be fully commissioned. The turnaround time for submissions to be evaluated is 45 days. It's early days for this process and I don't know anyone personally who has had a project commissioned this way – generally Amazon have worked with the big names, and producers or sales agents have brokered deals, and they also have a large, in-house production team. But keep an eye on output to see if they really are reaching out to a diverse number of companies.

The head of Amazon Original Movies is Ted Hope, who has produced countless dramas and docs including *The Devil in Daniel Johnston* and *Thumbsucker*.

TRADITIONAL BROADCASTER COMMISSIONING: HOW DO I PITCH MY IDEAS?

TV broadcasters in the UK and internationally fund their content in various ways:

- **Commissioning independent companies** – this means paying companies to make a programme for them
- **Commissioning individuals** – usually for new talent slots or news only, and will often place with a production company
- **In-house production** – the BBC and ITV in the UK do a mixture of making content with in-house production staff and working with independents, Channel 4 work only with independents. Netflix, Amazon, Discovery Channel and Sky all have a mixture of in-house and indie production
- **Investing in independent companies for slate funding** – for example Channel 4's Growth Fund
- **Funding development** – which means paying for taster films or pilot scripts and episodes
- **Acquisitions** – which means buying in finished content from domestic and international suppliers
- **Co-productions** – which means co-funding with other broadcasters, studios or companies

Broadcasters are usually structured with:

- Editorial departments, commissioning content
- Production departments, making content
- Acquisition departments, buying in content
- Business affairs departments, working on the legal and contractual side
- Finance departments

In larger, multigenre broadcasters, each genre has its own commissioning team. They vary slightly but generally are made up of these subgenres:

- Drama
- Documentaries
- Arts
- Comedy
- News and current affairs
- Features
- Education
- Factual entertainment
- Specialist factual
- Events
- Sport
- Film
- Online
- Branded
- Natural history
- Music
- Acquisitions

Most programmes for broadcasters are still commissioned for time slots, although this model is changing and becoming less relevant as viewers watch online or with catch-up. However, there is still a core audience of older viewers and families that sit down to watch a drama at 9 pm, documentary at 8 pm, entertainment at 7 pm or comedy at 10 pm.

Other networks, such as current affairs network Al Jazeera English, commission by strand. Al Jazeera English includes the *Witness* observational documentary strand, *People and Power* investigative strand, and *Viewfinder*, global perspectives from filmmakers across the world.

Other news broadcasters often work with individuals for either foreign or domestic stories. The Channel 4 News Film Fund is a good example of this.

Independent content creators can pitch through online platforms for most broadcasters. This is a good way of keeping a record of your pitch, and is supposed to ensure that clients have to get back to you within a certain time period.

In my experience, things do not actually get commissioned much this way, though. A percentage may get off the ground through the website, but the best way is to network by attending industry events, festivals, open days, etc., find out who the commissioners are (you can generally discover this on their websites) and organise a meeting where you pitch a few ideas at once.

Even better, team up with someone who has experience with the funders and clients you are targeting, and a personal relationship with them, so they can send them an email or call them direct. This cuts out the middle man and means you get in front of funders much more quickly.

A lot of time can be saved by spending a bit of money on a part-time development executive with good contacts, who can get you through the door. You can advertise for this person through all the appropriate industry job websites.

INTERVIEW WITH KLAUDE THOMAS,
HEAD OF DIGITAL AT ABC AUSTRALIA

What do you do at ABC?

I manage digital product development and general digital transformation of ABC's commercial division.

Do you work with independent producers and agencies?

I occasionally work with agencies. The ABC often enters into co-productions and broadcast arrangements with linear media producers (video, audio), and, rarely, with non-linear media producers (games).

Do you have an in-house team?

Yes, we have an in-house digital team in commercial and the ABC has a digital division comprising multiple development teams. The ABC maintains teams for news, radio and TV.

How is gaming integrated into your digital output?

At present it is generally supplementary, e.g. Peppa Pig games that supplement the Peppa Pig video IP. That said, once you get beyond pre-school the most successful games succeed foremost as games: the IP becomes secondary. In commercial we more often use gamification rather than true games: using the techniques of games such as chance and score to create and sustain engagement.

Can you identify any big forthcoming trends for the digital video and gaming markets?

Sure. The crossover between messenger services and bots is leading to conversational UIs for everything. Deep-learning AI is some short decades away from taking over a great many specialised but essentially routine knowledge-jobs. The problems of comfort and interactivity in VR are being/will be solved over the next several years; I believe the first payoffs for VR will be in the form of commercialisable AR (augmented reality) and industrial uses of VR, e.g. architecture.

What should digital creative entrepreneurs be thinking about if they want to work with you?

The ABC has strengths and weaknesses as to what it can offer. It can offer a tremendously strong trust-brand in Australia, and linear media channels and distribution. It understands broadcast, streaming, etc., extremely well. And is coming to understand social channels well. If you approach the ABC with a video or audio proposal it can expertly assess it and know what to do with it. For digital, the ABC is presently bootstrapping reasonably speedily: and in that aspect is a consumer of SaaS and PaaS to automate or more coherently perform various functions, e.g. social media governance, media asset management, rights management, analytics, CRM and so on. A whole new digital infrastructure is being created to overlie or replace the old broadcast infrastructure. For now, the ABC lacks the ability to expertly evaluate and distribute non-linear dynamic media (e.g. games). That capability is held by games publishers and indies, etc. So for now and likely the next five years at least the ABC is perhaps better seen as a partner who can abet the success of creative digital, rather than a source of funding or distribution for same. Notwithstanding that partnership with the ABC might give access to funding from other sources. The exception is kids and pre-school. The ABC has tremendous strength with families and a developing expertise with kids and pre-school games. So for that specific niche one might think about seeking a co-pro or funding from the ABC for creative digital.

HOW DO I PROTECT MY IDEA?

The short answer is, you can't. It is always possible that someone else has had the same idea at the same time, unless there is something about your project that is particular to you. This might be that it involves you personally, your family or friends, or something that you are personally organising; you have gone quite far down the road with developing it; you have signed exclusivity agreements with the subjects and/or non-disclosure agreements with those to whom you have pitched, or with whom you have discussed the idea – and everyone has stuck to those agreements.

The law is very grey in this area, saying that copyright can cover 'the expression of an idea' but not the idea itself. Formats for a TV programme can be a bit more robust in their structure and therefore slightly easier to safeguard through taking steps such as registering relevant trademarks, domain names and social media accounts. It is difficult to license a format without it first having been successfully broadcast. If you think it really is hot property you can also register your format idea with the Format Recognition and Protection Association (FRAPA).

The question is, though, are you willing to enforce these agreements, if they are broken? Do you have the contacts or financial and legal clout to do so?

In my experience, it's pretty rare that someone actively sets out to 'steal' your idea. However, it can happen in a roundabout way. Funders of creative projects get pitched a lot, and although they may say 'no' to your idea when you pitch it, the same idea might spring to their mind in the future during casual conversation with a regular client. Suddenly, you see your idea on-screen a year down the line. Alternatively, they might like your idea but not trust a small company to carry it off – so ask another trusted company to do it. In the first scenario, there is very little that you can do – every idea has its time and people will not necessarily remember who pitched them in the first place. In the second, it's a case of being realistic before pitching. If your idea is big and ambitious but you are a small start-up, think about approaching a bigger company that has done similar projects before to co-produce with you before pitching. This is called 'warehousing'. In this case you need to have a development contract in place between you and the bigger company, to do as much as you can to protect yourself as the originator of the concept. You need to trust this company not to exclude you or be overly harsh on terms, so if at all possible approach producers whom you already know, or at least have a connection in common with, who can introduce you. This brings an element of obligation and loyalty into the process that can work in your favour.

The bar for pitching ideas has been raised significantly in the digital age; now, pilot or taster films are considered the norm, and a lot of work is often put into a proposal before putting it in front of a funder. Sometimes crowdfunding campaigns have kick-started the project, and enabled the production of a pilot before pitching. These are all strong ways of protecting the concept because it is a much more substantial proposition with access secured and production crew, contributors and/or talent attached.

In terms of recourse if you think your idea has been stolen, an emailed pitch or pitching via one of the broadcaster sites like the

BBC's ecommissioning or Channel 4's 4producers makes a record of your pitch. It is debatable how watertight this is in practice, however. You are unlikely to go up against a big network in court, unless you have a lot of cash to spare – and there is no real way to prove that someone else did not pitch this in a private verbal meeting.

In today's world of digital stars, it often helps to have on-screen talent attached. If you have their buy-in, then funders will trust you more.

Essentially, the more work you do, the more indispensable you become, but the trick is not to be too precious about your ideas; they are probably less unique than you like to imagine!

With digital innovations and creative tech, it may be possible to patent your idea. A patent is a government licence conferring the sole right to exclude others from making, using, or selling an invention. The patent would need to be held within all the global territories where you want to sell your product.

CREATIVE CONTENT COMPANIES – WHO ARE THEY?

There are many hundreds of production companies and digital agencies in the UK; indeed there are hundreds in London alone. As the digital revolution is global, of course, it all applies to the UK and that means small, digital creative companies are emerging all over the place

However, the industry here is still more closed and hierarchical than all of this might suggest. The largest, highest-turnover companies with the largest staff and resources still dominate. These companies still get the bulk of their funding from TV broadcasters but they also get funding from film studios, online studios such as Netflix and Amazon, and from corporate clients including brands. They also get revenue streams from global distribution of the content they own, both online and TV, and from selling formats for programmes worldwide.

At the top of the production food chain there are very large 'superindies' that are generally conglomerates. This means there is a large parent company that owns several smaller businesses.

There are also very large parent company or high-turnover digital agencies that dominate the landscape.

Under these in the pecking order are independent companies that are not owned by anyone else. These vary in size from large to medium to small and micro. There are many more small and micro creative businesses in the landscape now than there were even five years ago.

SUPERINDIES AND INDEPENDENTS

As content goes global, consolidation has followed, with large networks buying up companies and networks, merging with or creating indies, and this has significantly affected the kind of content that is being created, particularly in the mainstream market.

In the last decade the biggest parent companies, or umbrella groups, buying up smaller indies have included Endemol, Freemantle Media, All3Media, Tinopolis and Shine TV. Broadcasters have included ITV Studios, NBC Universal, Warner Brothers and Discovery Channel. These are large global media companies with enormous reach, and for that reason they enjoy a huge share of the market across all kinds of content.

We will look at consolidation in a bit more detail in the last part of this book.

A list of the main UK superindies is below, although consolidation moves at such a pace that some of this information may have changed by the time you read this!

- All3Media Group ([Discovery/Liberty Global] North One, Bentley, Optomen, Lion, Company, Lime, Maverick, Objective, Studio Lambert, Neal Street, Little Dot)

- Argonon (Leopard, Leopard Drama, Remedy, Windfall, BrightSpark, Transparent, Blacklisted Films)

- Avalon (Avalon TV, Liberty Bell, Flame, Topical)

- Tinopolis (Firecracker Fiction Factory, fFatti fFilms, Rain)

- Warner Bros (Wall to Wall, Ricochet, Twenty Twenty, Shed, Renegade, Headstrong, Watershed, Yalli)
- William Morris Endeavour
- IMG
- Zodiak/Banijay (RDF, IWC, Bwark, Touchpaper, Comedy Unit)
- Foundation, Red House

The figure on the opposite page shows a list of true independents in the UK indie landscape over a certain turnover. Again, this list is subject to change at any time as indies get bought up or shift position.

MOST INFLUENTIAL DIGITAL AGENCIES

Compiled by the Recommended Agency Register (RAR) for 2014 and 2015, below are some of the most influential digital agencies:

- Mediacom North
- Jellyfish
- Brass
- BWP Group
- Tangible
- Media Agency Group
- HRG UK
- Home
- Icrossing
- Stein IAS
- Pancentric Digital
- TH_NK
- Analogue Folk
- Catch Digital
- Navigate Digital
- Big Group
- Manifesto Digital
- Passion Digital
- E3 Media
- Hugo & Cat

THE TOP TRUE INDEPENDENTS

INDIE		£	INDIE		£
1	Avalon	87.1m	27	Oxford Film & TV	4.1m
2	Hat Trick	47m	28	Minnow Films	3.6m
3	Red Planet	16.7m	29	Knickerbockerglory	3m
4	Zig Zag	15.6m	30	Back2Back	2.7m
5	Input Media	14.6m	31	3DD	2.6m
6	Rondo Media	14.1m	32	Magic Light	2.54m
7	Off the Fence	13.5m	=33	Quicksilver Media	2.5m
8	Atlantic	12.5m	=33	Pilot	2.5m
9	Arrow	10.9m	=33	Thumbs Up	2.5m
10	October Films	10.8m	36	Sixteen South	2.3m
11	Keo Films	10.1m	37	HCA Entertainment	2.2m
12	True North	9.4m	38	JJ Stereo	1.8m
13	Drama Republic	8.8m	39	Rawcut TV	1.75m
=14	Icon Films Ltd	8.5m	40	Testimony Films	1.5m
=14	Blink	8.5m	41	Woodcut Media	1.42m
16	Nutopia	8m	42	Lambent	1.4m
17	Wag TV	7.6m	43	Sweet TV	1.3m
18	Wild Pictures	6.4m	44	Lupus Films	1.2m
19	Tern TV	5.5m	45	If Not Us Films	1.01m
20	Burning Bright	5.2m	46	Hardcash Films	1m
21	Eleven Film	5.1m	47	Clean Cut Media	941k
22	Outline	4.9m	48	ClearStory	845k
23	Attaboy	4.7m	49	Firecrest Films	700k
24	Pacific	4.5m	50	Amos Pictures	637k
25	Rollem	4.4m	51	Illuminations Media	560k
26	Kindle	4.2m	52	Caledonia TV	460k

YOUR **FIRST** PROJECT

When you have a funder in place for your project, there are lots of things to think about.

HOW MUCH STAFF YOU WILL NEED

Will you use freelance or permanent staff? This depends on schedule and budget. You must make sure you have budgeted enough for salaries and holiday time per staff member. For a very long-term project it can be a good idea to make staff PAYE because it is cheaper overall to do so for a long period, but for shorter-term ones freelancing is generally easiest and is becoming more and more the norm. You may want to think about how to best use staff across projects if more business comes in, for example, making a freelancer permanent if they are very good and looking for a longer-term role.

WHICH ROLES ARE MOST IMPORTANT?

Which roles do you need to hire in first? Remember that some key staff members are responsible for hiring in other members and so they must be prioritised. Others are responsible for running the project logistically or creatively from beginning to end and should be involved as early as possible.

HOW YOU WILL HIRE YOUR STAFF

Word of mouth, advertising on job websites, industry press, digging out your old contacts book? Make a plan well in advance as this can be a very time-consuming and often frustrating process. Sometimes people can be very flaky! You think you've got the perfect candidate and you get gazumped at the last moment by another tempting offer, or they fail to show up altogether on the designated day. Have a back-up plan, for example, a second candidate you have not yet spoken to, for each key member of staff. Always get back to candidates who have applied for the position, but do not tell second- or third-choice candidates they haven't got the job until you know your first choice is definitely on board. Make sure you draft employment contracts for all staff and give them a copy.

HOW YOUR SCHEDULE WILL WORK

Make sure everyone on the team has access to a centralised schedule that has been created on a platform like iCloud, Basecamp or Google Docs and can be edited as necessary. Be realistic about what can be achieved in the time and be honest with your clients about milestones. It's better to finish early because you have overestimated the time needed than have to continually call them begging for an extra week.

Schedule in contingency time for any unforeseen technical, logistical or personnel issues and ALWAYS have a bit of money put aside for these things, too. Around two to three per cent of your budget is a good ballpark figure.

BUDGET DRAWDOWN AND CASH FLOW

As discussed in the last chapter, how the funder distributes the funds to you for making your project is extremely important. For example, there might be 30 per cent paid on signature of contract, 30 per cent on beginning of principal photography (when you start filming), 30 per cent on beginning of post-production and ten per cent on delivery of the finished product. How will you make this work with all your project outgoings – staff, equipment, insurance, premises, travel, expenses and all the rest? Don't guess; make sure you're on top of this. Create a cost report and have your project manager update it every day.

FREQUENCY OF MEETINGS/COMMUNICATION WITH STAFF

How often do you plan to get your whole team, or sections of your team, together for a meeting? Don't do this on an ad hoc, making it up as you go along, basis. If your team are constantly being interrupted for meetings on a whim, it will irritate them and affect their ability to work, but it is also important to get the team together on a regular and predictable basis (i.e. once a week) so that everyone can reconnect, ask questions and air their opinions. Have small senior meetings on a more frequent basis, but make sure you or another elected person on your senior team are always accessible to everyone, including the most junior staff. You should be overseeing the professional development of your team, as well as their work on any particular project, and you should be a mentor and positive role model to junior staff. Bear in mind here the personalities of your staff, too. Some will want a lot of interaction, others are happier working alone. The current obsession with open-plan spaces and constant interaction is not necessarily best for creativity, productivity and not wanting to strangle your co-workers!

INTERNS

Interns, or work experience staff, are always a tricky area in popular industries like media. Unfortunately, film and TV, fashion and publishing all have very bad reputations for exploiting super-keen graduates and school leavers by allowing them to work for months, or even years, on end, without pay. Apart from being highly exploitative of the individual, this also means that those from less-well-off backgrounds are barred from the creative industries because they cannot afford to work for free. Legislation around this is nebulous as it depends on the employment status of the intern and whether they are at school, school leavers or graduates, as to whether they are actually entitled to the minimum wage. Many think the legal limit for unpaid internships should be four weeks, although this has not actually been introduced into law and there is no official regulation of internships in the way that apprenticeships, for example, are regulated. I have always encouraged work experience and mentoring as it can be so bewildering for young people trying to break into the media industry. By all means give them a chance in your company on a work-experience contract, and if they are good then start paying them! Early positive mentors can make all the difference to confidence and achievement and all the better if it can be young people who may not get a chance otherwise because they don't come from the right background. You can do your bit for diversity by casting your net wide for interns from all walks of life.

THE APPRENTICESHIP LEVY

This generally applies to medium- and larger-sized companies. From spring 2017, employers in all industries with a pay bill of over three million per year in the UK will be required to pay 0.5 per cent of their annual pay bill towards an apprenticeship levy. Your pay bill means the total amount of earnings subject to Class 1 Secondary National Insurance contributions, so including wages, bonuses and pensions that you pay NIC on. Funding for taking in apprentices can then be accessed via a digital service account, so you can bring apprentices into your company and pay them using this fund.

WORKFLOW AND DELIVERY SPECIFICATIONS

This means having a plan for how your project will come together technically and logistically, and delivering it to your client according to their technical specifications. In the digital space this generally means you will be creating written, graphics, animation, stills or video content for delivery online.

Work out where you will store important documents, footage, images, graphics, demos, etc., in one central space, how it will be uploaded, how you will keep it confidential, and if and how clients will access it.

For footage stored on the Cloud that is secure you can use places like Dropbox or Vimeo Pro with password protection, for data and documents iCloud, Google Drive, Basecamp, Salesforce Chatter and many more. I always found Vimeo Pro a very easy and non-confusing method of sharing works in progress with clients as it is a simple link that can be clicked on, and I have always used Basecamp for projects, although it is not always easy to convince your staff to do the same!

Remember to keep passwords secure and change them fairly regularly. With data that is confidential, make sure everyone on your team who is uploading or saving data is doing it correctly or, even better, limit the number who can do so to two people to limit mistakes. We once got into hot water because an editor mistakenly uploaded a highly confidential video for a large corporate client publicly and one of their team came across it!

Some free online storage services:

- Google Drive: 15GB free
- Box: 10GB free
- oneDrive: 5GB free
- iCloud: 5GB free
- Amazon Cloud Drive: 5GB free
- Dropbox: 2GB free
- Flickr: 1TB free photo storage

From the paid-for options, from my experience, for video Vimeo is by far the cheapest, and easiest to use. I also used platforms like Sharefile for corporate clients, but it was comparatively very expensive:

- Vimeo Plus $59 per year
- Vimeo Pro $199 per year

- Vimeo Business $599 per year
- Citrix Sharefile $100 per month

PROJECT MANAGEMENT SYSTEMS

Project management systems also help considerably with the everyday running of projects, particularly if teams aren't always in the same space. Google Drive can work fairly well as a project management system for small individual projects and is free, but as mentioned before, my preferred project management system has always been Basecamp. It is simple, clear and has good features such as shared calendars and milestones, allocated to-do lists, a chat function, writeboards and an easy to use file upload system. You can keep a page for your company, and a separate page for clients, with different logins, too. Basecamp costs $29 per month for a team only, and $79 per month for team and clients.

Other systems mentioned by creatives include Teamwork Projects, Workamajic and Function Fox or, for larger organisations, Salesforce Chatter, but there are many more out there so shop around.

Technical specifications are just that, specific; so make sure the person delivering your project technically understands how they need to give it to the client.

CLIENT CONTRACTS

First off, do you have a contract in place with your client? Read it over carefully and have a lawyer do the same, if possible. Media lawyers are expensive but there are inexpensive membership organisations offering free industry legal advice to members, and this can be invaluable to the small creative business. Contracts can be opaque and full of jargon in order to bamboozle you into agreeing to stuff you are not quite aware of. Anything you are unclear on, or any small print you think might be compromising, have it checked out.

YOUR ROLE ON THE PROJECT

This is very important for setting the tone of leadership among your co-directors and staff. It will be a template for the company as you go forward with more and more projects on the slate. Of course, things can and will change and evolve a bit but you will find that, if you are very hands-off at the beginning, it will seem strange if you suddenly become a micro manager later on, and similarly, if staff get used to having you around and then you start disappearing all the time, it affects morale. So try to set your level of involvement and your accessibility and stick to it as much as you can. What this will be depends on what your overall role in the company will be. Working in the company too much on specific projects can mean you are never getting the opportunity to work on the company as a whole, getting development funding in and meeting new clients, which is essential to survival. Working on it too much can mean you become distanced from your staff and co-workers and things start happening without your being consulted. There is a happy medium to be found, but it will be dependent on your personality and management style, your co-directors and how much you are happy delegating in the early years of the company. If you find that the choice you have made is not working and you want to change it, then explain that to everyone so they do not take it personally and think they have done something wrong when your approach seems different all of a sudden.

THE POINT OF CONTACT FOR YOUR CLIENT

This is another very important decision to make. Some clients can be extremely demanding; others let you get on with it and only reappear when a milestone in the schedule needs to be met. It is always easiest if you have an extremely competent project manager, account manager or production manager who is there for the long haul across all your projects and in the office, full-time or part-time, to deal with clients. Continuity really helps to maintain client relationships. This way you can deal with all the high-level stuff – initial deal making, contract signing, wining and dining and kicking off the project – then hand over to that person to deal with the day-to-day questions and crises on the client end. If you try to take this role on yourself, it could become a constant headache as whiney clients call you at all hours of the day and night with issues and complaints. It could end up souring your relationship, and jeopardising future business with them. Better to keep that nitty-gritty stuff at a bit of a distance if you want to stay on an even keel with the top brass.

Another thing to bear in mind is availability. Because everything works at a 24-hour, seven-day-a-week global level these days, clients can expect an immediate response to their question sent from a hotel in Hong Kong at 3 am UK time. You need to clearly manage expectations here. It can be a slippery slope to staying up all night, under the duvet with your iPhone! I have found that if client calls or emails are left to the next working day, the world doesn't end and their business doesn't disappear. Try to have some perspective on this although, obviously, if it is a crucial time, i.e. online project launch, a big exhibition, broadcast or presentation where your last-minute input could make or break it, you need to make yourself available well outside hours for that period only.

WHEN CLIENTS WON'T PAY

This is a very common problem with all companies, and especially creative ones. Unfortunately, the larger the client is, the more likely they are to pay late or, in some cases, not pay at all. I have had this experience with broadcasters, large corporate clients and universities.

The most effective means I found to deal with it was to copy my lawyer into a formal email or letter to the client with terms and details of interest accrued after the payment deadline.

If this isn't effective try your bank; they generally have a department that will send out a threatening letter although you do, of course, have to pay a fee!

Finally, you can get a lawyer to formally chase for you, which is much more expensive. Taking a client to court is also a possible but very expensive option. You can go public about such treatment, but obviously this will blacklist you with the client so it depends if you want repeat business from them or not.

INVOICE FACTORING

This is a service that banks, and various other lending companies, provide to a business – again for a quite sizeable fee. Factoring means that the provider will give you cash up front on the strength of invoices in the processing pipeline for payment to your company, for cash-flow purposes.

Say, for example, you have work for £250,000 broken up into five milestone payments of £50,000 but your outgoings for the first quarter are £75,000 and you have no other revenue coming in at that time. A factoring provider will give you the additional £25,000 for a percentage of that amount. The fee depends on the provider, so shop around for the best deal.

I would only advise using this service when you have a lot of business coming in, as it is fairly expensive.

STAFF AND TALENT

HIRING STAFF AND STAFF MANAGEMENT

For small creative companies, flexibility is key. Having worked out how you want to structure your own salary and those of your business partners, you need to make decisions about when and how to hire staff.

Usually the majority of key positions, such as producers/directors, assistant producers, editors, animators and camera operators, can be hired on a project-by-project basis, keeping costs down.

There are some staff you may want to have employed on a PAYE basis or on a long-term freelance basis, for example, development producers and researchers, production managers and bookkeepers.

Do some thorough research on market norms before hiring so you have an idea what to expect in terms of salary payments. Salaries vary widely across different genres and different kinds of creative role, but with creative projects there is a spectrum because people are aware that the budget for a big drama or natural history programme will be very different from a campaign, educational project or current affairs series. Talk to companies that are doing similar things to you, to get an idea of realistic rates for attracting good talent. Check with unions such as BECTU and PACT as to what their rates are, although they often differ from the market reality, in my experience. Good talent is always worth the money in terms of overall quality and if they are good, they will know their worth. That said, you have to be realistic about what you can afford in the budget you have and they will understand that. Lots of content creators are squeezed today because of competition – the sheer volume being produced.

If you are using interns you need to be aware of the rules around unpaid work experience.

For all of your staff you have to be aware of the rules on employment contracts and things like holiday entitlement, sick leave and pensions.

Many creative companies employ people on a flexible part-time basis, often fitting around families, which can work well, particularly for development of ideas or with longer-term projects that are more fragmented. I have often hired part-time development producers and production managers who organise their hours around their kids, and it has worked for everyone.

Managing your staff is another consideration. Remember those horrible bosses and managers you had in your jobbing days? Remember the bullies and drama queens, the passive aggressive head screwers and those people with the tact, warmth and people skills of spanners? Well, don't be one of them! Think about how you were treated in the past, both good and bad, and emulate the good. Work, particularly this kind of work, should be enjoyable and collaborative, not testing and combative. If people management isn't your forte, turn to one of your partners for help in this area and think about employing a talent manager as you grow.

WORKING WITH TALENT

By talent I mean both on-screen presenters and off-screen experts, academics, consultants and established creatives and writers who might want to collaborate with you.

Let's start with the on-screen presenters. There are lots of reasons why you might want a high-profile person or expert to lead your project on-screen. They can impart knowledge, bring subjects and situations to life, contribute expertise and contacts and a loyal audience of followers. They can spearhead campaigns that are close to their heart, and bring a human element to the most abstract of ideas. They can make audiences laugh and engage.

On-screen talent can also be high maintenance, because there is a lot at stake for them as well as for you. They will probably have an agent you have to negotiate with, or if not they will expect you to invest a lot of time in getting them out there.

If it is a big online star, like a YouTuber, or Instagram influencer, they will already have an extremely strong brand and following and you will, to some extent, have to create the project around them if you are going to harness that following. They will most likely be young, used to calling the shots, and inexperienced outside of their particular field, so you need to plan for some hurdles in the collaborative process, too.

Make sure both of you are aware of the parameters and have a clear contract between you, whether that's at idea development or production stage, particularly if the idea and access has come from them. This chapter includes examples of development and production contracts for on-screen talent.

If you are working with an expert and/or academic, there are different considerations. Often there is a rather large gulf between an expert who has specialised deeply in one area and the fickle, short-attention-span, intellectual magpie that is the modern producer. You need to get onto the same page and understand the other's way of understanding information and communicating it. The culture of academia is very different to the cut and thrust of the media industry and this is something else you must tread carefully with. If an academic gives you her time and you promise the earth then never call her again, you are not progressing the already fractious relationship between experts and producers.

Issues of intellectual property and project ownership may also come up here – particularly if you are co-producing with another company.

....

> **Examples of an Option Agreement (p.304) and Deed of Assignment (p.307) can be found in the Appendices at the end of this book**

....

PART **THREE**

GROWTH AND MOVING ON

GROWTH STRATEGIES AND FUNDING

At the end of your first two years' trading, it's time to think about growing and evolving as an organisation.

First, think about whether this is something you want to do and your company is capable of doing. With growth comes responsibility, and some like to stay small and agile.

Has your turnover increased or fluctuated? How was that impacted by the various projects you chose to pursue? Although the bottom line is not the sole purpose of the creative company as previously outlined, it is important.

Identify the ways you could be more forward-looking. If you have been doing a lot of digital projects could you team up with a cutting-edge tech start-up for a new, ambitious web platform? Did you find working with talent the most exciting part of the last two years, and if so should you think about representing talent and building relationships with brands?

Have you got the team in place to help you grow, or do you need to restructure and hire new blood?

If you decide that growth is a good idea, review the projects you have under your belt, and think about the areas you would like to expand into. Spend some time researching companies that grew from your size to something more ambitious. How did they get there?

Next you need funding for growth. Where you go for this depends on your current size and turnover, and the new directions you want to take. Some of the options we looked at in the earlier funding chapter still apply here and in fact may be easier for a more established company. This point in your business cycle is where private investment becomes very useful. You could choose to increase your shareholders, and get some equity into the business to help it grow.

After a few years you might find yourself in a commercially successful enough position to consider merging with another company or selling to a larger company. If your company structure is very robust and you have at least £50,000 in capital, you might even look at an Initial Public Offering, or IPO, which means floating your shares on the stock market for public ownership. Alternatively, you might look to buy up another company to increase your reach.

So, when growing your business you can consider:

- private equity and more company investors
- merging with another company
- warehousing
- selling your company
- buying another company
- growth loans and grants
- mentor schemes
- crowdfunding for growth
- specialist consultants in company growth and exit
- Initial Public Offering (IPO)

THE CURRENT CLIMATE – SOME INDUSTRY CONTEXT

Production companies and digital agencies have been undergoing a consolidation process for some time, but the last eight years has seen a huge increase. Consolidation is the merger and acquisition of many smaller companies into larger ones.

Since 2008, US media groups such as NBC Universal and Warner Brothers have acquired several UK production companies, and today, according to Ofcom, seven of the ten largest UK producers are owned by large foreign media corporations. The BBC and ITV are now the only remaining British-owned broadcasters and many believe the US may have ITV in its sights, too.

In a step further, the traditional production industry has seen a lot of 'vertical integration' – this means broadcaster/producer co-ownership of other independent producers.

There has also been a new trend of broadcasters such as Channel 4 taking up to 25 per cent stakes in a production company through their Growth Fund, rather than acquiring it outright – this usually happens with smaller growing indies and gives some hope to the tiny but scrappy independent producer up against the industry behemoths (an interview with the head of the Growth Fund, Laura Franses, is included at the end of this chapter).

And the deals just keep getting bigger and bigger. In 2016, Liberty Global and Discovery created a joint venture company to buy All3Media, itself a media giant, in a deal reported to be worth £500 million plus.

Viacom recently acquired Channel 5, and two of the UK's biggest production companies, 21st Century Fox-owned Shine and Endemol, are currently in a joint venture to form a £1 billion-turnover 'mega-indie'. Mega-indies are, it seems, a burgeoning trend that will continue and increase. Great news if you are owned by one of them, less so if you are on the outside looking in.

Some of the few remaining truly independent producers in the UK do admit to concerns. Small and medium-sized indies worry they don't have the financial resources or network of customers to be able to compete with the superindies, and that broadcasters who have bought into the sector may prefer to commission their own production companies.

DIGITAL AGENCY CONSOLIDATION

Things are no less complicated in the market for digital agencies.

As with traditional production companies, media is splintering across so many different devices, platforms and channels that it is almost impossible to keep up, and creating a huge mega company that is all things to all people is seen as the answer. Media agencies of all flavours, shapes and sizes are being forced to refine their structures to ensure that one 'brand experience' reaches consumers across all channels. This means consolidation and often the merging of companies that offer both digital and creative production services.

As famous ad man Martin Sorrell says in this article for *The Drum*:

The thinking about scale is that it comes back to the digital world. It's highly fragmented and fragmenting further, getting more complex for agencies, media and owners and brands to operate. The leverage of scale is more powerful in a fragmented landscape than it ever has been in a traditional marketplace.

In other words – go big, or go home.

Media agencies are being forced to collaborate more with creative, digital technology and data-driven disciplines. This can mean working together, but more often it means buying up these skills and integrating them into your bigger company.

Agencies such as Razorfish, which offer both digital and creative services, have in-house media buying teams and so can offer an integrated service to clients under one roof. For example, M/Six is a joint venture between one of the UK's creative agencies, Chi & Partners, and media network Group M.

Publicis Groupe recently consolidated six agency brands (Starcom, Mediavest, Spark, Zenith, Optimedia and Blue 449) into four global brands – Starcom; Zenith; Mediavest/Spark and Optimedia/Blue449, although its proposed merger with giant Omnicom collapsed last year.

As digital technology increases in sophistication the lines between categories within the digital sector itself are getting blurred. Media agencies now face challenges from corporations like Google and Facebook, and this shows no signs of slowing down.

In view of this, it's understandable that many smaller companies think 'if you can't beat 'em, join 'em' – and look to sell their business, merge with another one or even buy one.

YOUR GOALS AND PRIORITIES WHEN MERGING OR SELLING YOUR COMPANY

You can decide what level of involvement, if any, you want to have in this new venture and it's best to do this before negotiating with the other party. Do you see this as an opportunity to expand and collaborate, or an opportunity to move on and make some cash for the next adventure, while seeing your baby continue to thrive?

Merging can be a big commitment if you are staying at the helm of your company, or even taking a step back and letting someone else take the reins. It's important that both entities are on the same page, not only creatively and in terms of reputation but also in ensuring that they share the same values and that there aren't any major personality clashes on the horizon!

Whether you are going to stay involved long-term or not, make sure you put enough time and effort into any merger as it is still your reputation and the company you founded that is continuing its life elsewhere.

If you are lucky enough to be approached by a potential buyer, it can be even more complicated because that parent company will want to make sure that you represent it as the umbrella organisation, giving you a bit less wiggle room. It is still crucial to have thorough conversations about brand identity and content, as well as the money side of it and your role in the whole enterprise.

Both of these ventures will include a lot of media-lawyer time so make sure you have budgeted for this! Some member organisations do help with free legal advice but mergers and acquisitions are much too complex and important to leave to these sorts of services.

WAREHOUSING

Warehousing is a low-risk way of merging with a larger organisation on certain projects, or for a certain period of time. You offer a viable idea and a good team; they offer the infrastructure and support. This often means being able to cash flow a project, having ready access to legal advice and the relevant business affairs and finance departments to handle complex project administration. A larger company also has credibility, which will convince investors that the project is in a safe pair of hands. You get to associate your name with the project – and will often be based in premises with them. The finished project or projects are credited as co-productions between the two companies. The good thing about this is that you're building up your experience and credits; it effectively allows you to take on larger-scale projects that you wouldn't be able to do alone – until such a point whereby you're perceived as having experience on these types of projects; then you go solo. An example of this might be Simon Chin who produced *Man on Wire*: his new company Red Box Films had no credits as such to its name – it partnered or warehoused with another, well-established company called Wallet Wall. The success of this feature documentary obviously catapulted his company into a position where it can stand a little more on its own two feet the next time around. Now they're a hugely successful company, outputting some of the best feature docs that come out of the UK.

➤ **An example of a Standard Collaboration Agreement (p.313) can be found in the Appendices at the end of this book**

CASE STUDY – MOSAIC FILMS, FACTUAL PRODUCTION COMPANY

Andy Glynne is managing director of Mosaic Films, which merged with DFG Films several years ago. Andy says:

> Some time ago, I ran a tiny production company which made tiny films for tiny audiences. Everyone in the company worked really really hard – and although we grew in size (and indeed in stature) we felt that we could only grow so big. We wanted to make longer content, bigger content, and content which could scale up – not just short films but longer ones, features films and series. It felt like we were caught

in a vicious cycle; being small meant we were perceived as being small; therefore no one would give us the real jobs that would allow us to grow – without those jobs, we stayed small … you get the picture!

The solution was to merge with Mosaic Films, which had an established record of more traditional and longer-form content with a very similar subject matter and outlook. This allowed the company to thrive using complementary skills and experience, and take the step up to feature-length documentary projects and international co-productions. DFG Films had a reputation for producing cutting-edge shorter-form projects, including BAFTA award-winning current affairs and human-rights-based short animations, and Mosaic had produced award-winning, longer-form mainstream factual content. Andy says:

Mergers are often based on the 'two heads are better than one' philosophy; two companies who are on the same trajectory (although often with complementary skills) can come together and pool resources. The good part of this is, hopefully, growth of a company, with their ability to often undertake projects (and get finance for) the type of projects that neither company by itself could take on alone.

....

The obvious downside to an official merger is that, in some cases, two heads are not better at all – personality clashes and different objectives for your company may cause more long-term headaches than trying to steer the course solo.

So how do you become a business that someone wants to buy, or invest in?

First, think about who you would want as an investor, partner or buyer. That will depend on the type of business you do. If you are making digital content, TV and film, it will probably be a competitor, or large media group, that you want to attract.

Other investors, like business angels, venture capitalists and venture philanthropists, may be interested, too, if only to help you expand so that you can then can get noticed and eventually sell to a bigger company or network.

If you are fairly successful in the business of digital innovation and creative technology, one of the many big venture capital firms is likely to be interested in you, along with your competitors.

Make sure that anyone you approach or attract understands how creative businesses work and the inherent unpredictability of the business model. This should already be the case with your competitors, but with venture capital firms, business angels or high-net-worth individuals it might not be. You have to make sure expectations are realistic from their end.

All voting shareholders in the business have input into this decision and proposals must be put to them for a vote. Your board of directors and advisory board are also instrumental in this decision and can offer help and advice.

Also make sure that they are right for you in terms of working practices, personality and level of involvement. Having investors breathing down your neck every five minutes or being called to weekly board meetings with a team of accountants may not be what you had in mind.

Second, make sure your business is solid and scaleable. That means you can demonstrate a growth in output and profit over time, give or take a few inevitable blips along the way, which the right investors will understand is part of being a creative company. Do your website, business plan and company accounts show a growing maturity and quality of content, an increase in clients, and an ability to balance the books and hopefully make a profit that goes up year on year? Is your team solid and is there continuity with your staff and executives? Does your advisory board include people with a good mix of relevant skills and experience, who have been successful themselves? Investors and buyers will look for all of these things.

Third, get your company independently valued. This can be done by media lawyers, accountants and regulated media-business brokers.

Creative companies making digital content often have more of what are termed 'intangible assets' because their products are ideas, the expressions of those ideas, and finished content that is sold or licensed – and the intellectual property inherent in all of those things. They may also have patents for digital technology, for example. This makes them harder to put a value on, but other considerations would be the worth of reputation, contacts in the industry and relationships with clients. Buyers will also look at location, premises, equipment value, debtors, employees and what similar-sized businesses in the same field have sold for.

Fourth, study the competition and your place in the market at that time. This helps to work out who might want to buy you, but also how you can differentiate yourself from competitors in the eyes of other buyers. Look at your competitors' output, structure, staff and acquisition strategies. Have they bought companies like yours, and if so, how was it done? Would you be happy approaching them or would you want an intermediary to do it? Do you have contacts within the company that might help in the first instance?

Going back to your role, make sure you have decided whether you want to be involved or not, and to what extent. Are you happy for a buyer to take complete control, or do you expect to stay at the helm? If it's the latter, make sure you can show that you are the best person for the job. This might seem like an odd thing to say given that you have built the business up to this point, but often buyers will want to put their own stamp on things, and have their own executive team, so there is no room for confusion here.

Finally, get all your processes in order. This means:

- current shareholder valuation (business brokers, your lawyer and accountant can help with this)
- assets
- sales, turnover and profit
- payroll
- dividends payments
- bonuses
- historical accounts
- management accounts

- bookkeeping records
- company paperwork
- legal contracts
- loans
- leases and mortgages
- company expenses
- staff contracts
- health and safety policies
- insurance policies
- recruitment policies
- diversity commitments
- press and advertising
- workflows, digital storage systems and project management systems
- any legal issues, historical or current
- why you are selling

Have immediate knowledge of your current financial situation including cash flow, debt and creditors, money owing to you, returning clients, projected sales and distribution revenue.

If you are selling your company rather than just bringing an equity investor in, think about the staff and your board of directors in the deal, too. Can they expect to keep their jobs, and if not what will happen to them? Some may want to leave of their own accord, and others not have their contracts renewed, but this all has to be clarified before the deal goes through. If you have to make them redundant then you need to have all the necessary administration in order or make it clear that this will be taken care of by the new owners in due course.

Make sure to update your business plan, taking all of the above points into consideration. This is the time that you may have to stand up on that shiny corporate floor and dazzle those jaded suits, so attention to detail is essential. The plan will probably be a good deal longer than when you started out and that's fine, as long as everything is relevant and there is no repetition or obfuscation. If there are any big regulatory or funding changes in your sector, make sure you are across them. For example, how Brexit will affect your business might be one concern for buyers now.

Once buyers have made an offer to you and you have agreed a price through a process of negotiation, they will begin a process of due diligence, which means formally investigating all of the above elements, and also possibly talking to clients and staff. This usually takes four weeks or more.

Completion comes once you have met the conditions of sale, including:

- all financials verified
- leases, contract and licence transfers done if appropriate
- all financials transferred
- transfer of VAT registration

It can be hard to know where to start in making it clear that you want to sell, and finding out how much your company is worth in the marketplace, or indeed you may want to do it all discreetly. By now you will have built up a network and you can start to call upon them for ideas for buyers and market advice, and give yourself plenty of time for research; LinkedIn also has many experts in this area.

Once you are sure you want to sell, you may find it helps to use a business broker who specialises in the media industry. These organisations are a bit like estate agents or head-hunters – they are experts in valuing and marketing businesses. Like head-hunters and estate agents, though, they have wildly varying levels of competency and integrity. Look for ones that are members of a trade organisation like the Institute of Commercial and Business Agents or the International Business Brokers Association.

Make sure that you and your team are emotionally prepared for the changes ahead. If you are selling to or merging with a rival company, it can be like negotiating a new stepfamily for your team and there are bound to be a few hiccups along the way. If you are letting go it will be hard, and if you are taking on a bigger team and having to get used to bosses after being on your own for so long, that can be hard, too. But given that you will have put a lot of thought and planning into this, you should be ready.

PRIVATE EQUITY STAKES

Investment deals, mergers and acquisitions (M&A) in the creative industries have been booming in the UK.

According to research by ICAEW's Corporate Finance Faculty and Experian's Corpfin team, there were more than 70 big company transactions, worth a total of £3.9 billion, in 2014 alone.

Equity investors will pay for a share of your business, which means that you have access to growth funding without having to sell up completely. Often angel funds, venture capital funds and high-net-worth individuals take smaller stakes in lots of different businesses, spreading their risk in the hope that a few will give them a handsome return. Many of these angels and funds are now working across equity crowdfunding models. Equity crowdfunding was worth £84 million of UK investment in 2014, according to NESTA. Make sure that you go with a reputable equity crowdfunding platform that will have the necessary vetting process in place for its investors.

Media networks are in on the action now, too, with Channel 4, the BBC, Discovery and Sky all investing in companies over the last few years. The new and very encouraging trend is for taking minority stakes in early stage companies, and helping them towards exit, rather than buying up established ones. Channel 4's Growth Fund takes up to a 25 per cent stake in creative content companies with good growth potential; Laura Franses from the fund talks in more detail about how they are working with companies at the end of this chapter.

How much equity investors agree to pay, and how deeply they are involved with you thereafter, will depend on many different factors. If you are going to a media network, they are likely to have much deeper input because they have the experience in your sector, and a reputation to maintain. Business angels may not have similar experience and may just be looking to an eventual exit across their investment portfolio.

Business angels can operate as individuals, or more commonly within syndicates. A cursory search on Google will come up with scores of options all over the UK, including the aforementioned Angel Investment Network and AngelCoFund, a partner of the British Business Bank. When using business angels, make sure they are right for you as well as vice versa – what commercial experience are they bringing to the table? After all, they will own part of your business and so you are involved with them over a fairly long period of time, even if they are planning on a swift exit! Angel investors need to be self-certified as either 'sophisticated investors', depending on their financial and commercial experience, or as 'high net worth', based on their personal wealth.

Private investors will be looking for the following things in your business profile:

- a very robust business model and business plan
- information about the business, its development and planned investments
- a realistic risk profile – potential obstacles in the way of the return backers want to see on their investment and how you would deal with them
- an experienced, commercially driven management team
- what you are offering in terms of their involvement, for example a seat on the board (many will be non-executive directors in a company)
- share ownership details including voting rights

Investors and lenders who are making investments will usually have their accountants and legal advisors to check the financials, accounts and contractual position of the business, as well as speaking to staff and the executive board.

Equity investors are taking more risk than lenders, so will typically seek a return that is significantly higher than normal interest rates charged by banks.

If you are raising funds from private investors you must comply with the law on 'financial promotions' and with prospectus rules of the Financial Conduct Authority. The official approval of HMRC may also be required, in order to benefit from various tax incentives for investors.

BUYING AN EXISTING BUSINESS

You may have some spare capital, or access to it, and be interested in buying one of your competitors. If so, where do you look and what do you need to consider before making an approach?

The same general rules apply as when buying, but in reverse. There are several listing websites that feature businesses for sale, and you can also advertise as a buyer on listing websites. Go to industry conferences and events, and contact all your existing network, so that you can get the word out there. If you know any companies that have been bought up by a parent company, ask if you can talk to one of the executive team.

It's not hard to find brokers specialising in media out there – there are scores of agencies and individuals, but take your time finding the right one. Talk to them about how they work, and what kind of deals they have done in the past in your sector. They can help you to approach competitors that might not obviously be for sale, and also help you with access to finance to complete the buying process.

Create an information sheet about yourself and what you are looking for, your skillset and your ability to fund. You can then circulate this to agents so that they can find suitable matches. You may already have your eye on a competitor or a small business working in an area of digital that you would like to expand into, and you can also approach them directly to gauge interest, whether they are for sale or not, but be discreet about it.

Once you have identified a business, made an approach and received an expression of interest in reply, you can start the negotiation process, the due diligence process, get financing in place and finally make an offer.

Make sure you then begin a comprehensive process of due diligence, as outlined above in the selling process, taking all the same things into consideration.

The vendor should willingly give you all the information you need if they are a healthy business; however, if you want to do some preliminary research before approaching them you can download company information including accounts on the Companies House website, for a small fee. They might ask for a down payment while the due diligence process is taking place, and you should seek professional advice about this from your accountant, lawyer and/or broker.

If there are premises involved, the process may take quite a bit longer as you would need to do an independent evaluation and survey of those premises before taking them on.

Financing for business acquisition can come about through many of the channels we have already discussed throughout, such as bank loans and government loans, private equity or friends and family.

You should meet with the executive team of the business you want to buy several times during this process, and also negotiate a handover period so that you and your team can familiarise yourselves with the present owners in place, if you are taking over completely.

You may choose to buy the business but leave the current executive team and staff in place, in which case it is essential that you get to know them before taking the company over.

Financiers will look for all of the information from you that you would need to prepare for a sale of your own business, as they need to be confident that you can manage this process financially, legally and in terms of your existing board, staff and resources. They will also want to see the figures from due diligence of the company you are looking to buy.

The due diligence process includes legal, financial and commercial due diligence and you will be expected to research all of these thoroughly. Get your accountant, lawyer and broker, if you are using one, to manage this process as it is extremely important that nothing is left out and you have an expert, independent picture of where the business is really at. You may have met with the executive team a few times by now and be getting excited about the sale, so you may have rose-tinted spectacles on at this point!

Don't make a formal offer until the due diligence process is completed, you have confirmed financing and you are happy that it is viable for you to take over the business. After this, formal completion can take place.

INITIAL PUBLIC OFFERING

Initial Public Offering, or IPO, means floating your shares on the stock market for public ownership. This used to be the preserve of big, established companies with a strong financial history because of the level of regulation, but the digital boom of the late nineties and early noughties saw relatively smaller companies seeking to expand their businesses this way.

In 1995 the London Stock Exchange introduced the Alternative Investment Market, or AIM, geared towards smaller businesses with projected sales of under £1 million which want to float in order to grow. AIM is much less prescriptive in its requirements on turnover, profit and trading record than the main London Stock Exchange; in fact there are no requirements to be of a minimum size in order to get listed. There is a strict formal process your company needs to go through before being considered, however, and this process can take a lot of time, resources and most of all money. Your company must have a very robust business model and financial projections, and a skilled and experienced board of directors. Once listed you are required to make quarterly financial reports which are public.

There is debate about whether smaller companies getting involved in the stock market has been a good thing, as many of these companies were not considered profitable or robust enough to handle being a public company and the costs involved. The main thing is that you must have demonstrably large growth in your business to make it worth your while.

WHY GO PUBLIC?

As long as your business is ready for it, going public means that you have highly valued shares available and can raise a lot of cash for the growth of your business. You can offer staff share options as an incentive, too. Being publicly traded carries a lot of prestige and gravitas – it opens many financial doors and raises your profile, exposing you to the top talent in your industry.

As long as there is public demand for your stock, more shares can always be issued and projected share growth can be part of your company's external valuation process.

Once floated, shares on AIM can be raised without going through the laborious procedures of the main Stock Exchange, and companies looking to buy can find you easily. These shares come with many tax reliefs, too – including inheritance tax relief, gift relief on Capital Gains Tax, EIS reliefs, reliefs for losses, for VCTs and for corporate venturing schemes.

WHAT ARE THE DRAWBACKS?

Going public may not be worth it for a small company, because the process of evaluation, paying for listing and publicity spend is so costly and time-consuming. There needs to be a significant public appetite for what you are doing and a very healthy growth projection in order to justify the initial outlay.

Listing itself is extremely costly. It varies depending on circumstances but there is an estimated £250,000 minimum spend attached, plus a commission fee from funds raised.

Some analysts predict that floating on AIM can cost anywhere between £400,000 and £1 million all in – and that for companies with a projected market cap of lower than £25 million it's probably not worth their while.

If you think floating might be an option, speak to a nominated advisor (NOMAD) who specialises in the creative industries and has helped companies like yours in the past. This will be an investment bank, corporate finance firm or accountancy firm, approved by the London Stock Exchange, and they must be Financial Services Authority regulated. As with most things finance-expert-related, personal recommendations are best if possible. They will be able to give you realistic advice about whether there would be enough public interest in your company to support an application for listing.

THE PROCESS

Once you have decided to apply for listing on AIM, and your chosen NOMAD has agreed that it is viable, they will begin the admission process.

Alongside them will be other advisors such as brokers, accountants and lawyers.

The NOMAD has responsibility beyond listing, too, to ensure that the executive team in your business is fully aware of all its responsibilities as a publicly listed company.

Your executive team and advisors will then spend three to six months preparing materials for admission including details on company directors, financial position, business activities growth strategy and publicity spend – essentially a very sophisticated business plan.

OTHER SOURCES OF GROWTH FUNDING FOR CREATIVE BUSINESSES

Many of the funding sources detailed in the growth-funding section of this book also have growth funding available.

Some others, specifically targeted towards growth, include:

EDGE CREATIVE ENTERPRISE FUND

Edge Creative Enterprise Fund is aimed at fast-growing, creative SMEs which have scaleable intellectual property, and are ready to start bringing in investors. The fund comprises private-sector funding from financial institutions and high-net-worth individuals, and has also received funding from the British Business Bank. It is targeted specifically at the creative industries. According to its website, the fund's purpose is:

> to nurture and assist creative businesses to grow. By their nature, many of these companies start with a small number of employees, and a high degree of entrepreneurial flair. Edge provides the crucial capital and mentoring skills to stimulate growth and innovation at these firms. In this way, Edge will create growth and returns for both the management teams of its portfolio companies and its investors ... (it) is targeting a minimum three times return for its private investors over its 7–10 year life.

So you had better be a pretty safe bet – or as safe as it is ever possible to be with companies that have IP rather than tangible products at their core!

LENDINGCROWD

This functions much like Crowdcube or Funding Circle, and is specifically targeted at growing businesses – so you should have been trading for a minimum of two years and be able to demonstrate growth in that time. Successful applications launch on their loan market where investors compete to fill loans at the best possible rate. Loans are for between £25,000 and £250,00, with variable interest rates.

MARKET INVOICE.COM

Founded in 2010, this company pitches itself as an alternative to the high-street banks for growing small to medium-sized businesses. Market Invoice frees up cash for your business by selling your invoices, for a fee, so that you can access money immediately rather than waiting for your client's payment schedule. You can sell up to 90 per cent of the value of the invoice depending on your circumstances. For example, if your company turnover is between £500,000 and £1 million, and the invoice is worth £100,000, you can be advanced a maximum of £82,485 within a matter of hours and will pay a fee of £2,983. When you register with them they set up a Barclays trust account for you into which money is paid. They pay in the money up front then, when your client pays the invoice, they take their fee and forward the remainder to you.

This is a really clever and simple idea for growing businesses. Often when you reach the growth stage, your biggest problem is not necessarily turnover, but cash flow. As mentioned before, clients can be very bad at paying or have ridiculously long payment terms of up to 90 days, leaving you high and dry with immediate outgoings. Or you may need to spend a sizeable amount on research and development up front to bring ambitious projects forward and keep the flow of ideas coming. You may find that because you are growing you have to upsize your premises, and this alone can cost a fortune. Cash-flow problems have led to many otherwise healthy creative businesses getting into debt or even having to fold. It can be incredibly frustrating to have lots of business in the pipeline but be unable to pay your staff and bills and the stress can impair your ability to work, so this is a good solution.

A word of warning, though – if you use this facility a lot it represents a serious outgoing in your company through fees and you need to be absolutely sure that you can afford it. There is no point in crippling yourself financially to deal with a short-term cash-flow issue!

SOLENT GROWTH HUB

This is a valuable network for business growth, which can be tailored to your sector and includes local networking events, business networks and mentoring services to help growing businesses get to the next stage of development.

INTERVIEW: LAURA FRANSES,
HEAD OF THE CHANNEL 4 GROWTH FUND

What's your role within the fund?

Finding the companies we want to invest in and trying to identify the talent, and understand the landscape. So I have a lot of meetings with companies that I think are interesting. I then make them an offer for C4 to buy part of their company and then once that deal is done I sit on pretty much all the boards of the companies and help them grow and get to their exit situation. So I'm quite hands-on. You invest in companies and then you're part of that company.

Sometimes VCs or private equity orgs split the roles so that the people who do the deals aren't necessarily the people who manage the relationship post-investment, but because I have a background in independent TV production and running those kinds of companies, actually you realise that sitting on the boards is very useful to the companies. It turned out that if we were going to try and nurture those companies we needed somebody who had been through those hurdles.

How do you become involved in a company?

We take a minority stake in the company – 25 per cent is the maximum stake C4 are allowed to take. Generally the companies are set up in a fairly similar way – most companies seem to be run by two creatives who own the equity; there's rarely an outside investor there. The creatives get to the point where they think: we want to grow, and we need a bit of outside help and particularly commercial help. For that reason people are quite keen on C4. The other reason is that we don't take more shares than 25 per cent so the owners and creative founders still retain control of their company. There's a reason that people went out and set up companies and left bigger companies – because they want to retain control.

What were the aims of the fund when you started out?

I think C4 had quite a lot of different ambitions for it. It was something they had wanted to do for a very long time. There were two main aims: to create a return on investment, and an aim to support interesting companies and strong creative talent. C4 felt strongly about finding interesting voices, seeing if we could grow those kinds of companies and deepening its relationship with independent producers. That's been a really interesting part of it – C4 buys from independent producers but it's an arm's-length commissioning relationship and understanding those businesses close up and the creatives in them and how they grow has been something that a lot of people in C4 and particularly the chief exec have found very interesting – understanding our suppliers on that level. As time has gone on this has become more and more important to C4 – understanding these creative entrepreneurs close up.

What are the criteria for participating in the fund?

We are broad in our criteria. The most important thing is growth potential. We'll make an assessment and ask: are there more stages of growth this company can go through and can we help them get there? So a company that has been around for 20 years and stayed in a steady state, we'll think we can't really help, but if we see a company that is in year two or three, that has had a series on air that's been well received and interesting things in the pipeline, that would be interesting to us. Companies with ambitious founders, highly motivated, hard-working founders, is the number-one criterion because those are the companies most likely to grow. Companies must have a commercial ambition, too – we're trying to create companies rather than programme makers so that's a little different. Companies that we think we will work with well. I don't mean as C4 commissioners; I mean companies that will be open to having an outside investor involved. So if somebody is very protective because it's their baby, that probably wouldn't work. It's a certain mindset that's needed to let someone into your house and sit at your table. UK-based and creatively led, i.e. the creative talent is the most important – what credits do they have, what have they made, do we like the content?

Is there a specific commitment to diversity?

There has been a big commitment to ethnic diversity so last year we invested in three BAME-led companies – Voltage, Whisper and Renowned. In terms of the regions and nations aspect we have invested in a company called True North, which is Leeds-based, and we'd love to find another one. We have consistently been looking outside of England but what we haven't found yet is a company that needs our help and that can scale – we found some smaller ones but not ones that are on a growth trajectory.

A lot of the companies we invested in don't have content on C4, that's not a requirement. They've just got to have content that resonates with broadcasters somewhere, whether it's US broadcasters or anywhere.

When deciding on a company we'll look at what their output is, what they've got commissioned, how many hours, how much of that is series. We'll look at their financial accounts, making sure that turnover is growing and it's profitable. It's problematic for us to invest in a company that is consistently loss-making. But before we even look at the accounts we look at the content and what's in the pipeline.

In terms of genre, we are pretty open. There are a lot of factual companies we've invested in because factual is so much a part of the market. We've got a drama, comedy and sports and youth company, and we would invest in most genres. We would like to find an entertainment company – there are very few little entertainment companies.

Who was your first sign-up?

Popkorn were our first company. They literally filled in the application form. We hadn't heard of them; they hadn't done anything for C4 in three or four years so they didn't have a relationship with C4 at the point they applied. They were tiny, and had just done the series *My*

Violent Child on C5. I think they are a good example of what we look for. We liked the team a lot. Rory and Colin were really strong; they had made good stuff, they had a really good balance of creatives with Emma as the highly experienced production manager. They just needed a bit of cash because they wanted to hire a development team. At the moment they applied those three were just doing everything – Rory was execing, Colin was the editor and Emma was the PM. They came to us with a plan to build a development team and they made some really good hires around that; they were smart about how they directed their investment. We made that investment a year and a half ago and they've now got a 20-part series with UKTV and a second series of *My Violent Child*. They're making 30 hours this year. So it's working!

How often would you see them, and are there other people at C4 who sit on their board?

I see them every month – either they come here or I go there. We've recently brought in someone to work with them more closely who sees them once a week and looks at their cash flow and business plan so I'm now moving down to seeing them once a quarter. I think they think of it as a combination of the commercial arm of their company and a financial director. I don't think there will be a day when we're not in contact with them.

Every company has different needs. Popkorn want more help on finance; some companies may not have a commercial legal team so they want more help on that; some may want more strategy help. We adapt to what each company needs but we speak to them all once a week and meet them all formally once a month to go through their management accounts.

They formally have to produce management accounts and we formally sit down with them and tell them what it all means. Creatives without a finance background understand their company in a very different way within six months.

Have there been any teething problems?

How you relate to three or four companies is very different from how you relate to nine. I think we were very ad hoc at the beginning, i.e. send us stuff when you get a chance, etc., but now we have to be 'we need your accounts, plans and board materials on this day', so we've had to formalise reporting deadlines and how we interact with companies. We know what things we need to do up front a lot sooner and if they're missing certain people in the team we need to help them get that in. We realised pretty quickly that we need to help the companies come up with a plan as to how to spend the investment, and if they didn't have a plan, that money sitting in the bank could sometimes be confusing for companies that were used to running in a very tight way. If they didn't have a plan for where the money was going, it evaporated; so now we're pretty structured about where's that money going, what's your monthly overhead, etc. So we became more formal over time.

How does a company register interest?

They drop a note to us via the Growth Fund email account or email me or call me directly or speak to someone in commissioning who refers them to me. So we get a lot of enquiries – in the last month we've had about 15/16 enquiries to follow up on. We probably ask the person enquiring what their slate is and what's in production. We'll always look at the website. We had someone email us today and they didn't have a website, they just had a holding page, and that's a fundamental thing. You've got to send a message that you are open for business. If we think there's something there, someone on my team will meet them, find out more about their background, look up their accounts and shareholding structure, then if we are really interested they will talk to me and I will meet them, and if I really like them I'll have Lorraine Heggessey who is on our board as a creative advisor meet them. I can normally get a sense of their business and commercial aptitude and what they will be like to work with but I really rely on Lorraine's take as to how strong they are creatively. Then I will do more background checks on them and then I will put a proposal in front of the C4 Growth Fund advisory board where I table investments. Then the chief exec of C4 is on that board and will look at it and say OK let's make an offer, and then the chief exec, head of finance and head of legal will also meet those companies.

Do you do an independent share valuation and invest on that basis?

The normal way of valuing companies is to look at their net profit and do a multiple of that. This is hard with very small companies because sometimes they are not making profits. So you have to use it as a guide but we'll also try and project where the business is going and put a value on that.

Are applications rolling, and how long will the fund continue?

At the beginning C4 had this idea that we would have two sets of deadlines a year where people could apply, but now we're always open. As with anything, there are some periods of the year when we are more actively looking, but we are always looking. I think the fund will keep going; there's still more money to invest, but also it's possible that some of our companies will start to exit and that money will come back into the fund, so C4 will continue to back it. The limiting factor is whether we can find enough exciting companies out there. It really crosses over with different departments in C4, i.e. talent, research, legal and finance and commissioners.

If you're a big broadcaster you're always wondering about who's making these shows; you know, what's their life like? So people at C4 are very curious and supportive.

What are your priorities for the next couple of years?

A bit more drama, a nations and regions company, and working out what's the digital play, i.e. do we invest in a platform or online company? Dabbling on the fringes of our comfort zone, into technology.

The challenge for us with a digital agency is that it's not creating any content that it owns and can then sell on different platforms. So a digital company that was making content we would be interested in but not if they are basically platforms or putting other people's content out on the web. We understand content exploitation so I think we'll always stay on that side. Content is attractive because you own the IP and those companies sell on quite high valuations – I'm not sure what the market is like for a pure digital agency. Maybe that's something we will see as time goes on, when there is a more established market, and within two years things probably will change.

How do you think the Growth Fund will change the landscape over the next decade?

I don't think the fund will change the creative landscape exactly, but we will certainly accelerate and facilitate change. I think strong creative entrepreneurs will always be successful; we just get them to a successful point sooner. We're accelerating success rather than owning that success ourselves.

We have already brought change to the fore and given opportunities to people, for example in the BAME space, sooner. We did bring in a sports company as a direct challenge to Sunset and Vine and IMG and hopefully we're seeding a lot of creative entrepreneurs who can go on and challenge established organisations in the industry. With Eleven Film, they will go on in time to challenge Kudos and Carnival. We're bringing in fresh blood, fresh ideas and taking over the older companies.

Consolidation is baked into the industry. What I'm seeing that's interesting is that in the last year you're seeing consolidators taking minority rather than majority stakes, i.e Freemantle and Full Fat TV or Justine Gorman's company; you see Sky now taking a minority investment in Sugar Films and BBC Worldwide, too, and All3 as well. It's seeing it like this: the interesting talent is in growth mode, so we need to get in earlier; we don't want to buy a company when it's in full flight and it's going to cost us £40 million for a 100 per cent shareholding. What's happening in the landscape is that if you start a company when it's young you collaborate, you guide them, you influence them.

DON'T BE AFRAID OF CHANGE:
WINDING UP AND MOVING ON

The first couple of years of running your own creative company are a very steep learning curve. Put aside some time at the end of this period to take a clear-eyed look at what you did right, and also what you did wrong.

Have there been any negative patterns across your company and projects: relationships with clients, staff management, cash flow, accounts, administration, marketing issues, industry reputation or creative conflicts? Are you happy with your output in general and if not how would you change the things you are not happy with?

Include in this review your own performance as a company director, boss and creative leader and your relationship with your partners in the company.

If there are things holding you back at this stage they will probably continue to do so into your company's future, unless they are addressed now.

There are many things I would do differently if I had the time over again. For example, I would choose a business partner who had a different skillset from my own so that we complemented each other and the growth of the business, and so I didn't have to shoulder all the responsibility on my own; make sure to hire a solid and trustworthy bookkeeper immediately, and an accountant with more experience of the media industry; think more deeply, earlier, about the exact direction I wanted to take and market the company accordingly; be more cautious when choosing premises; network more and be more aggressive in certain competitive situations!

Sometimes it becomes clear that the best thing you can do for yourself and your company is to wind it up and move on to other things.

There could be many reasons for this. Perhaps you have grown in a different direction or gone through a life change that has changed your priorities. Perhaps you have had an experience that has inspired you to change your life completely, or you have reached burn-out. Perhaps a large client has defaulted or gone into liquidation, leaving you with unpaid debts, or you have accrued debt some other way. Perhaps there is a dispute with a business partner or one of you wants to leave. Alternatively it could just be too difficult to continue as you are – financially, emotionally or in terms of balance with the rest of life if your business and client relationships have not worked out and the work has dried up.

If you are sure that you do not want to continue trading through difficult times, you have various options when it comes to ending the life of the company. You can wind the company up if you have no debts and there is straightforward agreement between the partners. You can go into liquidation if there are more complex issues to work out but you can effectively manage the financial and contractual situations. If you find yourself in financial trouble there is the option of insolvency, which is similar to the personal option of bankruptcy.

COMPANY STRIKE-OFF OR MEMBERS' VOLUNTARY LIQUIDATION

If your company is solvent, meaning it has no debts or is in a position to pay off its remaining debts, and all the directors and shareholders are in agreement, you can wind the company up for a £10 fee by filling in a DS01 form, called a company strike-off form.

This decision should be agreed by the board and passed as a resolution. Generally you will need some help from your accountant to complete this process, particularly if there are several directors and/or shareholders.

In order to strike off in this way you must have ceased trading for at least three months. This means that you have no contracts for business in the pipeline, and all current contracts have ceased.

You will need to chase all debtors for payment before winding the company up, as you will lose that money once it ceases to exist as an entity. Make sure you get all the money that is owed and make sure that you deal with your premises, leases, furniture and equipment.

Then pay all outstanding debts and cancel or transfer any other financial agreements.

At the same time, you have to inform all your creditors that you intend to close the company down. This would include any banks, financial, public or private institutions or individuals that you hold accounts or business loans with, and anyone else to whom you might owe money.

If anyone objects, the process will have to be stalled as they have a right to pursue money owing to them that has not been paid or that they think is owing to them even if you disagree. In this case they will file an objection against the strike-off of the company.

If there is capital in the company once all debts are paid it will have to be split among the shareholders appropriately according to their share, and the same should be done with company assets.

You also have to inform employees, shareholders and any board members who did not sign the strike-off form.

You must make PAYE employees redundant or pay their final salary and taxes and any other outstanding company rates and taxes.

You must also inform HMRC of your intention to wind up, and close your payroll and VAT accounts down.

Finally you have to file final accounts to HMRC, but not to Companies House.

After two months, if no one has objected and all the boxes have been ticked, your company will be dissolved.

VOLUNTARY LIQUIDATION

Creditors' voluntary liquidation usually happens when the company has become insolvent. This means that it has more debts than assets, and is unable to repay outstanding debt. Usually the company directors know that the company is no longer viable, and cannot trade its way out of debt or be restructured in order to keep trading. It is then their legal duty as company directors to act. If directors leave it too long to make a decision and continue when the company is no longer viable, they could be charged with wrongful trading, so the decision really does have to be made rather than avoided.

Sometimes you can meet debts by restructuring, for example cutting company running costs and cutting directors' salaries. Always consider this as an option as it gets you out of the process faster – even if it means financial pain for you in the short term.

You should not be paying yourself a salary from the company if it is insolvent, and if it can be proved that you have been doing so then you can be fined, made personally liable for company debts and disqualified as a company director. Often bodies who have been brought in to investigate company insolvency, such as insolvency practitioners, uncover evidence that this has been happening.

In the liquidation process assets are sold and turned into cash for the creditors. Creditors must be paid on an equitable basis, with no preference shown, so repayments have to be worked out for everyone before being distributed.

According to insolvency practitioner KSA Group, creditors' voluntary liquidation is the most common form of liquidation in the UK:

> in the 2nd quarter of 2016 the total number of companies that went into liquidation was 2,501. Around 10,000 companies will be closed this way per year.

In order to carry out voluntary liquidation, an insolvency practitioner is usually employed. If you do choose to use one, make sure that they are licensed. Insolvency practitioners generally charge a minimum of £5,500 plus VAT (often it's quite a bit more) and they often expect their fee up front if you may not have sufficient assets to pay them and all the creditors. You might find one that will take their fee from the distribution of monies from the liquidation process, which, as long as you have sufficient assets, is preferable. For this reason they are not always a realistic option for a company that is really struggling with debt and directors who do not have a lot of funds themselves.

The process begins with company shareholders nominating a liquidator, and directors giving that liquidator a list of all company creditors. The nominated liquidator then writes to all creditors to arrange a meeting, and at this meeting the creditors vote to appoint the liquidator. If a majority does not agree, then another one has to be found.

The liquidator then gets to business. He or she will investigate the conduct of the company directors, do all the admin, cancel leases, deal with staff, collect assets, sell them at auction and distribute the payments to the creditors. Usually payments are small because there is limited time to find buyers for assets so creditors expect to receive only a percentage of the debt owed to them as a result of this process. The directors have to give them the company accounting books and records for use during this process. This is a legal requirement.

OTHER OPTIONS FOR INSOLVENT COMPANIES

Appointing a liquidator is NOT a legal requirement for insolvent companies. Some practitioners you speak to in your hour of need may claim it is, but in fact all that is required by law is that the insolvent company ceases to trade, and that all creditors are then treated equitably. This means directors must immediately begin a formal or informal procedure that will result in the repayment of outstanding debts, or an agreement to write those debts off. It also means that you cannot pay some creditors but not others. The company does not have to be formally liquidated. Obviously, whether you choose to use a professional liquidator or not will depend on the size of your company, how many creditors and employees you have, and what your assets and debts are – it has to be a manageable process for the directors if they choose not to liquidate.

If you want to manage it yourself, you should take all the steps in the company wind-up procedure and then write to your creditors to suggest a clear debt settlement or repayment plan. Banks will often agree to write off a portion of your overdraft fee or other outstanding debts in return for immediate payment, called full and final settlement. You may have to go through a lengthy formal process to get to this point, though, as it has to be dealt with by the collections department rather than your business manager, and your business manager may initially refuse. Other creditors will generally do the same or may even agree to write off the debt if it is small enough. Creditors will only go to the bother and expense of objecting to your strike-off and taking the matter to court if the debt is large enough to make it worth their while; they will be aware that the money they get back is only likely to be a proportion of the entire debt owed.

If you owe HMRC money then they will certainly expect payment – but again, you can write to them suggesting that a proportion of the debt is paid or work out a repayment plan. They are well used to companies in this situation.

CORPORATE VOLUNTARY ARRANGEMENTS

A corporate voluntary arrangement is when a company makes an agreement with its creditors by proposing a 'composition in satisfaction of its debt' or a 'scheme of arrangement of its affairs'. This means an arrangement, approved by the court, in which the company has formally agreed terms with its creditors for the settlement of its debts.

This arrangement can be proposed by the company directors, an official liquidator or an official administrator.

Once the proposition has been approved and the courts have been notified, the proposal is put to a vote of the company's creditors at an official meeting and all creditors are bound to abide by the agreement.

COMPANY ADMINISTRATION

Administration is when a person, 'the administrator', is appointed to manage a company's affairs, business and property for the benefit of the creditors. The person appointed must be an insolvency practitioner and has the status of an officer of the court (whether or not he or she is appointed by the court).

Often this process is put in place if there is a chance the company might be able to trade through its financial difficulties, or find a buyer to bail it out and appoint a new executive team. Administration is also useful if the company has tangible assets such as property, where a good price might be found if there is enough time to do so (and where there would not be sufficient time in a winding-up process).

An administration order can be made by the court, or an administrator can be appointed by company directors to evaluate the company position and decide if administration is appropriate.

If the administrator decides it is appropriate, any actions against the company, for example a winding-up petition by a creditor or any other legal proceedings, can be temporarily suspended.

The appointment of an administrator expires after one year; however, the process can sometimes take longer in which case an extension can be granted by the court, with the permission of the creditors involved.

ADMINISTRATIVE RECEIVERSHIP

In a similar process, an administrative receiver can be appointed by a creditor. The receiver must be an insolvency practitioner (IP). Before a receiver can be appointed, a document, called a debenture, which gives the creditor charge over company assets, must be granted by the company. Once granted, the company is in administrative receivership. The receiver's job is to recover money for the creditor. The creditor may then try to supervise the continued trading of the business in order to help it out of financial difficulties and return the money owed, sell all or part of the company, or cease trading and sell off company assets.

COMPULSORY LIQUIDATION

Compulsory liquidation is where a court order has been made for your company to be made bankrupt (that is, wound up). A winding-up petition can be presented in the High Court, or the district registry of the High Court, for the area in which your company is registered or trading.

The winding-up petition can be presented by the company directors or shareholders, a creditor, an insolvency practitioner, a receiver or administrator, the Secretary of State for Business, Innovation and Skills or the Financial Conduct Authority.

In a compulsory liquidation the cost of issuing a winding-up petition (roughly £1,490–£1,990) is covered by the creditor, and the liquidator is appointed by the court or the creditor.

For this reason, creditors do not normally pursue compulsory liquidation unless it is financially worth their while to do so, but they are allowed to do it for any debt over £750.

HOW THESE DIFFERENT ROUTES AFFECT YOU AS A COMPANY DIRECTOR

As long as you have followed one of these legal processes accurately and informed all of your creditors, you should not find yourself in serious trouble.

Directors are liable for debts where they have signed a personal guarantee, for example, with most business bank overdrafts and also many loan agreements. This means that, even if you have successfully wound up your company, creditors could still chase you if they feel they have not been treated properly or if you have not worked out a payment plan with them.

One of the biggest risks for company directors in the liquidation process is the official investigation process, where their conduct might come into question and lead to them being fined, prosecuted or disqualified as a company director.

CONCLUSION

There are many ways you can start, growth routes you can take and end points to your journey as a founder/managing director of a creative company today. This book has only covered some of them but it has hopefully inspired you to take the next step and make your own mark in the creative industries. As your company evolves, you will evolve along with it and life experiences will shape your decisions, too. I have now decided to move on from the company that I established to set up a non-profit social campaigning organisation, Mental Abuse Matters, raising awareness about emotional and psychological abuse. It will start with a wide-reaching campaign, and an educational outreach project, communicating with families, educators, the police and legal profession and communities across the board. In doing this I will be able to use my skills as a company director and content creator as well as all the collaborative, technological and network opportunities afforded by the digital age, while also fulfilling an ambition to be more directly involved in cultural change. It's an exciting time to create, and to add your voice to the global community, because the galvanising power and reach of digital is unprecedented in human history. Once you have the skills to cut through the volume of content and find your audience, much can be achieved. After many years of telling stories about people working to create a more progressive society, which is in itself an important way to facilitate change, I want to be doing it in a more fundamental way. The message will still be communicated through the visual image, video and animation because this is the most powerful way to cut across divides. The people I have worked with and things learned along the way will be invaluable to this next chapter. Whatever route you take, I wish you good luck, fulfilment and prosperity on your journey, too.

RESOURCES

YOUR USP

Companies House information
https://www.gov.uk/choose-company-name

Creative thinking
https://www.theguardian.com/media-network/2016/may/18/born-creative-educated-out-of-us-school-business

Finland education system
http://www.independent.co.uk/news/world/europe/finland-schools-subjects-are-out-and-topics-are-in-as-country-reforms-its-education-system-10123911.html

SETTING UP YOUR LIMITED COMPANY

Company director responsibilities, Companies House
https://www.gov.uk/running-a-limited-company/directors-responsibilities

Private Limited Companies
http://www.nabarro.com/downloads/corporate_governance_directors_duties_uk_handbook.pdf

Difference between shareholders and directors
http://www.companylawclub.co.uk/what-is-the-difference-between-shareholders-and-directors

Director responsibilities

http://united-kingdom.taylorwessing.com/synapse/duties_personal_liabilities.html

How do voting rights work?

http://www.companylawclub.co.uk/what-voting-rights-do-shares-have

Memorandum and Articles

https://www.gov.uk/limited-company-formation/memorandum-and-articles-of-association

Limited Liability Partnerships and CIOs

http://www.companylawclub.co.uk/types-of-registered-companies

HMRC COMES CALLING!

Tax on dividends, Companies House

https://www.gov.uk/tax-on-dividends/how-dividends-are-taxed

Tax rate thresholds 2016/17

https://www.gov.uk/government/publications/tax-and-tax-credit-rates-and-thresholds-for-2016-17/tax-and-tax-credit-rates-and-thresholds-for-2016-17

Paternity pay rules

https://www.gov.uk/employers-paternity-pay-leave/eligibility

Shared parental leave

http://www.maternityaction.org.uk/wp/advice-2/mums-dads-scenarios/shared-parental-leave-and-pay/

Childcare vouchers

http://www.childcarevouchers.co.uk/parents/parents-how-it-works/#.VqDUIxy1kgA

Maternity allowance

https://www.gov.uk/maternity-pay-leave/overviewLegislation%20Changes2.pdf

https://www.gov.uk/maternity-allowance

VAT registration
https://www.gov.uk/vat-registration/how-to-register

Annual accounts HMRC
https://www.gov.uk/first-company-accounts-and-return/overview

START-UP FUNDING IN THE DIGITAL AGE

SEIS
https://www.gov.uk/guidance/seed-enterprise-investment-scheme-background

https://www.gov.uk/guidance/seed-enterprise-investment-scheme-how-companies-qualify

Crowdfunding
http://www.growthbusiness.co.uk/growing-a-business/business-finance/2483726/top-10-crowdfunding-platforms-for-business-finance.thtml

crowdfunder.co.uk/film

www.crowdcube.co.uk

Brexit: creative industries
https://inews.co.uk/explainers/iq/brexit-mean-uks-arts-media-industries/

http://creative.wardwilliams.co.uk/eu-referendum-affect-creative-industries/

Brexit: employment law
http://united-kingdom.taylorwessing.com/download/article-brexit-employment-law.html

PREMISES, BUDGETS AND CASH FLOWING

Creative hubs for offices
http://startups.co.uk/the-best-clubs-hubs-and-co-work-spaces-for-entrepreneurs/

Quiet: The Power of Introverts in a World That Can't Stop Talking, Susan Cain, published by Penguin Books, 2012

New companies embracing flexible working
http://www.fastcompany.com/3059295/your-most-productive-self/inside-three-companies-that-are-innovating-flexible-schedules?partner=bigthink

PUBLICITY AND ADVERTISING

Future of digital marketing
http://www.mediavisioninteractive.com/blog/digital-marketing-2/digital-marketing-predictions-2015/

Digital agencies
www.found.co.uk

PITCHING FOR BUSINESS

Types of digital content now
http://www.zazzlemedia.co.uk/blog/digital-content-types/

How media consumption has changed in a decade
http://themediaoctopus.com/how-media-consumption-and-use-has-changed-in-a-decade/

PACT and Ofcom reports
http://old.culture.gov.uk/images/consultation_responses/CR2011-PACT_Annex1.pdf

http://downloads.bbc.co.uk/commissioning/site/Terms_Of_Trade.pdf

http://media.ofcom.org.uk/news/2015/psb-review-statement/

http://stakeholders.ofcom.org.uk/binaries/consultations/psb-review-3/responses/Pact_Annex.pdf

http://media.ofcom.org.uk/news/2015/psb-review-statement/

Netflix
https://www.midiaresearch.com/blog/netflix-gets-ready-to-disrupt-tv-commissioning-in-2016/

YouTubers
http://uk.businessinsider.com/how-to-make-money-as-a-youtube-star-2015-12

http://www.investopedia.com/articles/personal-finance/032615/how-youtube-ad-revenue-works.asp

GROWTH STRATEGIES AND FUNDING

Growth
https://www.marketinvoice.com/pricing

http://www.peraconsulting.com/sme-growth/

https://www.nibusinessinfo.co.uk/content/buy-existing-business

Sweden, six-hour days
http://indy100.independent.co.uk/article/what-happened-after-sweden-introduced-a-six-hour-work-day--W1bR6djCD_b

Consolidation
http://insight.globalwebindex.net/hs-fs/hub/304927/file-1414878665-pdf/Reports/GWI_Media_Consumption_Summary_Q3_2014.pdf

WINDING UP AND MOVING ON

Winding up
https://www.businessdebtline.org/EW/factsheets/Pages/limitedcompany/closingalimitedcompany.aspx

https://www.gov.uk/strike-off-your-company-from-companies-register/apply-to-strike-off

http://www.companyrescue.co.uk/creditors-voluntary-liquidation?gclid=CI7V3Jb6_84CFUU8GwodEUgCHQ

APPENDICES

All the templates can be downloaded at www.kamerabooks.co.uk/ceresources

APPENDIX 1
SHAREHOLDERS' CONTRACT

DATED _____ 2008

(1) PARTY 1

(2) PARTY 2

(3) PARTY 3

(4)COMPANY NAME

**SHAREHOLDERS' AGREEMENT
RELATING TO
COMPANY NAME**

THIS AGREEMENT is dated

PARTIES

(1)

(2)

(3)

(4) **COMPANY NAME** (Company Registration Number) whose registered office is situated at .... ('**Company**').

BACKGROUND

(A) The Company is a private company limited by shares incorporated and registered in England and Wales.

(B) The authorised share capital of the Company is £............ divided into .... A Shares of £ each and ... B Shares of £ each which are allotted to the Shareholders (as defined below) as more particularly set out in Part 1 of Schedule 1. The other principal details of the Company are set out in Part 2 of Schedule 1.

(C) The Shareholders have agreed to enter into this agreement for the purpose of controlling their capacity as shareholders of the Company.

AGREED TERMS

1. **Interpretation**

1.1 The definitions and rules of interpretation in this clause apply in this agreement.

'**A Shares**' means the A Shares of £ each in the share capital of the Company from time to time.

'**Articles**' means the articles of association of the Company from time to time;

'**Auditors**' means the auditors of the Company for the time being.

'**B Shares**' means the B Shares of £ each in the share capital of the Company from time to time.

'**Business Day**' means a day (other than a Saturday or Sunday) when banks in the City of London are open for business.

273

'**Deed of Adherence**' means a deed in the form set out in Schedule 2 or a deed in such other form as the Shareholders may agree;

'**Shareholder**' means any of X, X and X as the context requires, and Shareholders means all of them together.

'**Shares**' means shares in the capital of the Company of whatever class.

1.2 Clause and schedule headings do not affect the interpretation of this agreement.

1.3 A person includes a natural person, a corporate or unincorporated body (whether or not having a separate legal personality).

1.4 A reference to a particular law is a reference to it as it is in force for the time being taking account of any amendment, extension, application or re-enactment, and includes any subordinate legislation for the time being in force made under it.

1.5 Writing or written includes faxes but not e-mail.

1.6 Documents in agreed form are documents in the form agreed by the parties and initialled by them for identification.

1.7 Words in the singular include the plural and in the plural include the singular.

2. Business of the Company

The Shareholders shall, for as long as they hold shares in the capital of the Company, procure (so far as is possible in the exercise of their rights and powers) that the business of the Company is carried on in accordance with the objects in the memorandum of association as adopted by the Company for the time being.

3. Directors and management

3.1 x shall be entitled under this Agreement to remain the managing director of the Company for so long as she remains a Shareholder. She shall exercise the normal functions and have the normal responsibilities of such office including the sole and exclusive day to day conduct of the management and affairs of the Company without involvement from the other Shareholders (including but not limited to the right to assign any intellectual property rights in any of the projects carried out by the Company) subject only to the provisions of this Agreement

3.2   x shall be entitled under this Agreement to remain a non-executive director of the Company for so long as she remains a Shareholder. X shall be entitled to attend and observe (but not to vote) at all meetings of the board.]

3.3   x shall, for as long as she is the managing director of the Company and so far as is possible, ensure that all Shareholders are kept informed of the following matters involving the Company:

   (a)   any purchase, lease or other acquisition of assets or any interests therein which exceed the value of £50,000.

   (b)   any sale or disposal of the whole or any part of the Company's undertaking, property, assets, or any interest therein or contract to do so.

   (c)   any contract, transaction or arrangement of a value exceeding £50,000.

   (d)   any loan made to or by the Company in excess of £50,000.

4.   Transfer of Shares

4.1   No Shareholder (other than X) shall sell, transfer, assign, pledge, charge or otherwise dispose of any share or any interest in any share in the Company except as permitted by this agreement or with the prior written consent of the Shareholders. The provisions contained in clauses 4 to 7 of this Agreement and the restrictions relating to the transfer of shares contained in the Articles shall not apply to the transfer of any Shares held by X.

4.2   Except for transfers for which the other Shareholders give their prior written consent, no Shareholder shall transfer any shares unless she transfers all (and not some only) of the shares held by her.

4.3   A Shareholder wishing to transfer shares (Seller) shall give notice in writing (Transfer Notice) to the other parties (Ongoing Shareholders) specifying the details of the proposed transfer, including the identity of the proposed buyer(s) and the price for the shares.

4.4   Within 3 (three) months of receiving the Transfer Notice, the Ongoing Shareholders shall give a notice to the Seller saying that they wish to:

   (a)   purchase a proportion of the shares in the Transfer Notice, which the number of ordinary shares held by her bears to the total number of ordinary shares held by the Ongoing Shareholders, at the price specified; or

(b) purchase a proportion of the shares in the Transfer Notice, which the number of ordinary shares held by her bears to the total number of ordinary shares held by the Ongoing Shareholders, but that the price specified is too high.

4.5 If the Ongoing Shareholders wish to purchase the Seller's shares but consider the price specified to be too high, the parties shall endeavour to agree a price. If the parties fail to reach agreement within 3 (three) months of the Transfer Notice, the Auditors shall determine the fair value of the shares in accordance with clause 7.

4.6 If the Seller does not agree with the Fair Value as certified in the Auditors' written notice, she shall revoke the Transfer Notice by notice in writing to the Ongoing Shareholders within 7 (seven) Business Days of delivery of the Auditors' written notice. If the Seller revokes the Transfer Notice, she is not entitled to transfer the shares except in accordance with this agreement.

4.7 If the Ongoing Shareholders do not agree with the Fair Value as certified in the Auditors' written notice, they shall give notice to the Seller within 7 (seven) Business Days of delivery of the Auditors' written notice.

4.8 Subject to the Seller not exercising her right to revoke the Transfer Notice, and unless the Ongoing Shareholders give notice in writing to the Seller within 14 (fourteen) Business Days of the date of the Auditors' written notice that they do not wish to purchase the shares, completion of the sale of the shares comprised in the Transfer Notice at the Fair Value, or price specified and agreed pursuant to clause 4.4(a) (as the case may be), shall take place in accordance with clause 6.

4.9 If the Ongoing Shareholders fail to give notice under clause 4.4, or give notice under clause 4.7:

(a) the Seller is entitled to transfer her shares to the third party buyer identified in the Transfer Notice at a price not less than the price specified in the Transfer Notice (or the Fair Value, if lower); and

(b) the Seller shall procure that any buyer of shares that is not a party to this agreement shall, at completion, enter into a shareholders' agreement in relation to such shares with the parties to this agreement on the same terms that apply to the Seller.

5. Events of default

5.1 A Shareholder is deemed to have served a Transfer Notice under clause 4.3 immediately before any of the following events of default:

(a) his death; or

(b) a bankruptcy order being made against her, or an arrangement or composition being made with her creditors, or where she otherwise takes the benefit of any statutory provision for the time being in force for the relief of insolvent debtors.

5.2 The deemed Transfer Notice has the same effect as a Transfer Notice, except that:

(a) the deemed Transfer Notice takes effect on the basis that it does not identify a proposed buyer or state a price for the shares and the parties shall refer the question of a valuation to the Auditors under clause 6;

(b) the Auditors are required to determine the Fair Value for the shares;

(c) the Seller does not have a right of withdrawal following a valuation;

(d) on the completion of any sale in accordance with this clause, the buyer is not required to procure the discharge of any security given by the Seller or to procure the release of any debts of the Company to her; and

(e) if the Ongoing Shareholders do not accept the offer in the deemed Transfer Notice, the Seller does not have the right to sell the shares to a third party and the Company shall be wound up forthwith upon the Ongoing Shareholders giving notice in writing to the Company within 10 (ten) Business Days from the delivery of the deemed Transfer Notice or written notice of the Fair Value, whichever is the later.

6. Completion of Share process

6.1 Completion of the sale and purchase of shares under clause 4 and clause 5 of this agreement shall take place on 3 (three) months after:

(a) the day of delivery of the Transfer Notice, unless the Auditors have been requested to determine Fair Value; or

(b) the day of delivery of the Auditors' Fair Value notice.

6.2 At such completion:

(a)   the Seller shall deliver, or procure that there is delivered to the Ongoing Shareholders, a duly completed share transfer form transferring the legal and beneficial ownership of the relevant shares to the Ongoing Shareholders, together with the relevant share certificates and such other documents as the Ongoing Shareholders may reasonably require to show good title to the shares, or to enable them to be registered as the holders of the shares;

(b)   the Ongoing Shareholders shall deliver or procure that there is delivered to the Seller a bankers' draft for the purchase price.

6.3   The shares are sold by the Seller with full title guarantee.

6.4   If any Ongoing Shareholder fails to pay the purchase price on the due date, without prejudice to any other remedy which the Seller may have, the outstanding balance of the purchase price shall accrue interest at a rate equal to 1% above the base rate of Barclays Bank Plc from time to time.

6.5   The parties shall procure the registration (subject to due stamping by the Ongoing Shareholders) of the transfers of shares in the Company effected pursuant to this clause and each of them consents to such transfers and registrations under this agreement and the Articles.

7.   Fair Value

7.1   The Fair Value for any shares to be transferred under this agreement is that proportion of the amount the Auditors consider to be the fair value of the entire issued share capital of the Company that the Seller's shares bear to the entire issued share capital of the Company (with no discount for the size of the Seller's shareholding).

7.2   In determining the Fair Value of the entire issued share capital of the Company, the Auditors rely on the following assumptions:

(a)   the sale is between a willing seller and a willing buyer;

(b)   the shares are sold free of all restrictions, liens, charges and other encumbrances; and

(c)   the sale is taking place on the date the Auditors were requested to determine the Fair Value.

8. Issue of further shares

8.1 If the Company wishes to issue further shares, the Shareholders shall procure (so far as is possible in the exercise of their rights and powers) that the Company gives notice to each Shareholder stating the number of shares to be issued and the price of the shares.

8.2 Each Shareholder shall have the option, but not the obligation, to subscribe for, at the price stated in the notice, that proportion of the shares proposed to be issued which the number of ordinary shares held by her bears to the total number of ordinary shares in issue at the time the Company gives its notice. Each Shareholder may exercise the option by giving notice to the Company, at any time within 15 (fifteen) Business Days following the Company's notice, accompanied by a banker's draft made payable to the Company in respect of full payment for the shares to be subscribed for.

8.3 Any shares referred to in the Company's notice, in respect of which the Shareholders do not exercise their options, may be issued by the Company in accordance with its notice, provided that any such issue is completed within 20 (twenty) Business Days after the Company's notice.

9. Further Shareholders

The Shareholders shall procure that before any person (other than a person who is already a party to this Agreement) is registered as the holder of any share in the Company such person shall enter into a Deed of Adherence. The Company shall not register any such person as the holder of any share until such a deed has been executed and exchanged. Upon such registration, execution and exchange that person shall be deemed to be a party to this Agreement.

10. Payment of dividends

10.1 In deciding whether in respect of any accounting reference period the Company has profits available for distribution the parties hereto shall procure that the Auditors of the Company shall certify whether such profits are available or not and the amount thereof (if any). In giving such certificate the Auditors shall act as experts and not arbitrators and their determination shall be binding on the parties hereto.

10.2 No dividend shall be declared by the Company:

(a) which is prohibited by any legal commitment binding upon the Company;

(b) which would render the Company unable to pay its debts as and when they fall due;

(c) the amount of which should reasonably be retained as a provision for corporation tax or other tax liabilities or for other actual liabilities of the Company;

10.3 The Company shall pay a dividend to the Shareholders in the proportion of their shareholding in the Company as follows:

(a) on a yearly basis to X;

(b) on either a monthly or quarterly basis to X and X.

11. Accounts

11.1 The Company undertakes to, and covenants with, X that (unless X gives its prior written consent to the contrary):

(a) the Company shall provide to X any financial and other information concerning the Company as X may from time to time reasonably require, and (in that regard) permit any authorised representative from time to time, upon reasonable prior notice and at her expense, to inspect and take copies of any books, papers, documents and other records of the Company, as she may stipulate.

(a) the Company shall provide to X a copy of the accounts for the Company in respect of each financial year within 4 weeks of the accounts being concluded.

12. Termination

12.1 This agreement terminates immediately upon the occurrence of any of the following events:

(a) a resolution is passed for the winding up of the Company; or

(b) a receiver, administrator or administrative receiver is appointed over the whole or any part of the assets of the Company or the affairs, business and property of the Company is to be managed by a supervisor under any arrangement made with the creditors of the Company.

12.2 Termination of this agreement shall be without prejudice to the rights of any Shareholder accrued prior to such termination, or under any provision which is expressly stated not to be affected by such termination including in respect of any prior breach of this agreement.

12.3 On a winding-up, the Shareholders shall endeavour to agree a suitable basis for dealing with the interests and assets of the Company and shall endeavour to ensure that:

(a) all existing contracts of the Company are performed so far as resources permit;

(b) no new contractual obligations are entered into by the Company; and

(c) the Company is wound up as soon as practicable.

13. Confidentiality

Each Shareholder undertakes that she shall not at any time after the date of this agreement use, divulge or communicate to any person (except to her professional representatives or advisers or as may be required by law or any legal or regulatory authority) any confidential information concerning the terms of this agreement, the business or affairs of the other Shareholders or the Company which may have (or may in future) come to her knowledge, and each of the Shareholders shall use her reasonable endeavours to prevent the publication or disclosure of any confidential information concerning such matters.

14. Notices

Any notice given under this agreement shall be in writing and shall be delivered by hand, transmitted by fax, or sent by pre-paid first class post or recorded delivery post to the address of the party, or to such other address notified to the other parties. A correctly addressed notice sent by pre-paid first class post or recorded delivery post shall be deemed to have been received at the time at which it would have been delivered in the normal course of post. A notice sent by fax to the fax number of the relevant party shall be deemed to have been received at the time of transmission.

15. Severance

15.1 If any provision (or part of a provision) of this agreement is found by any court or administrative body of competent jurisdiction to be invalid, unenforceable or illegal, the other provisions shall remain in force.

15.2 If any invalid, unenforceable or illegal provision would be valid, enforceable and legal if some part of it were deleted, the provision shall apply with whatever modification is necessary to give effect to the commercial intention of the parties.

16. Costs and expenses

Each Shareholder shall pay the costs relating to the negotiation, preparation, execution and implementation by her of this agreement in the same proportion to which she holds shares in the Company.

17. Governing Law and Jurisdiction

17.1 This agreement and any disputes or claims arising out of or in connection with its subject matter are governed by and construed in accordance with the laws of England.

17.2 The parties irrevocably agree that the courts of England have exclusive jurisdiction to settle any dispute or claim that arises out of or in connection with this agreement.

18. Status of this agreement

If any provisions of the memorandum or articles of association of the Company at any time conflict with any provisions of this agreement, this agreement shall prevail and the Shareholders shall, whenever necessary, exercise all voting and other rights and powers available to them to procure the amendment, waiver or suspension of the relevant provision of the memorandum or articles of association to the extent necessary to permit the Company and its affairs to be administered as provided in this agreement.

19 Counterpart

This agreement may be executed in any number of counterparts all of which taken together shall constitute one and the same instrument. Any party to this agreement may enter into this agreement by executing any such counterpart.

20. No partnership

The Shareholders are not in partnership with each other, nor are they agents of each other.

21. Determination of disputes

In the event of any dispute under or arising out of this Agreement (other than one for which a separate method of resolution has been provided):

21.1 The Shareholders shall take the matter before an independent mediator in accordance with the procedures of ADR Group, London, with the intention that the matter shall if possible be resolved by mediation.

21.2 The mediator shall be agreed by the Shareholders, or failing such agreement within 15 Business Days of one Shareholder requesting the appointment of a mediator, shall be appointed on the application of any of the Shareholders in accordance with clause 21.6.

21.3 Unless otherwise agreed the costs of the mediation shall be paid by each of the Shareholders in the same proportion to which she holds shares in the Company but any Shareholder which may of her own volition incur any additional costs shall be responsible for them.

21.4 The doctrines of laches, waiver or estoppel shall not be considered in any such mediation.

21.5 In the event that the mediator appointed as above shall certify in writing his opinion that the dispute is not capable of resolution by mediation, or that the mediation has not been concluded within 60 days of the agreement of the Shareholders as to the appointment of the mediator or a request by any of the Shareholders for such an appointment, then it shall be referred in accordance with the Arbitration Act 1996 to a single arbitrator to be appointed, in default of agreement, upon the request of the Shareholders in accordance with clause 21.6, and the decision of the arbitrator (including any decision as to costs) shall be final and binding on the Shareholders.

21.6 An appointment of a mediator or arbitrator shall be made upon the request of any of the Shareholders by the president or other chief officer for the time being of the Relevant Institution or any deputy duly authorised by the Relevant Institution in that regard.

21.7 Nothing in this clause 21 shall preclude the making of an application to the Court for injunctive relief to restrain a breach or apprehended breach of this Agreement.

EXECUTED as a deed in the originals the day and year first before written

EXECUTED and DELIVERED as a deed
By **XX**
in the presence of:

Signature of Witness:
Name of Witness:
Address of Witness:

Occupation of Witness:

EXECUTED and DELIVERED as a deed
By **XX**
in the presence of:

Signature of Witness:
Name of Witness:
Address of Witness:

Occupation of Witness:

EXECUTED and DELIVERED as a deed
By **XX**
in the presence of:

Signature of Witness:
Name of Witness:
Address of Witness:

Occupation of Witness:

EXECUTED as a deed **COMPANY NAME**   ) and
)
signed by two duly authorised officers on its behalf   )
                                                        Director/Secretary
                                                        Director

SCHEDULE 1
PART 1
SHAREHOLDERS AND SHAREHOLDER NUMBERS

EXISTING SHAREHOLDERS	NUMBER OF A SHARES HELD	NUMBER OF B SHARES HELD
X X	-	-
X X	-	-
X X	-	-

PART 2
PRINCIPAL DETAILS OF THE COMPANY

Directors

X X
X X
X X (non-executive director)

Company Secretary

X X

Accounting Date

31 March

SCHEDULE 2
DEED OF ADHERENCE

THIS DEED OF ADHERENCE is made on this   day of   20[ ]

BY

[   ] of [   ] (the 'Covenantor')

SUPPLEMENTAL to a Shareholders' Agreement (the 'Shareholders' Agreement') dated [   ] made between (1) [DETAILS OF THE PARTIES] [as modified by [HERE SET OUT THE DETAILS OF ANY INSTRUMENT MODIFYING THE ORIGINAL AGREEMENT]].

THIS DEED WITNESSES as follows:-

1.   The Covenantor confirms that [she] [it] has been supplied with a copy of the Shareholders' Agreement and undertakes with each of the other parties to the Shareholders' Agreement from time to time to observe, perform and be bound by all the terms of the Shareholders' Agreement which are capable of applying to the Covenantor and which have not been performed at the date of this deed to the intent and effect that the Covenantor shall be deemed with effect from the date on which the Covenantor is registered as a member of the Company to be a party to the Shareholders' Agreement and to be a Shareholder Party (as defined in the Shareholders' Agreement).

2.   This Deed shall be governed by and construed in accordance with the laws of England.

EXECUTED as a deed on the date specified above.

EXECUTED as a deed by [   ]   )
LIMITED and signed by two   )
duly authorised officers on its behalf   )   Director/Secretary:

EXECUTED and DELIVERED as a deed by [   ]
in the presence of:

Signature of Witness:
Name of Witness:
Address of Witness:

Occupation of Witness:

APPENDIX 2
START-UP COMPANY RESOLUTION

The Companies Acts 1985 - 2006
Private Company Limited by Shares

WRITTEN RESOLUTION OF
(the "Company")

Passed on

I, the undersigned, being the only member of the Company who at the date of this resolution am entitled to attend and vote at general meetings of the Company, hereby RESOLVE in accordance with Regulation 53 of the Company's Articles of Association, and agree that such resolution for all purposes be as valid and effective as if the same had been passed at a general meeting of the Company duly convened and held:

ORDINARY RESOLUTION

SPECIAL RESOLUTION

Dated:
Signed:

....

APPENDIX 3
BUDGET EXAMPLE

Details	Amount	N°	Unit	Unit Price	Budget
Pre-production and production roles above the line					31,200.00
Development					2,350.00
Executive Producer	1	28	days	400.00	11,200.00
Producer/Director	1	13	weeks	1,350.00	17.550.00
Casting Workshop Expenses	1	20	wkshps	50.00	1,000.00
Licences/CRB checks	1	1	allow	200.00	200.00
Education consultant	1	5	days	250.00	1,250.00
Artists					3,000.00
Actors	5	2	days	250.00	2,500.00
CONTRIBUTOR FEE				£500	500.00
Production Staff					27,550.00
Production Manager	1	8	weeks	1,000.00	8,000.00
Shooting AP	1	6.5	weeks	900.00	5,850.00
Production Assnt	1	4	weeks	400.00	1,600.00
1st Assnt Dir	1	2	days	300.00	600.00
Production Accountant	1	1	allow	750.00	750.00
1 set runner	1	10	days	100.00	1,000.00
2 Runner/Driver	2	10	days	100.00	2,000.00
Camera Op	1	5	days	300.00	1,500.00
Assistant Camera	1	5	days	200.00	1,000.00
Gaffer	1	2	days	300.00	600.00

Recordist	1	5	days	300.00	1,500.00
Assistant Sound/Boom OP	1	5	days	150.00	750.00
Wardrobe/Make-up assistant	1	2	days	150.00	300.00
Make-up Artist	1	2	days	200.00	400.00
Production designer	1	2	days	350.00	700.00
Voice over TBC				1,000.00	1,000.00
Post Production					**16,950.00**
Editor	1	6	weeks	1,350.00	8,100.00
Editing Equipment – Offline	1	5	weeks	800.00	4,000.00
Digitising	1	2	days	150.00	300.00
Drives	2	1	allow	150.00	300.00
Grade	2	1	days	500.00	1,000.00
Online & titling	7	1	hours	250.00	1,750.00
Sound Mix	1	1	allow	1,000.00	1,000.00
VO record				500.00	500.00
Materials					**400.00**
Props – purchased	1	1	allow	200.00	200.00
Costumes/Make-up	1	1	allow	200.00	200.00
Production equipment					**13,950.00**
Camera + lighting Equipment schools shoots	1	15	days	200.00	3,000.00
Multi camera rig inc. extra crew and set up				10,000.00	10,000.00
Walky Talkies	1	1	allow	200.00	200.00
Sound equipment (+ radio mikes)	1	5	days	150.00	750.00
Other production					**4,450.00**
Location Fees	1	1	allow	500.00	500.00
Cast/Crew Transport (park, permits, con charge, petrol)	2	15	days	50.00	1,500.00
Vehicle hire	1	15	days	60.00	900.00
Shoot consumable	1	1	allow	150.00	150.00
Catering	5	10	days	20.00	1,000.00
Catering (50 x 7)			allow		400.00
Film/Tape stock					**670.00**
Cards	1	10	card	50.00	500.00

Post Prod Stock	1	6	tapes	20.00	120.00
Misv DVDs etc	1	1	allow	50.00	50.00
Music					**1,500.00**
Music	1	1	allow	1,000.00	1,500.00
Office Overheads Etc					**7,755.00**
Mobile Phones	1	1	allow	500.00	500.00
Desks, fax, internet etc	1	10	weeks	150.00	1,500.00
Computer Equipment/ Peripherals	1	1	allow	500.00	500.00
Prod Insurance	1	1	allow	1,500.00	1,500.00
Couriers	1	1	allow	200.00	255.00
Holiday pay					3,500.00
Sub-Total					**108,600.00**
Contingency	1	1	allow	4,000.00	**4,500.00**
Production Fee					**15,000.00**
TOTAL					**128,100.00**

APPENDIX 4
PRODUCER/DIRECTOR CONTRACT

Date:

Dear

We write to confirm the agreement reached between us as follows:

1. Engagement

We hereby engage you to be the Producer/Director of a programme of .... minutes' duration which we propose but do not undertake to and provisionally entitled ..... ("the Programme") and you hereby agree to render to us your services as Producer/Producer/Director of the Programme on the terms and conditions set out in this agreement.

2. Term

Subject always to Condition 9 of this agreement, we shall be entitled to your services throughout the period from   to   and thereafter if necessary subject to your prior professional commitments and a negotiation between us in good faith concerning your remuneration during any such additional period.

You will be engaged throughout this period for a total of   , on the following basis:

a)   Exclusive:

Your rest days will be such days as shall be agreed between yourself and the nominated producer.

You will be expected to work on any public holidays during the term of the agreement.

3. Remuneration

3.1 Subject to the provisions of this agreement and to the due performance by you of your obligations hereunder, we shall as inclusive remuneration and as full equitable and complete consideration for all services rendered and for all rights, consents and benefits assigned and granted by you to us hereunder pay to you

per day

You shall be entitled to paid holiday calculated at the rate of five point six weeks per annum, pro rata to the length of engagement hereunder and your leave year shall commence on the date of commencement of your engagement. For the avoidance of doubt any paid holiday provided for under the provisions of this agreement shall be inclusive of any entitlement which you may have under Regulation 13 of the Working Time Regulations 1998 (or any modification or re-enactment thereof). You may be required (for no additional payment) to work on bank and public holidays if necessary to meet the production and delivery schedules for the Programme. You acknowledge and agree;

(a) that you have elected to receive and we shall pay you, in respect of any such holiday pay entitlement, on a monthly basis throughout the Term until such time as you notify us to the contrary. Under this contract term you are entitled to 4.4 days paid holiday, at a total of £

(b) that by virtue of the fact you will receive advance payment of holiday pay throughout the Term, you will have no further entitlement to any additional payment in respect of holiday pay at the expiry of the Term; and

(c) any holiday taken during the Term this agreement can only be taken with our prior written agreement. We reserve the right to schedule certain periods during the Term as holiday by giving you twice as many days' notice of the scheduled holiday as the holiday to be scheduled. For the avoidance of doubt in the event that you are able to take all or part of your holiday entitlement during the term of your engagement and in respect of which you receive an advance against your holiday credit entitlement then we shall be entitled to deduct the same from any payments otherwise due hereunder

3.2 The holiday entitlement shall be paid pro rata at a rate of:
4.4 days

4. Conditions of Engagement for Producer/Directors ("the Conditions")

The attached Conditions are hereby incorporated in this agreement. In the Conditions we are referred to as the "Company" and you are referred to as the "Producer/Director".

5. Special Provisions

5.1 The Company's single nominated Executive Producer is

5.2 Our base shall be

5.3 You will direct and deliver the Programme in accordance with the agreed schedule that has been provided to you.

5.4 You will be invited to supervise the edit wherever reasonably practicable where re-editing of the programme is required by the original commissioning broadcaster, or if not available, to give guidance on how it should be carried out for no further payment.

Kindly indicate your acceptance of the above by signing and returning to us the enclosed duplicate of this letter.

Yours sincerely   Read and agreed by:

_____   _____

for and on behalf of   duly authorised for and
                                             on behalf of

To be completed by the Producer/Producer/Director:
VAT No:

APPENDIX 5
INVESTMENT AGREEMENT

INVESTMENT AGREEMENT

From: **XXX**

To: **XXX**
Address

For the attention of: X
('you')

Dated:

Dear Madam

'X' – Financing by X

Further to our previous correspondence with regard to my proposed contribution to the financing of the television documentary provisionally entitled 'X' based on a script by [XXX] to be directed by [XXX] and produced by [XXX] (the 'Documentary'), I set out below the terms upon which I have today agreed to provide such financing.

1. Financing

I hereby undertake to provide to you today the sum of (Sterling) £XXX (the 'Finance') by making available such funds to the Production Account (see below). Whether and if so to what level I am prepared to increase the Finance in due course shall be at my sole discretion but in the event of me doing so, any further monies provided by me shall be on the same commercial terms as the provision of the Finance and in such a case the Finance shall be treated as an advance on my total equity investment in the Documentary.

2. Banking – Production Account

2.1 You confirm that you have set up a bank account in the name of [XXX] (the 'Production Account') into which the Finance will be paid and that all payments therefrom will be made in respect of expenditure necessary or desirable for the development, production of the Documentary.

2.2 You will maintain records and books of account relating to the production of the Documentary together with all invoices vouchers receipts and other records evidencing expenses and charges incurred in the production of the Documentary such records for the period of one year following delivery of the Documentary.

2.3 You acknowledge that I (or my advisers) shall have the right, once in every calendar quarter on reasonable prior notice, to inspect audit and take copies of all books and records relating to the Documentary.

3. Consideration for provision of Finance

3.1 I accept that the Finance shall only be repaid on a pari passu pro rata basis with any other equity investors contributing towards the final budget for the Documentary ('Budget') (but after all sales agent fees and expenses; distribution fees and expenses; all other customary 'off the tops'; marketing and sales costs and expenses; first position funding, together with related financing fees and interest; bank funding and any deferred fees payable) from the first (save as aforesaid) income (net of tax) received by you from the exploitation of the Film.

3.2 I shall also be entitled to a pro rata pari passu (with any other other equity investors) a share of your net profits received from the exploitation of the Documentary. It is currently anticipated that my share will be not less than 15% of 100% of your net profits received from the exploitation of the Documentary although this is subject to change depending on the overall financing required.

4. My Warranty

I warrant and undertake that I shall not reveal or make public any financial or other confidential information in connection with the Documentary or the terms of this Agreement save to professional advisers or as required by law.

5.   Your Warranties

You warrant and agree that you will:

5.1   Use best endeavours to raise the rest of of the required funding in order to complete and deliver the Documentary to its distributor(s);

5.2   Use the Finance only for development and production costs of the Documentary and for no other purpose.

6.   Credit

You shall take all reasonable measures to ensure that the Documentary contains a prominent screen credit on a favoured nations status with any other equity investors stating that I am one of the financiers of the Documentary.

Inadvertent failure to provide such credit shall be fully rectified prospectively on the next screening of the Documentary.

7.   General

7.1   The failure to exercise or delay in exercising a right or remedy provided by this Agreement or by law does not constitute a waiver of the right or remedy or a waiver of other rights or remedies.

7.2   Each party shall pay its own costs relating to the negotiation, preparation, execution and implementation by it of this Agreement.

7.3   This Agreement, and the documents referred to in it, constitutes the entire agreement and understanding of the parties and supersedes any previous agreement between the parties relating to the subject matter of this Agreement.

7.4   No variation of this Agreement shall be valid unless it is in writing and signed by or on behalf of each of the parties.

7.5   Any notice or other communication given under this Agreement shall be in writing and signed by or on behalf of the party giving it and may be served by delivering it personally or sending it by pre-paid recorded delivery or registered post or fax to the address and for the attention of the relevant party.

7.6   This Agreement shall be governed by and construed in accordance with English law and the parties submit to the non-exclusive jurisdiction of the English Courts.

Signed by **X**   )   ....

Signed by **X**   )
for and on behalf of   )   ....
X   )   Director

APPENDIX 6
PRE-SALES AGREEMENT

<u>**CO-PRODUCTION AGREEMENT**</u>

Dated as of the   day of 2017

PRODUCER NAME:

ADDRESS:

ATTENTION:

<u>**Re: [Project Name]**</u>

Dear Name:

Further to our recent discussions, this letter shall confirm the terms upon which X Limited ('X') will provide to Producer certain production financing services in relation to the Project, as defined below.

1. DEFINITIONS

'Project' shall mean an audiovisual programme or series of programmes developed and/or proposed to be produced by Producer under the working title [Project name], which has been commissioned by [BBC] (the 'Primary Broadcaster') but is not fully financed.

'Services' shall mean seeking, negotiating and contracting for the financing of the Project's production budget in any territory worldwide, whether through co-productions, pre-sales, sponsors, advertisers or any other sources of finance.

2.   ENGAGEMENT

(a)   Producer hereby engages X to provide the Services to Producer commencing on [DATE] and continuing for a period of three months up to and including [DATE] unless it is terminated earlier in accordance with this Agreement. If mutually agreed, the parties may extend this Agreement for an additional period of three months on the same terms. Where X is negotiating with any third party for any financing for the Project at the expiration of the Term or any extension, the Term shall be extended to allow X to finalise negotiations with a view to obtaining a firm commitment for such financing.

(b)   X shall provide the Services on a non-exclusive basis. For the avoidance of doubt, X shall be entitled during the Term to provide similar services to any other person or entity.

(c)   Unless otherwise expressly agreed in writing, X shall be exclusively responsible for seeking to secure and/or negotiate the terms of all financing agreements (other than the original UK commissioning agreement) in relation to the Project and the Producer shall not be entitled to employ and/or engage the services of any other person or persons to perform similar services with respect to the Project.

3.   X RIGHTS & OBLIGATIONS

(a)   X shall:

   (i)   provide the Services to the best of its ability and with all reasonable skill and care;

   (ii)   devote sufficient time to carry out the Services;

   (iii)   abide by the reasonable instructions of the Producer;

   (iv)   not incur any liability or bind the Producer to any obligation without Producer's prior written consent; and

(v)   not do anything which could, in Producer's reasonable opinion, bring the Producer or any aspect of its business into disrepute, or which could otherwise damage the Producer's goodwill.

(b)   The Services do not need to be performed at the Producer's offices or on particular days but X shall ensure its representative shall make herself reasonably available to attend meetings as and when required by the Producer.

(c)   If X is successful in securing the financing of the Project, X shall enter into all financing agreements directly, provided that any financing secured by X and the terms of any agreements relating to such financing shall be subject to Producer's prior written approval.

4.   PRODUCER RIGHTS & OBLIGATIONS

(a)   Producer shall supply X with all available materials relating to the Project, including without limitation any scripts, treatments, storylines and/or synopses, details of any committed contributors (including writers, actors/hosts, directors), the production budget, the level of financing committed by the Primary Broadcaster and the Primary Broadcaster's rights and holdbacks.

(b)   Producer shall keep X fully informed of any material changes to the Project, including without limitation any editorial or creative changes, or changes of key contributors, the production budget or financing structure.

5.   REMUNERATION

(a)   In consideration for the provision of the Services during the Term, if X is successful in securing production financing and the Project is produced, the Producer shall pay to X:

(i)   a commission equal to 15% of the gross sums secured by X;

(ii)   [x% of the Net Revenues from the Project. Net Revenues shall mean all gross sums derived from the exploitation of the Project in any media worldwide in perpetuity less the budgeted cost of production, industry standard distribution commission and expenses, any residual or clearances costs and taxes.]

(b) In addition to (a), it shall be a material term of the provision of the Services by X that if the Project is produced, X is granted the right to distribute all rights in the Project in all media (including without limitation all forms of television, video, and all ancillary rights in the project including merchandising, publishing, music publishing) worldwide for a term of 10 years, subject to the rights and holdbacks of the Primary Broadcaster and any agreed co-producers or pre-sale partners.

(c) Producer shall reimburse X for all reasonable out of pocket expenses properly and directly incurred in connection with the provision of the Services to the Producer including, without limitation, transportation, accommodation and other expenses incurred by X's consultant in attending sales markets or trade fairs PROVIDED THAT (i) X shall apportion such expenses on a fair and equitable basis between other parties for whom its consultant is providing similar services in relation to programmes at any such event, and (ii) X shall obtain Producer's prior written approval for any individual expenses greater than £500. If any of X's affiliated companies has any other programmes of the Producer under licence, X shall be entitled to recoup such expenses from gross receipts from exploitation of such programmes in lieu of billing Producer for such expenses.

(d) X shall contract for and collect all financing for which it secures a firm commitment during the Term (regardless of whether the contracts are completed and/or monies are paid or payable after expiration of the Term) and shall be entitled to retain its commission and any expenses as set out in (a) above on any part payment of any monies actually received. The remainder of the monies shall be paid over to Producer within 10 business days of X's receipt of monies, subject to receipt of a valid VAT invoice from Producer.

6. CREDIT

If X is successful in securing financing for the Project, X shall be entitled to a credit in the end titles of all copies of the Programme in a form to be agreed and subject to the practice of the person(s) commissioning or financing the production of the Programme.

7.   INTELLECTUAL PROPERTY

X hereby assigns to Producer absolutely the entire copyright and all other rights whatsoever in all products of X's services hereunder, including, without limitation, any material created by or on behalf of X relating to the Project.

8.   CONFIDENTIALITY

Neither party shall, whether during or after the Term, divulge to any person or company or otherwise make use of any trade secrets or confidential or commercially sensitive information of the other party (including without limitation all details of the Project) which may have come to the receiving party's knowledge during the Term, or the terms of this Agreement ('Confidential Information') except to its subsidiary companies and each of their employees and professional advisors and as is strictly necessary to carry out the Services and provided always any disclosees agree to be bound by this clause. This restriction shall continue to apply after the expiry of the Term without limitation in time, but shall cease to apply to any information or knowledge which subsequently comes into the public domain, other than by way of unauthorised disclosure by the X, or is legally required to be disclosed.

9.   REPRESENTATIONS & WARRANTIES

X represents, warrants and undertakes to Producer that:

(a)   It has full right and authority to enter into this Agreement and has not done anything and will not do anything which would hamper it from rendering the Services or be inconsistent with its obligations hereunder.

10.   TERMINATION

(a)   Producer shall be entitled to terminate this Agreement on written notice in the event that X is unable to provide a production financing expert to properly perform the Services.

(b)   On expiration or earlier termination, X shall promptly destroy or, if requested, return to Producer any materials relating to the Project and any other Confidential Information of the Producer which is in its possession or control.

11.   MISCELLANEOUS

(a)   Any notice to be given shall be in writing.   Notice shall be sufficiently served by being delivered to or sent by registered post addressed to the office set out in this Agreement. Any notice if so posted shall be deemed served upon the next business day following that on which it was posted.

(b)   Nothing contained in the Agreement shall be construed or deemed to constitute a joint venture, agency relationship or partnership between the parties.

(c)   No modification of this Agreement shall be binding unless in writing and signed by the parties hereto.

(d)   The provisions of this Agreement shall be deemed severable, and the invalidity or unenforceability of any provision shall not affect the validity or enforceability of the other provisions hereof.

(e)   Unless otherwise expressly provided in the terms of this agreement, the parties do not intend that a third party should have the right to enforce any term of this agreement pursuant to the terms of the Contracts (Rights of Third Parties) Act 1999.

(f)   This Agreement shall be governed by the laws of England and the parties hereto hereby submit to the exclusive jurisdiction of the English courts.

SIGNED by   ....
for and on behalf of
[PRODUCER NAME]

SIGNED by   ....
for and on behalf of
X LIMITED

APPENDIX 7
OPTION AGREEMENT

DATE:

Re: The Work X by X.

PARTIES:

(1) Company Name, of Company Address ('The Producer');
(2) X ('The Grantor').

1. INTERPRETATION

1.1 In this Agreement the following words and expressions shall have the following meanings unless the context otherwise requires:

Production Company: Company Name/Address

Property: Book title

Assignment: the assignment by the Grantor to the Producer of the Exclusivity Rights in Property; attached to this document

Option: the sole, exclusive and irrevocable option to purchase the Rights for the Purchase Price on the terms of the Assignment

'Option Period': the period commencing on the date of this Agreement and ending 12 calendar months from such date

'Option Extension Period':	12 calendar months from the expiry of the Option Period
'Option Price':	A nominal sum of UKP1.00
'Production':	the documentary intended for television broadcast and/or theatrical release which the Producer proposes to produce and which is currently in development; Working title X

1. OPTION

1.1 In consideration of the payment by the Producer of the Option Price (receipt of which the Grantor acknowledges) the Grantor grants to the Producer:-

  1.1.1 the Option

2. EXERCISE OF OPTION

2.1 The Producer will automatically exercise the Option on signing of this document by The Grantor and The Producer.

3. GRANTOR'S OBLIGATIONS

3.1 The Grantor warrants, undertakes and agrees with the Producer that:-

  3.1.1 It will not dispose of nor deal in any way with any of the Rights during the Option Period;

  3.1.2 the Grantor is the sole owner with full title guarantee of the Rights;

  3.1.3 no audiovisual work has been produced that is based on the same idea or substantially the same facts;

  3.1.4 the Grantor has the right to enter into this Agreement and the Assignment, there is no present or prospective claim to coverage of this subject;

  3.1.5 the Producer may at any time during the Option Period undertake production and pre-production activities in connection with the Rights, by mutual agreement;

3.1.6   the Grantor shall not disclose any confidential information concerning the business of the Producer or the contents of this Agreement;

3.1.7   If the television programme/film is commissioned, the Grantor shall indemnify the Producer against all claims, costs (including reasonable legal costs) awards, damages, actions and proceedings incurred by the Producer as a result of any breach by the Grantor of any of the Grantor's obligations contained in or implied under this Agreement.

4.   NO OBLIGATION TO EXPLOIT

Nothing in this Agreement shall impose upon the Producer any obligation to exercise the Option or to produce or exploit the Production. The Producer shall not be liable to the Grantor in respect of any loss of publicity or reputation arising from this.

Further the Producer warrants that they are a member of PACT.

4.1   Governing Law

This Agreement shall be governed by and construed in accordance with the Laws of England whose courts shall have exclusive jurisdiction.

Signed by or on behalf of the Parties on the date appearing at the beginning of this Agreement.

_____

Signed on behalf of the Producer

_____

Signed by the Grantor

APPENDIX 8
DEED OF ASSIGNMENT

Date:

<u>DEED OF ASSIGNMENT</u>

THIS DEED OF ASSIGNMENT hereby confirms that X (herein after known as the 'Grantor'), of X hereby grants and assigns the following rights as outlined in this deed over to X, (hereinafter known as the 'Producers'), X, under the following terms and conditions:-

1. Upon receiving payment, as herein agreed under clause 6, the Grantor hereby sells, grants, conveys and assigns the Producers, their successors, licensees and assigns, exclusively and forever, all documentary and drama documentary film rights, and including all television documentary and drama documentary film rights, and all video distribution, rental and sales rights, DVD distribution, rental and sales rights, internet rights, interactive and game rights, remakes, sequels and subsidiary, derivative and ancillary rights throughout the world, in and to the Property and in and to the copyright of it and all renewals and extensions of copyright of the Property. This extends to include copyright in the US.

2. The Producers hereunder (without in any way limiting the grant of rights hereinabove stated) are granted the following exclusive rights throughout the world:

    (i) to make, produce, adapt and copyright one or more documentary or drama documentary films, adaptations, whether fixed on film, tape, disk, cassette or through any other technical process whether now known or from now on devised, based in whole or in part on the Property, including remakes and sequels to any documentary feature film produced hereunder;

(ii) and to record and reproduce and license spoken words taken from or based upon the Property and any kinds of music, musical accompaniments and/or lyric to be performed or sung by the performers in any such film;

(iii) to exhibit, perform, rent, lease and generally deal in and with any documentary drama documentary film produced hereunder; by all means or technical processes whatsoever, whether now known or from now on devised including, film, tape, disc, cassette, television or otherwise; and anywhere whatsoever, including homes, theatre or elsewhere, and whether a fee is charged, directly or indirectly, of viewing of such a film;

(iv) to broadcast, transmit or reproduce the Property (including without limitations any film produced hereunder and/or any script or other material based on or using the Property), by means of television and any process analogue or digital thereto whether now known or from now on devised; and the exclusive right to exercise for television purposes all rights granted the Producers hereunder for film purposes.

(v) to use and exploit any merchandise and recordings of any sort and nature arising out of or connected with the Rights of the Property.

(vi) to use and exploit the rights for any purpose of advertising and/or publicity in any manner whatsoever.

RIGHTS TO MAKE CHANGES

3. The Writer agrees that the Producers shall have the unlimited right to vary, change, alter, modify, add to and/or delete from the Property, and to rearrange and/or transpose the Property and change the sequence of it and the characters and descriptions of the characters contained in the Property, and to use a portion or portions of the property or the characters, plots, or theme of it with any other literary, dramatic, or other material within the documentary or drama documentary.

4. The Writer hereby waives the benefit of any provisions of moral rights (droit moral) anywhere in the world and agrees not to permit or

prosecute any action of lawsuit on the ground that the documentary or drama documentary feature Film or other version of the Property produced or exhibited by the Producers, their assignees or licensees, in any way constitutes an infringement of any of the Writer's moral rights or is in any way a defamation or mutilation of the Property or any part of it or contains unauthorised variations, alternations, modifications, changes or translations.

DURATION AND EXTENT OF RIGHTS GRANTED

5.   The Producers shall enjoy, solely and exclusively, all the rights, licences, privileges and property granted hereunder throughout the world, in perpetuity, as long as any rights in the Property are recognised in law or equity, except as far as such period of perpetuity may be shortened due to any now existing or future copyright by the Writer of the Property anywhere in the world, in which case the Producers shall enjoy its sole and exclusive rights, licences, privileges and property hereunder to the fullest extent permissible under and for the full duration of such copyright or copyrights, and any renewals and/or extensions of it. All rights, licences, privileges and property granted herein to the Producers are irrevocable and not subject to rescission, restraint or injunction under any circumstances.

CONSIDERATION FOR THE RIGHTS

6.   As consideration for all rights granted and assigned to the Producers and for the Grantor's representation and warranties, the Producers agree to pay the Grantor, and the Grantor agrees to accept the sum of X. The payment of this sum shall be made as soon as sufficient development funds have been raised by the Producers, unless the Producers shall fail to exercise the Option before the expiration date in which case the rights herein shall revert immediately to the Grantor. The Grantor shall receive payment of this sum by a cheque made out in his name and sent to his home address.

6.1   As consideration for all rights granted and assigned to the Producers and for the Grantor's representation and warranties, the Producers agree to pay (or procure the payment of) four per cent (4%) of one hundred per cent (100%) of the total net profits received from the distribution, exhibition and exploitation of the Film and any remakes or sequels of the Film, to the Grantor and 'net profits' and the entitlements thereto shall be defined, calculated, reported and payable to Grantor on terms at such times and on a basis no less favourable than any other participant in net profits of the Film.

CREDIT OBLIGATION

7.   The Producers shall have the right to publish, advertise, announce and use in any manner or medium, the name, biography and likeness of the Grantor in connection with any exercise by the Producers of its rights hereunder, provided such use shall not constitute an endorsement of any product or service.

8.   The Grantor shall be accorded the following credit on screen and in paid ads controlled by the Producers in which the producers and/or Film director is accorded the credit: Based on the Novel by Roderic Knowles.

9.   Additionally, if the Producers exploit any other rights in and to the Property, then the Producers agree to give appropriate source material credit to the Property, to the extent that such source material credits are customarily given in connection with the exploitation of such rights.

ASSIGNMENT

10.   This Agreement and the rights herein stated and benefits thereof may be assigned by the Producers to any other person, association, firm or corporation, upon mutual agreement with the Grantor while the film is in development and pre-production.

10.1 The finished film may be assigned by the producers to any other person, firm or corporation.

11.   The Grantor represents and warrants to the Producers that the Grantor is the sole and exclusive proprietor, throughout the world, of the original literary material written by Roderic Knowles entitled X (the 'Property').

12.   The Grantor represents and warrants to the Producers that:-

    i.   The Grantor is the sole author of the Property.

    ii.   The Property was first published in x under the title of X, and was registered for copyright under the name of Roderic Knowles.

iii. No documentary film of the Property has been manufactured, produced, presented or authorised, no radio or television development, presentation, or programme based on the Property, or any part of it, has been manufactured, produced, presented, broadcast or authorised.

13. The Grantor represents and warrants to the Producers that:-

i. The Writer has not adapted the Property from any other literary, dramatic, or other material, nor, excepting for material which is in the public domain, has the Writer copied or used in the Property the plot, scenes, sequences or story of any other literary, dramatic or other material;

ii. The Property does not infringe upon any common law or statutory rights in any other literary, dramatic, or other material;

iii. As far as the Writer/Grantor has knowledge, no material in the Property is libellous, defamatory, or violates the rights of privacy of any person and the full use of the rights in the Property which are covered by and within the Option would not violate any rights of any person, association, firm or corporation;

iv. The Publishers of the Property have no interest or claim in the rights;

v. The Property is not under public domain in any country in the world where copyright protection is available.

14. The Grantor represents and warrants to the producers that:-

i. The Grantor is the exclusive proprietor, throughout the world, of the rights in the property which are covered within the option;

ii. The Grantor has not assigned, licensed nor in any manner encumbered, diminished, or impaired any of the rights herein granted;

iii. There is no outstanding claim or litigation pending against or involving the title, ownership and/or copyright in the Property, or in any part of it, or in the rights which are covered by the Option.

15. The Grantor further represents and warrants that no attempts hereafter will be made to encumber, diminish or impair any of the rights herein

granted and that all appropriate protection of such rights will continue to be maintained by the Grantor.

16. The Grantor agrees that the Grantor will not, at any time during the Option Period, exercise or authorise or permit the exercise by others of any of the rights covered by the Option.

17. None of the rights herein granted and assigned to the Producers have been granted and/or assigned to any person, association, firm or corporation other than the Producers. By signing in the spaces provided below the Grantor and the Producers accept and agree to all of the terms and conditions of this Agreement.

Signed by on behalf of X:

Signature _____

Name (printed) _____

Signed by the Grantor:

Signature _____

Name (printed) _____

Date _____

APPENDIX 9
STANDARD COLLABORATION AGREEMENT

COLLABORATION AGREEMENT

This collaboration agreement (the 'Agreement') is made and entered into as of DATE, by and between COMPANY NAME . and/or its designees and/or licensees ('X'), on the one hand, and *****, on the other hand, with respect to the development, production, and the grant of exclusive rights in a documentary-style programme to be developed for short-form electronic transmission (Internet, mobile, etc.), a broadcast and/or cable television series, one or more feature films and any and all other means of commercial exploitation of a show revolving around ****. For good and valuable consideration (the receipt and sufficiency of which is hereby acknowledged), X and **hereby agree as follows:

1. X and ** shall collaborate in the development of a television pilot and/or series based on the Concept ('Pilot' and 'Series', each a 'Project') with the working title X

2. The parties agree that X shall exclusively control the Concept with respect to any sale, option, license and/or other disposition of any and all rights in and to the Concept (the 'Disposition') and shall have the exclusive right to pitch/shop the Concept to potential Financiers (as defined below) and to negotiate any and all deals relating to the Concept and/or any program based thereon, subject to the terms hereof. In the event that X accepts a firm written commitment from

any third party network, studio, or other buyer or licensee (collectively, 'Financier') for the development or production of a Pilot and/or Series within the period commencing as of the date of full execution hereof and continuing for one (1) year ('Development/Pitch Period'), then the terms of this Agreement shall apply. In the event of a Disposition hereunder, the Development/Pitch Period shall be extended for the length of the Financier's development period not to exceed six (6) months, plus ninety (90) days to set the Project up elsewhere if such development period expires without a production order. If a Disposition is not made within the Development/Pitch Period (as it may be extended), then the parties shall have no further obligation to each other hereunder, but shall nonetheless retain their respective rights in the Concept and any of the material contributed to the development thereof.

3. The parties agree that in the event of a Disposition of the Concept within the Development/Pitch Period, X (or its authorized designee) shall be attached as the production company and copyright owner of the Concept and any Project(s).

4. The parties agree that in the event of a Disposition of the Concept within the Development/Pitch Period, X shall be shall be attached as executive producer and accorded credit as executive producer, X will be attached as co-director and X ...... as Associate Producer. X will negotiate all agreements with third parties. X shall not have the right to proceed with the further development, production, distribution and/ or other exploitation of the Concept and/or Project until ** gives his full and complete approval to the terms of its agreement(s).

5. In the event X produces the Pilot and/or Series, all executive producer fees, royalties, payments for rights, and related contingent compensation payable to the parties shall be allocated as follows:

    X   - %
    **   - %

    Any and all costs incurred by X and ** in connection with the Concept and/or Project shall be recouped 'off the top' prior to any payments to the parties pursuant to the above allocation.

6. All creative and business decisions, including, without limitation, any and all agreements (other than as set forth in paragraph 3) with the Financiers, shall be made by X following consultation with **. X and ** shall have mutual approval over the creative decisions, however, X final decision shall control.

7. ** hereby makes all customary representations and warranties with respect to their contributions to the Concept and/or Project. X hereby makes all customary representations and warranties with respect to their contribution to the Concept and/or Project.

8. All disputes which may arise between X and ** under or with respect to this Agreement shall be determined solely by arbitration in accordance with the rules of the American Arbitration Association, applying California law. The arbitration shall be held in Los Angeles, California, and the cost thereof, including reasonable attorneys' fees, shall be borne by the party which does not prevail therein. Such determination by the arbitrators or by the sole arbitrator, whatever the case may be, shall be final, binding, and conclusive upon the parties hereto, and shall be rendered in such form that it may be judicially confirmed under the laws of XXX.

9. ** agrees to execute and deliver to X all documents or do any acts which X reasonably deems necessary and which are consistent with this Agreement (subject to a reasonable period for review and good faith negotiation).

10. This Agreement shall be construed, interpreted and governed by the laws of XXX.

IN WITNESS WHEREOF, the parties have executed this Agreement as of the date first written above.

X..

By: _____
Authorized Officer

_____
X

_____
X

_____
****

About Us

In addition to Creative Essentials, Oldcastle Books has a number of other imprints, including No Exit Press, Kamera Books, Pulp! The Classics, Pocket Essentials and High Stakes Publishing
> **oldcastlebooks.co.uk**

Checkout the kamera film salon for independent, arthouse and world cinema > **kamera.co.uk**

For more information, media enquiries and review copies please contact Clare > **marketing@oldcastlebooks.com**